IMAGES
of America

MARSHFIELD

ON THE COVER: This photograph was taken in front of the Adler Opera House on East Second Street in 1898. The Elks Club had a minstrel group that would perform on stage, usually at the Opera House, and at times in blackface. The members of the group included many of the leading members of the business community in the city, including such people as John Stierle, a photographer and bird collector whose collection may be seen today at the Marshfield Public Library; Fred Beele, professional wrestling champion and the only Marshfield policeman killed in the line of duty; and Dr. H. Lathrop, one of the founders of the Marshfield Clinic. (Courtesy of the North Wood County Historical Society.)

IMAGES of America

MARSHFIELD

Kenneth J. Wood

ARCADIA PUBLISHING

ISBN 978-0-7385-8872-8

Published by Arcadia Publishing
Charleston, South Carolina

Printed in the United States of America

Library of Congress Control Number: 2011938362

For all general information, please contact Arcadia Publishing:
Telephone 843-853-2070
Fax 843-853-0044
E-mail sales@arcadiapublishing.com
For customer service and orders:
Toll-Free 1-888-313-2665

Visit us on the Internet at www.arcadiapublishing.com

To Lori

Without your long hours of assistance and advice,
this book would never have been completed.

Contents

Acknowledgments

I would like to acknowledge and thank the following people for their assistance in putting this book together: The North Wood County Historical Society (NWCHS) and especially its president, Tom Ptak, and archivist Kim Krueger, for not only giving me full access to their photo archives but providing a workspace in the Upham House Museum as well. I would also like to thank the board of directors of the NWCHS for giving permission to use the images found in this book; Alana Ziaya, archivist and manager of the George Magnin Medical Library at the Marshfield Clinic, who provided all the pictures of the doctors and the history of the Clinic; Shelby Weister for the photographs of the Northwood County Asylum (Norwood), Fire Chief Jim Schmidt for pictures relating to the fire department and the Great Fire of 1887; Mike Meyers of the police department; Sharon Tyrolt for providing the picture of St. Matthew's Lutheran Church; and my wife, Lori Belongia, for her encouragement and help throughout this project. I would also like to thank my grandmother Gertrude Wood, who, through stories from my early childhood of sailing ships, ancestors' run-ins with pirates, and their survival of the Great Chicago Fire of 1871, fostered my love and appreciation of history. This was certainly not a one-person job. Thanks to all who in any way contributed to this endeavor.

Unless otherwise noted, all photographs appear courtesy of the North Wood County Historical Society. Those pertaining to the history of the Marshfield Clinic were provided by the Marshfield Clinic Archives, and images of the North Wood County Asylum were provided by Shelby Weister.

This work could not have been prepared without the previous work of many others in the community. I would like to thank all those who included the identities of people in the photographs and the names and locations of structures, as well as the dates when donating them to the historical society.

I have attempted, to the best of my ability, to be accurate in my descriptions of the images. I am sure errors may have occurred, and I apologize if I have misinterpreted photographs or misidentified persons in them. My time in Marshfield only goes back 15 years, so I have relied upon earlier works that are located in the Marshfield Public Library.

I have viewed and scanned almost 1,000 images and was tasked with the very difficult choice of deciding which ones to include in this volume. I am sure I have omitted names and events of importance. The research was fun and increased my knowledge of my adopted city. I hope you enjoy the book as much as I enjoyed the writing.

INTRODUCTION

Marshfield is a unique Wisconsin city. It is the only city of its size in the state that is not located on navigable water. The city owes its existence to two factors: vast tracts of timber and the extension of railroads through central Wisconsin. This pictorial history of the city covers its beginning in 1872 through the development of timber-based industries and the evolution to other industries, including the emergence of the large medical complex the city is known for today.

In these pages, a young, rough-and-tumble logging town becomes a modern community. The photographs show the changes from a rough logging town of men, saloons, and mud streets to a refined city of schools, churches, parks, and businesses. The growth of the city was led by forward-looking civic pioneers who considered paved and brightly lit streets, electricity, and water in every home to be necessary for life. Those leaders valued education for all, including the deaf and those with special needs. Modern vocational training was a priority for all citizens. The progressive attitudes of the past continue today in this city that is rich with cultural and religious diversity.

Many of the early settlers were veterans of the Civil War. Their patriotic spirit continued with the formation of a National Guard unit in 1889 that served in the Spanish American War, the Mexican Border Crisis of 1916, and World Wars I and II. Many men and women also served in Korea and Vietnam and today continue the tradition with service in the Middle East.

Religion was also an important factor in the creation of the present city of Marshfield. The local Women's Christian Temperance Union was founded and led by Mary Upham in 1883, with the goal of reducing accidents at the mills by replacing the free sandwiches served with the purchase of beer at saloons with lunch at home.

The first hospital was established in 1890 by Catholic nuns and has grown into a large modern facility. St. Joseph's Hospital works closely with the Marshfield Clinic to serve the people of central Wisconsin.

Many fraternal groups have also helped develop the city's character. Groups such as the Masons, Knights of Columbus, Odd Fellows, Eagles, Elks, American Legion, and VFW have provided programs for youth, led charity drives, organized Christmas programs, and done their best to make the city a great place to live.

A walk through the main business district of South Central Avenue will show a variety of architectural styles from the late 19th century. A concerted effort is underway by the city and Main Street Marshfield to restore and preserve these early buildings.

Education also continues to be of importance. The facilities at North Wood County Technical College continue to expand and modernize to keep pace with the needs of today's businesses, as does the University of Wisconsin–Wood County two-year campus.

We would like to invite all of you to visit our city and see for yourselves its history, architecture, spacious parks, and zoo and experience for yourselves the friendliness of our citizens.

Welcome to Marshfield.

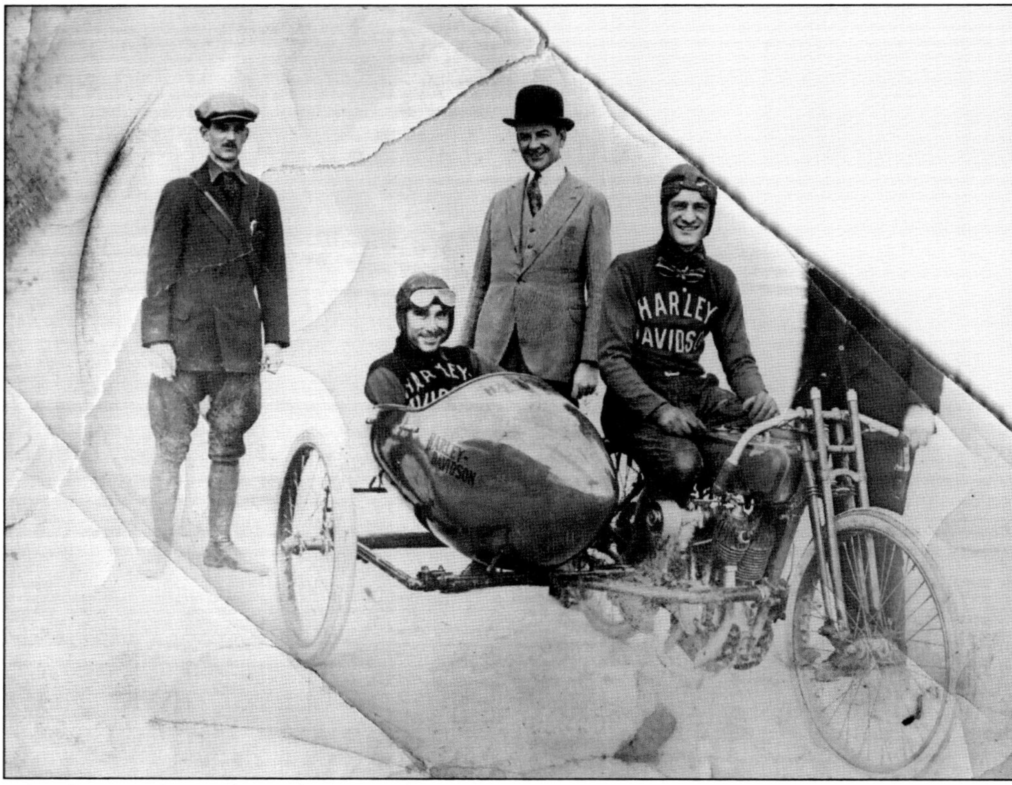

Like these early Harley riders, Marshfield got off to a rousing start with the coming of the railroads, roared with the lumberjacks spending their Saturday nights in town, made a big noise in the veneer and plywood world with Roddis Veneer in World War II, sped to the forefront in the mobile and modular home industry, and, as Harley-Davidson leads the motorcycle world, the Marshfield Clinic is among the leaders in the world in health care and medical research. The city will continue to strive to be the best place to live, not only in Wisconsin but also in the entire United States.

One

The Railroads Arrive

The Marshfield area was once inhabited by the Ojibwa, Winnebago, and Potawatomi Indians. In 1848, the tribes signed the Treaty of Poygan and gave up their rights to all land west of the Wolf River, including the Wisconsin River and its tributaries. The Yellow River, which begins in Clark County and enters the Wisconsin at Necedah, is one of these. In order to open the land to settlement to provide a defensive area between the settled portions of Wisconsin and the British in Canada, land was granted to railroad companies that they could sell to help pay for expansion. The Wisconsin Central Railroad Company was chosen to build a line from Menasha to Ashland.

Land ownership passed from the federal government to the Fox and Wisconsin Improvement Company, which in turn sold some of it to John Magee and Samuel Marsh. Records indicate that Louis Rivers, his wife, and their surviving child arrived from Necedah to begin building a log "hotel" in 1872. He was joined in this endeavor by his brother Frank, his in-laws the Manes family, and G.A. Lupient. Together, they built a two-room log hotel consisting of a large room with multitiered bunks and a large stove. The second room held long tables and benches for serving food and a long counter that served as both a bar and a grocery store counter.

The railroad arrived in Marshfield on July 4, 1872. The rails ran into the town at a heading of 285 degrees, and since all roads were laid out to intersect them at right angles, streets do not run true east, west, north, or south, making for some interesting intersections in newer areas of the city.

Between 1881 and 1891, four more railroad lines entered the city. In 1887, William Henry Upham built a line from the Wisconsin Central Depot to the Upham mill, then south along Spruce and Oak Avenues through what is today Wildwood Park to the Town of Richfield. He named it the Marshfield and Texas Railroad. Asked how far south it was going to run, Upham is said to have replied, "Probably to Texas." It was abandoned in 1900.

In 1893, a total of 1,000 freight cars and 28 passenger trains arrived and departed daily. Passenger service was totally terminated in 1965. Today, the remaining single set of tracks passing through the city is from the original Wisconsin Central Line.

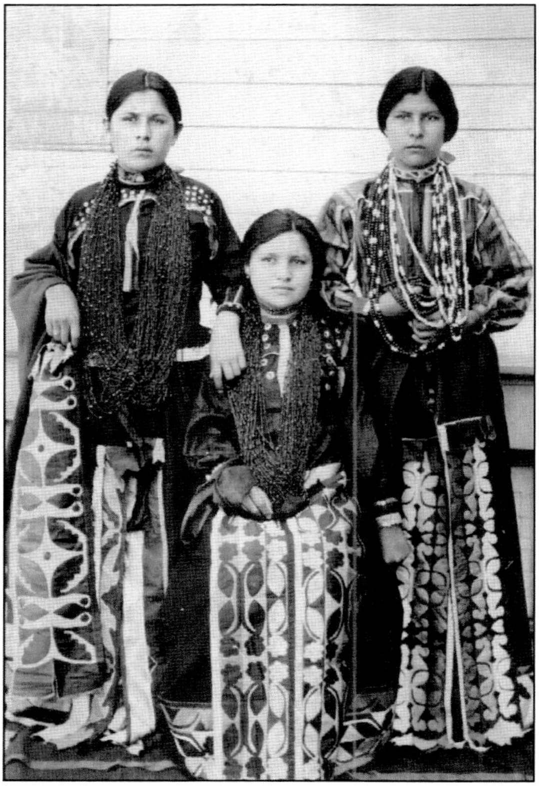

Before the white man came, the region was inhabited by the Chippewa and Potawatomi Indians. After the US government gave the land to the Fox and Wisconsin Improvement Company in 1856, it eventually passed to John Magee and Samuel Marsh. By the 1880s, when this photograph was taken, the Indian way of life had been replaced by the white man's.

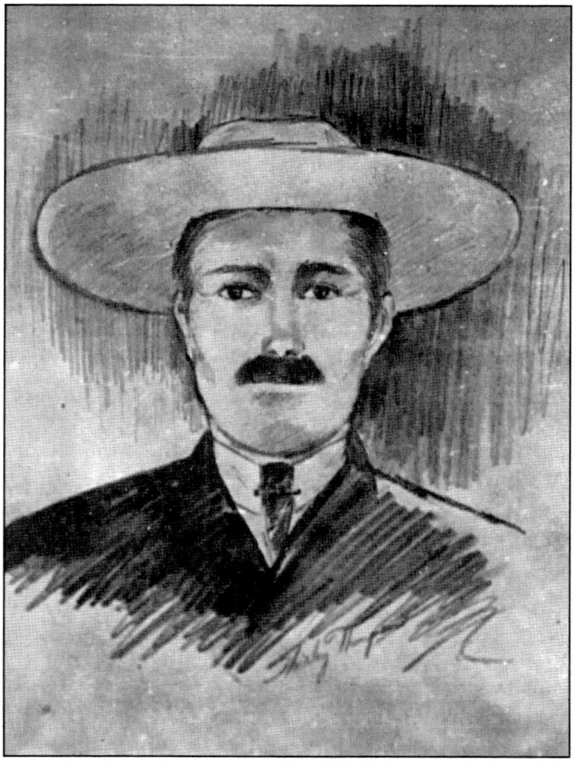

In 1868, brothers Frank and Louis Rivers from Necedah bought land here. Louis had heard that the Wisconsin Central Railroad was expanding its line from Stevens Point to Ashland, passing through the area. The Rivers built a log house that served as a dwelling, hotel, saloon, and, later, post office. In 1873, Louis applied to be postmaster. The office was granted in 1875, and Louis named it Marshfield.

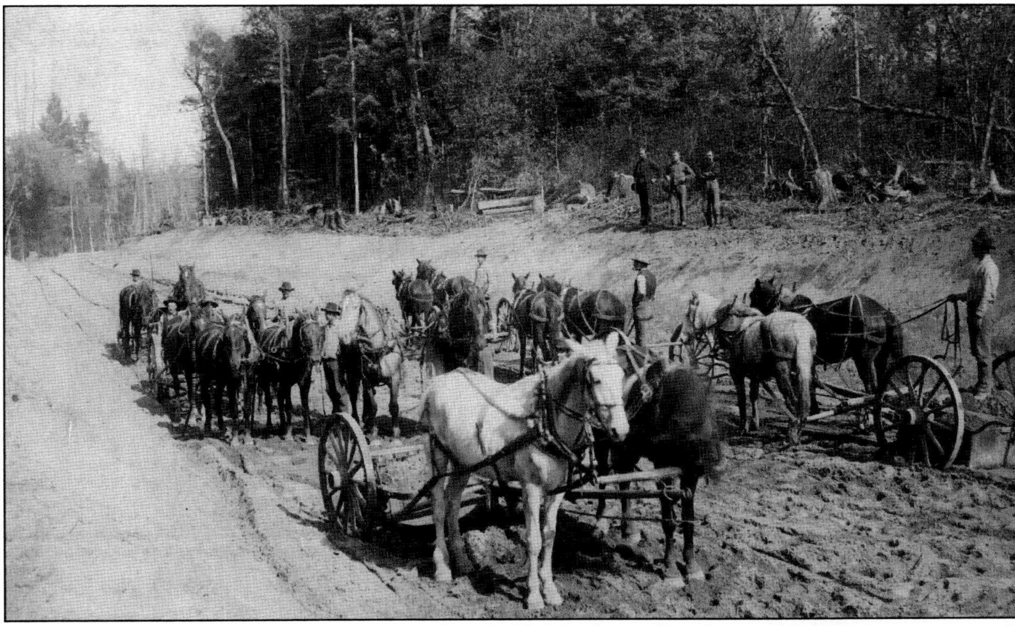

The first factor in the development of Marshfield was the railroad. Local lore says seven people greeted the first train, belonging to the Wisconsin Central Railroad, when it arrived on July 4, 1872. Construction had begun in Stevens Point in March and continued past Marshfield to Section 53, now known as Colby, by September. From there, it continued on to Lake Superior, arriving in Ashland in 1877.

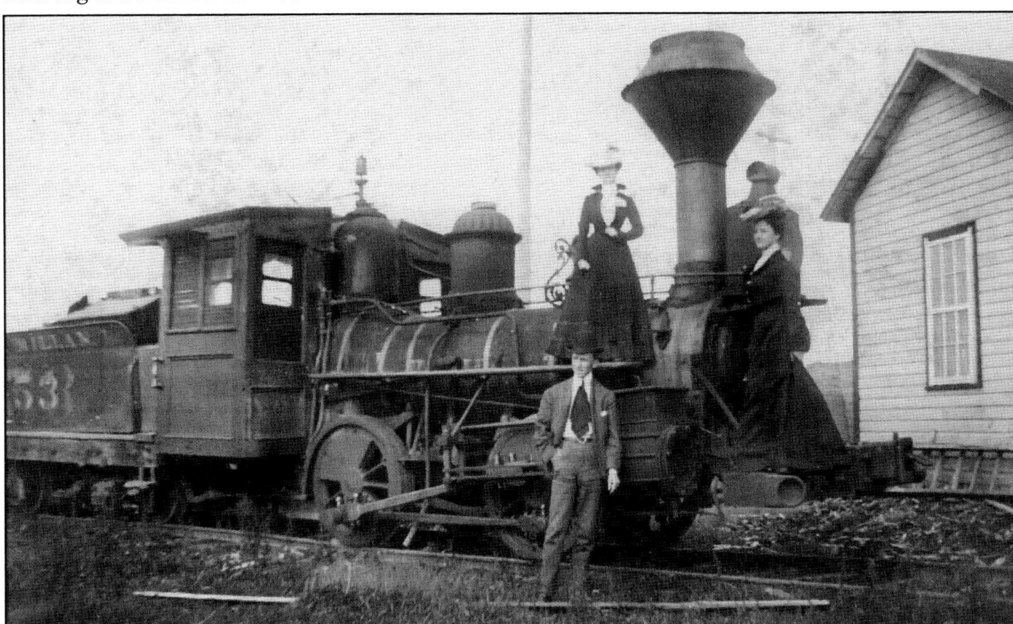

Benjamin and Charles McMillan built a sawmill north of Marshfield in 1873. They cut and hauled by sledge 800,000 feet of logs to the railroad stop just northwest of Marshfield called Mann. Wisconsin Central was asked to build a spur to the mill, but refused, so the brothers built their own line in 1881. Wisconsin Central bought it in 1891. This is McMillan Lumber Company Engine No. 53.

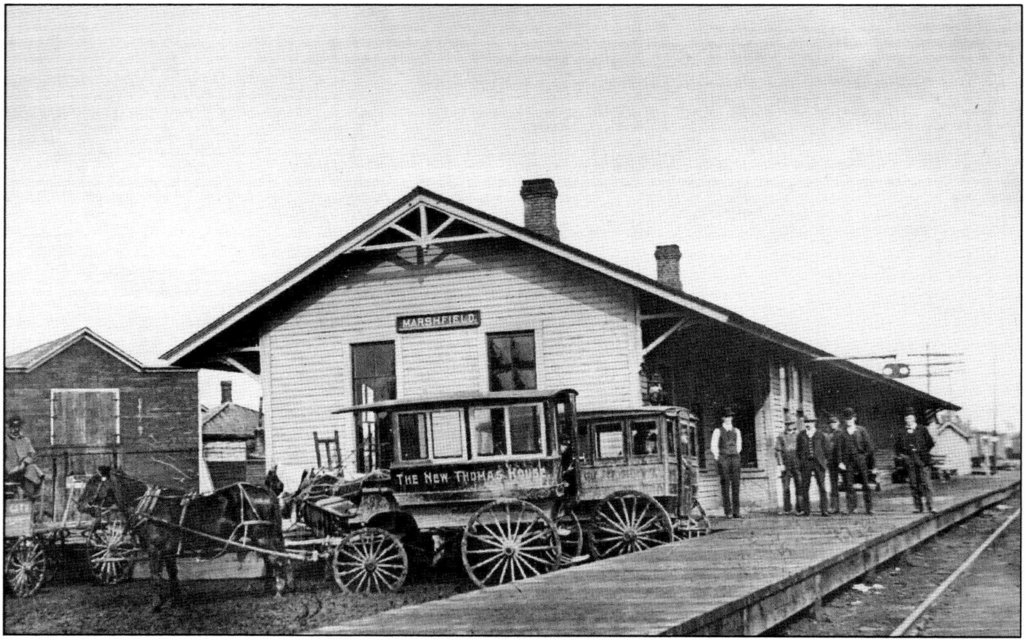

In 1890, the Chicago, St. Paul, Minneapolis & Omaha Railroad, called "the Omaha," had become part of the Chicago and North Western. A depot, roundhouse, and yard facilities were built in the area to the north of Hiller's Hardware in the 700 block of South Central Avenue. Remnants of the line can still be seen running to the southwest, just north of the Holiday Inn, parallel to Park Street.

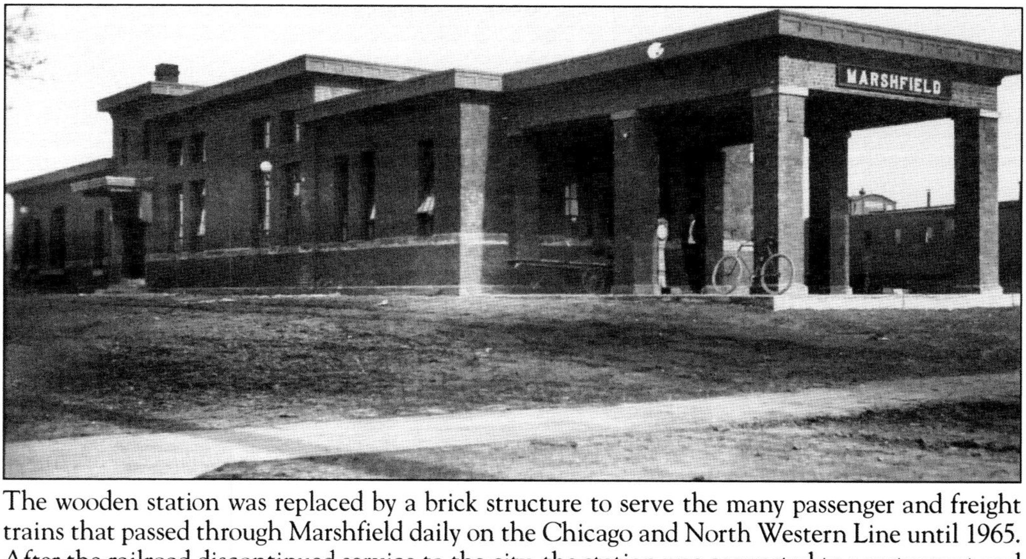

The wooden station was replaced by a brick structure to serve the many passenger and freight trains that passed through Marshfield daily on the Chicago and North Western Line until 1965. After the railroad discontinued service to the city, the station was converted to a restaurant and bar called The End of The Line. In 1996, Hiller's Hardware bought the building and razed it for the expansion of their hardware store.

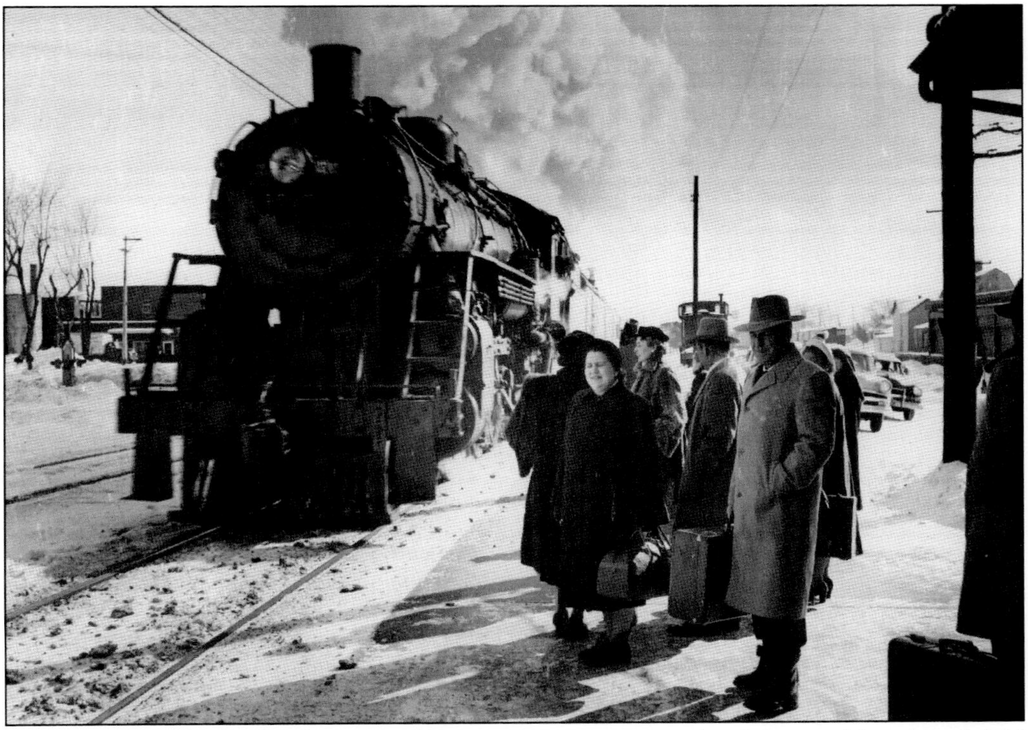

In 1893, a total of 1,000 freight cars and 28 passenger trains arrived and departed from Marshfield daily. By 1903, passenger trains had increased to 38 trains daily at the two depots. This freight depot was built to handle the shipments. You could board a train in Marshfield and go anywhere in the United States. By 1950, there were only eight trains: four South Line and four North Western. All passenger service ended in 1965.

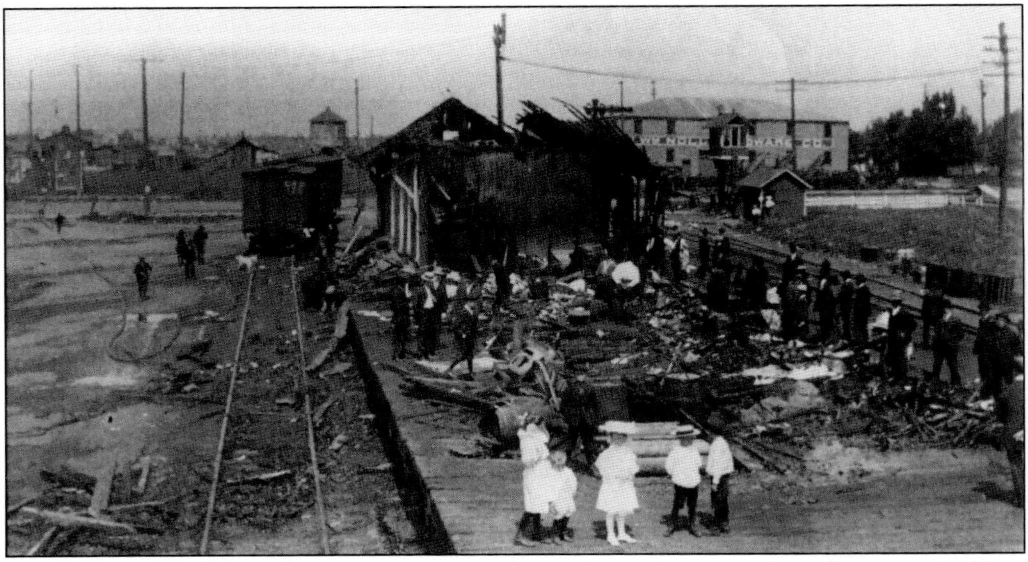

On June 16, 1907, the wooden Wisconsin Central depot burned. It was replaced by a stone building that served travelers until 1965. When Veterans Parkway was constructed through the city parallel to the existing railroad tracks, the depot was moved across the street, turned 180 degrees, and today operates as the Royal Tokyo Japanese Teppanyaki and Steak House.

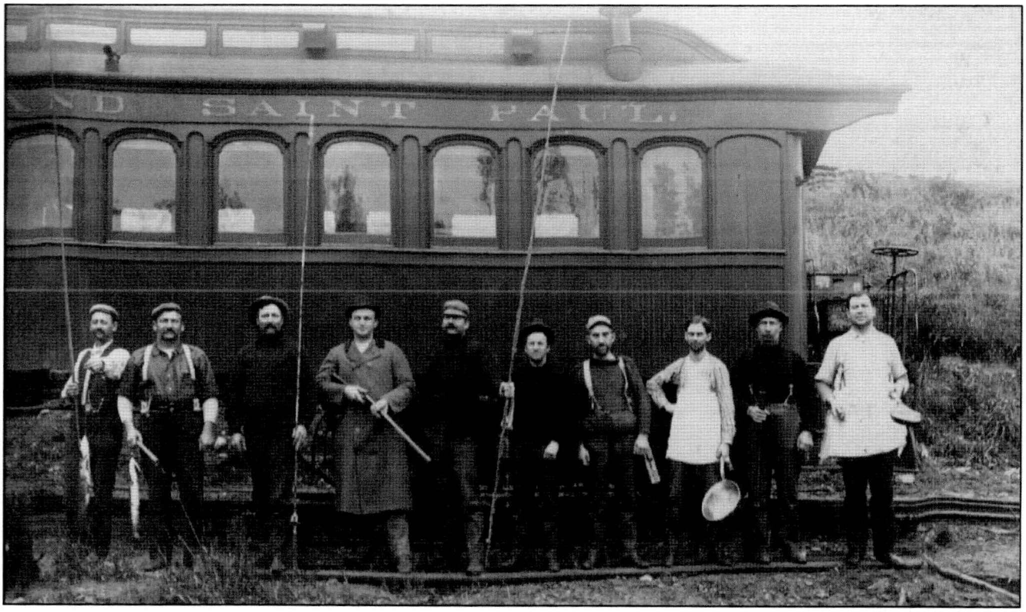

During the golden age of rail transportation, 1880 to 1916, many special trains were run, including funeral trains, trains carrying only delegates to conventions, tour groups, private cars for business executives and government leaders, and even, as shown here with their cooks, hunting and fishing parties. Since Marshfield was now connected to all the major cities of Wisconsin by rail, special trains often ran to and from the city.

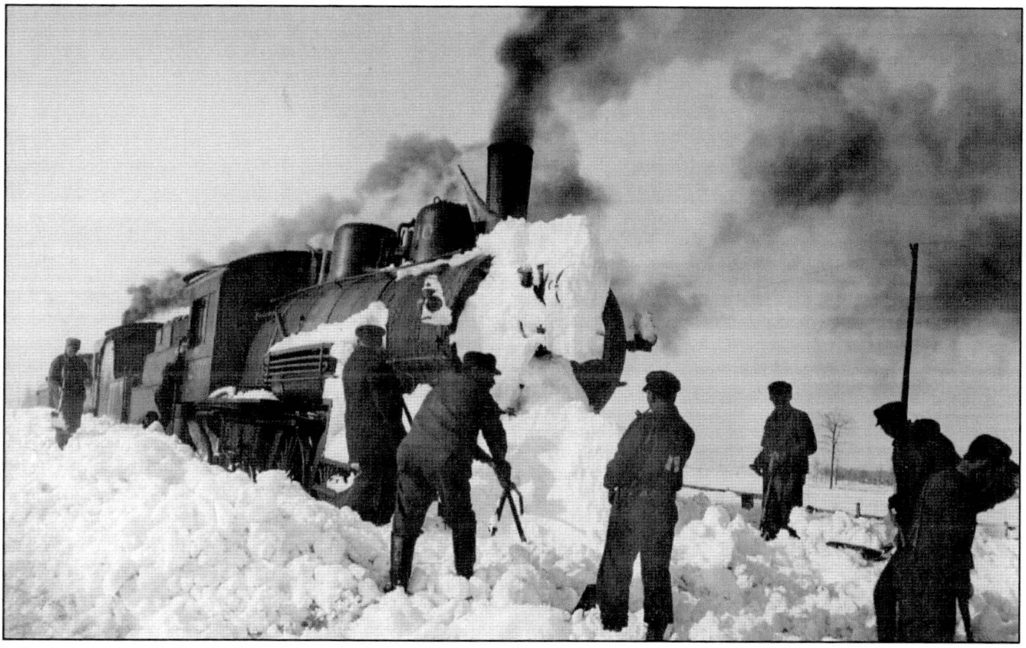

Many events disrupted train travel. In this case, a winter snowstorm has forced the crew to get out the shovels to clear a drift from the tracks. Other problems included both wild and domestic animals and even humans on the tracks, derailments, and vehicles either trying to beat the train or getting stalled at the crossing. Flashing lights and crossing bars became more common in the 1940s.

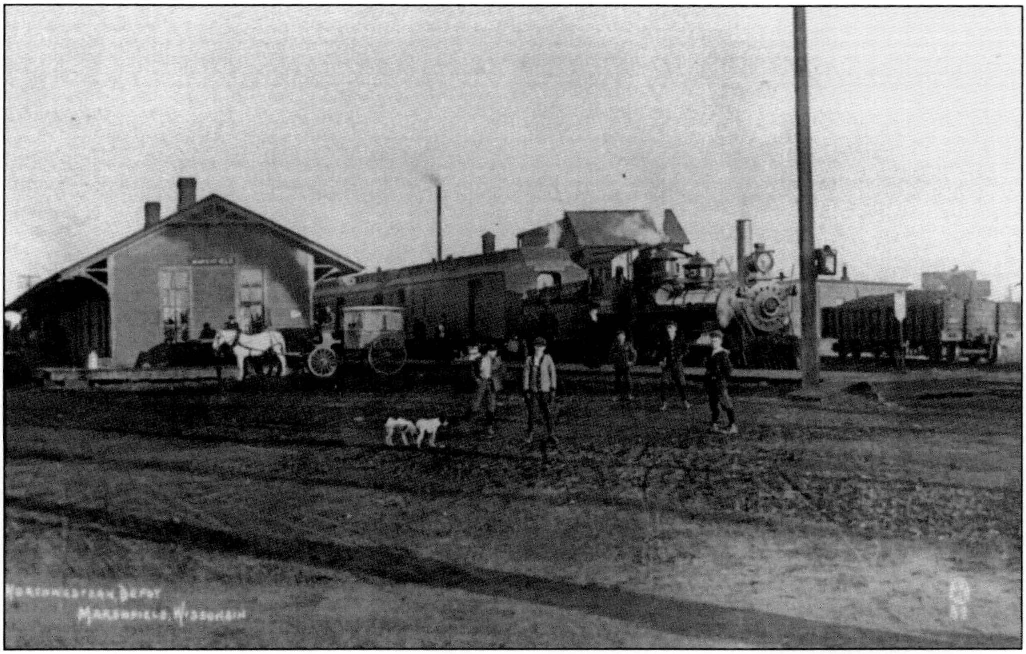

This group of boys and their dogs are at the North Western Depot and rail yard in the 700 block of South Central Avenue. The horse and buggy is waiting to take passengers to one of the many hotels in the city catering to the traveler. Today, this area is occupied by a small strip mall and Hiller's Hardware.

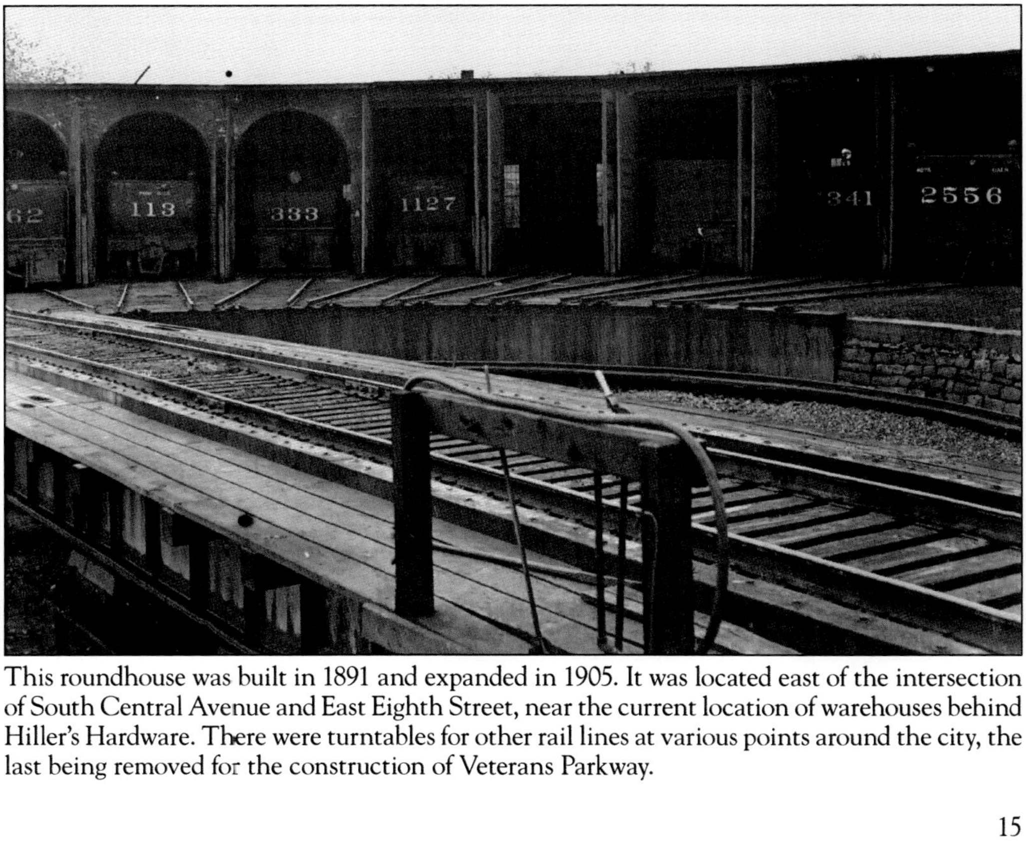

This roundhouse was built in 1891 and expanded in 1905. It was located east of the intersection of South Central Avenue and East Eighth Street, near the current location of warehouses behind Hiller's Hardware. There were turntables for other rail lines at various points around the city, the last being removed for the construction of Veterans Parkway.

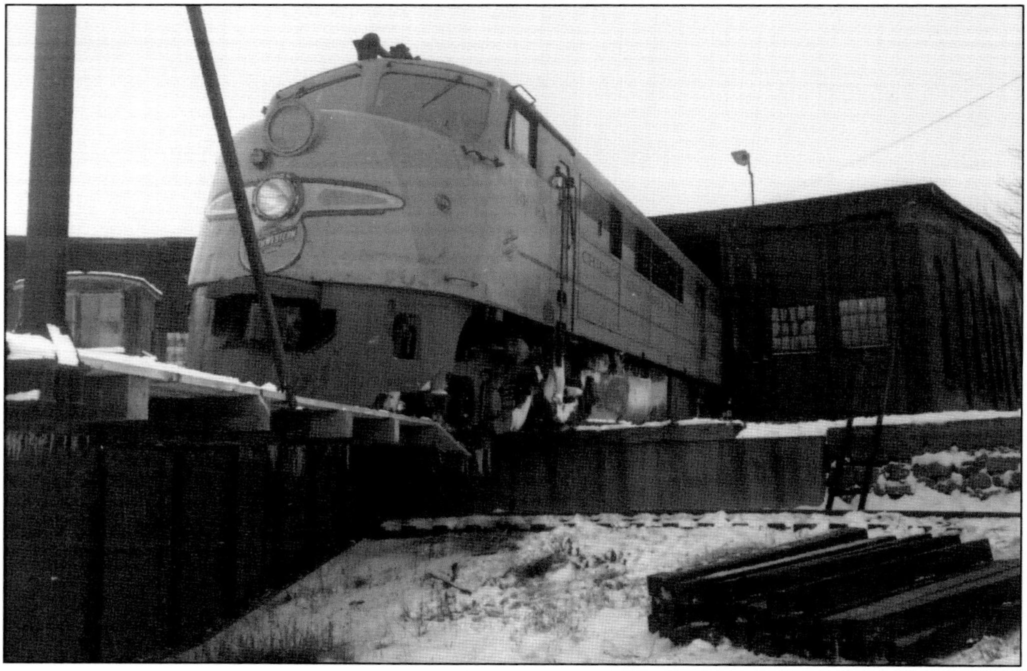

Derailments were an ever-present danger to the railroad men. Here, a locomotive from the Chicago and North Western line has jumped the track while leaving the roundhouse. If the rails were not exactly lined up, accidents such as these could occur.

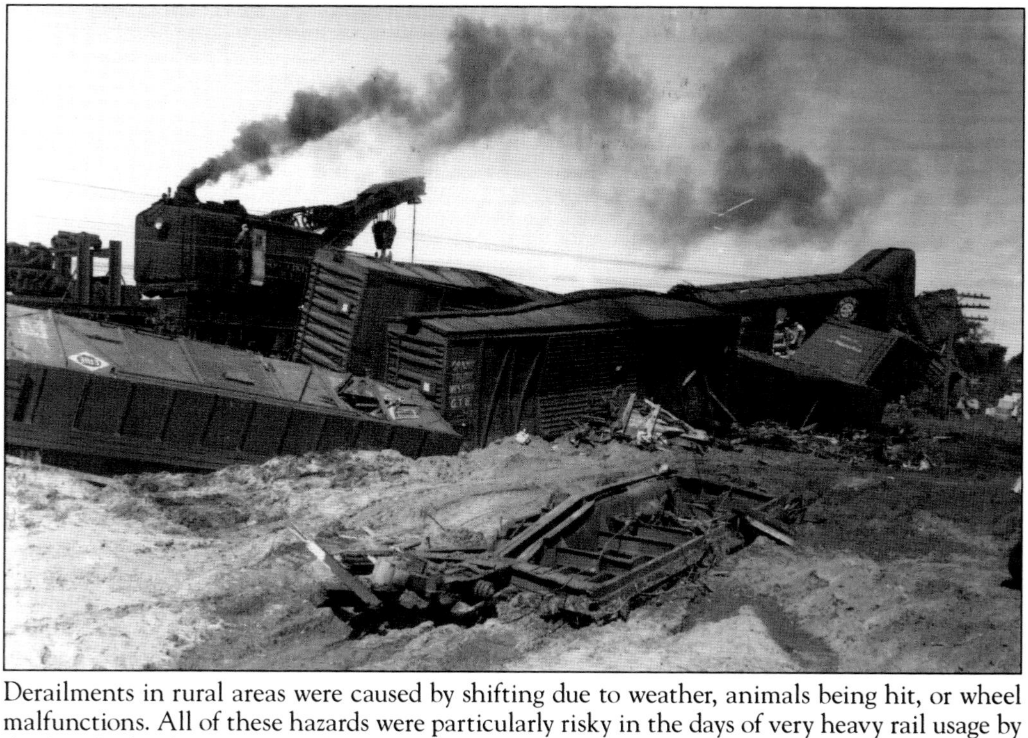

Derailments in rural areas were caused by shifting due to weather, animals being hit, or wheel malfunctions. All of these hazards were particularly risky in the days of very heavy rail usage by the hundreds of trains using them daily. Freight trains and passenger trains were subject to the same dangers.

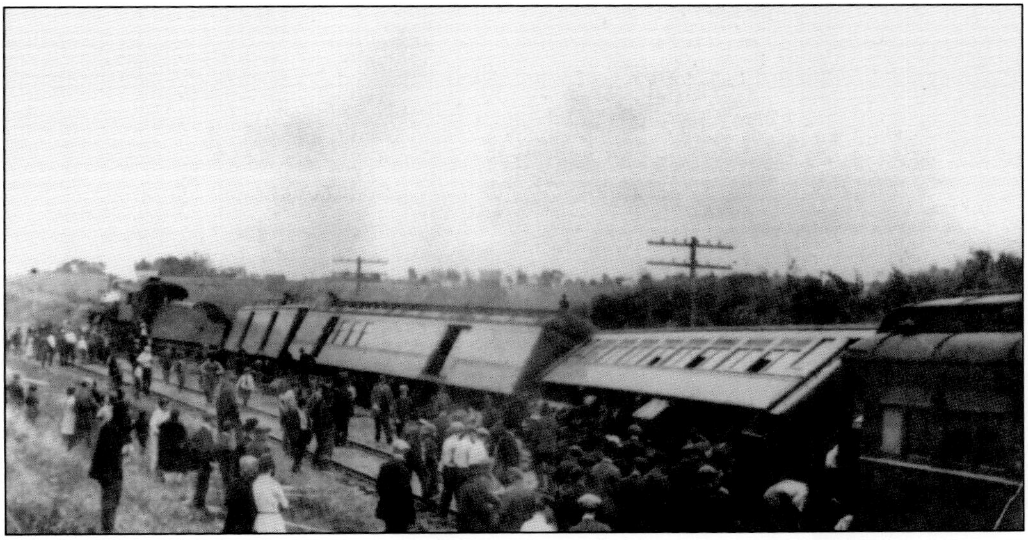

This passenger train derailed west of Marshfield on the run to Greenwood. No record could be found of the injuries, the casualties, or the cause of the accident. This type of accident was uncommon because the track crews, called gander dancers, worked constantly on the lines to ensure, as much as was possible, a safe journey.

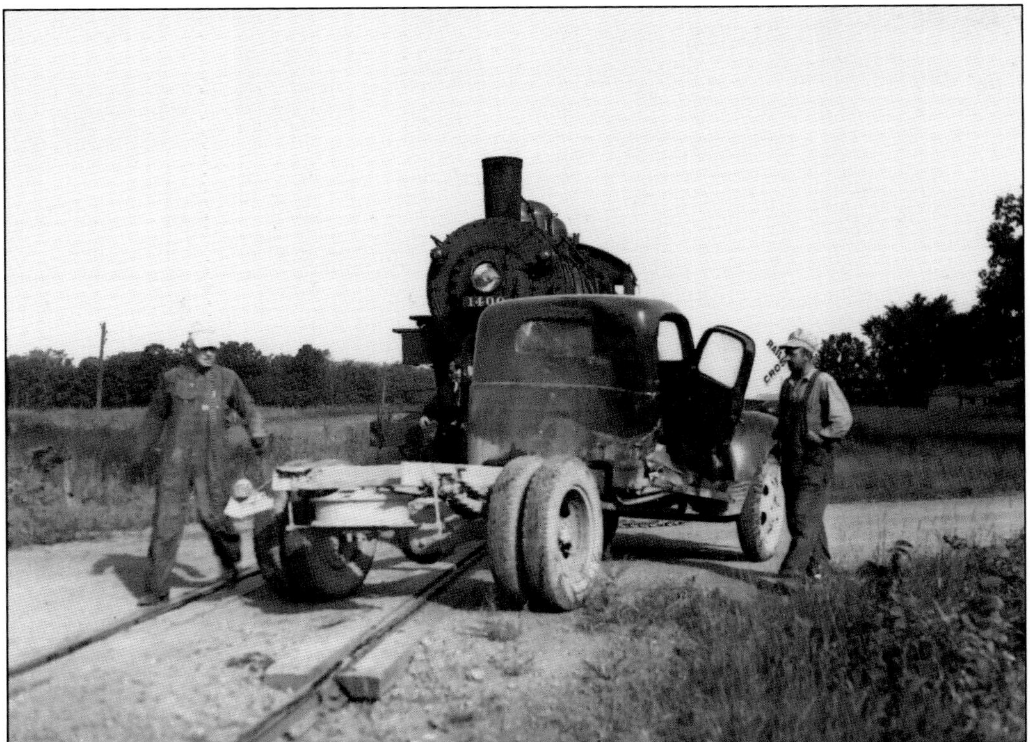

Not all accidents were caused by derailments. Trains often collided with other vehicles. Few railroad crossings had guards on duty. Trains sounded their horns, but vehicles were often struck at the crossing. In this case, the farm truck does not appear to be too badly damaged. The farmer and the engineer seem to be discussing the event, and there appear to have been no severe injuries.

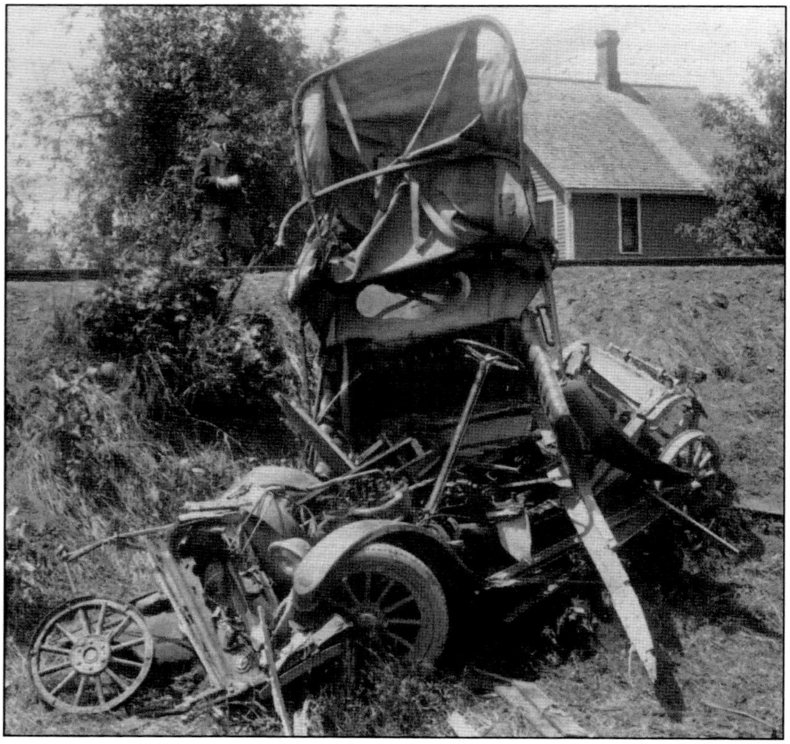

Considerable damage has been done to an automobile struck by a train. In the papers of the time, there are several reports each month of collisions between trains and trucks, cars, pedestrians, and horse-drawn wagons. This led to the development of warning signals replacing the unmarked crossings, or those in the city that had only a man waving a red flag as warning.

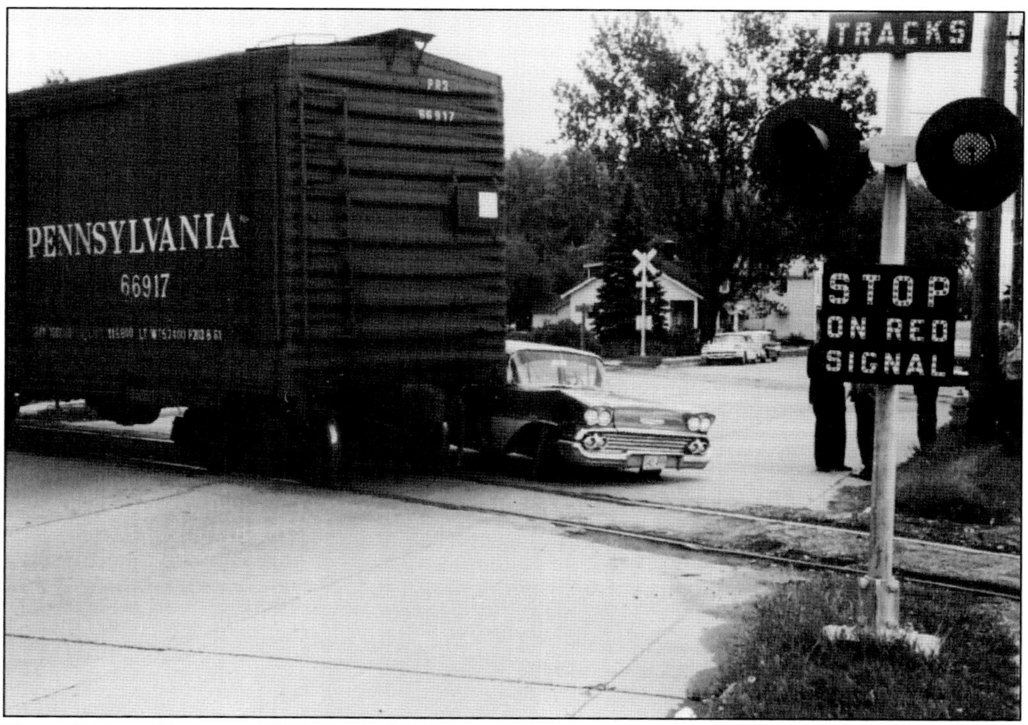

Even the installation of flashing red lights and crossing barriers could not stop accidents. This scene from the 1950s illustrates that there was always at least one driver who was sure he could beat the train to the crossing. This scene would be repeated many times and still occurs today.

Three young ladies await the arrival of their train and enjoy a bit of fun with the photographer. On the platform at their side are several boxes from the Vienna Bakery in Marshfield. Passenger trains often also carried freight and the mail. At smaller villages, the mailbags would be hung from a special arm. A hook on the mail car would pick it up.

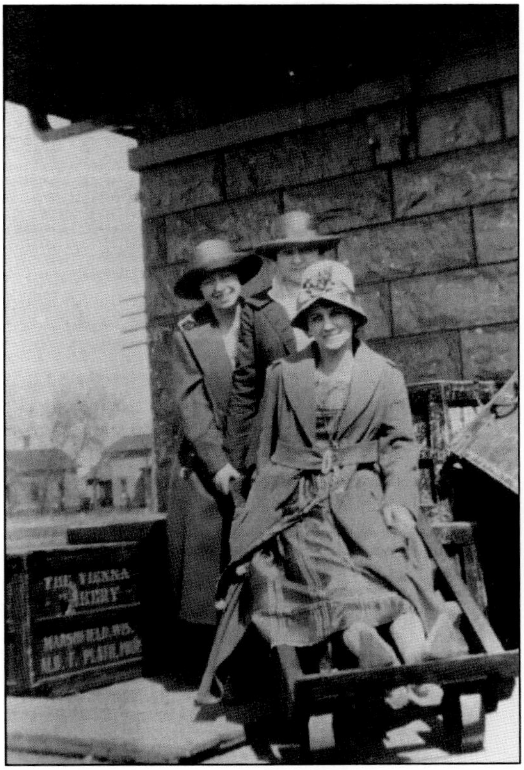

The circus came to town on the railroad. Here, a group of young people get a very close look at the elephants who served both as the star attractions at the Greatest Show on Earth and as the workhorses of the operation, providing the muscle power needed to erect the Big Top.

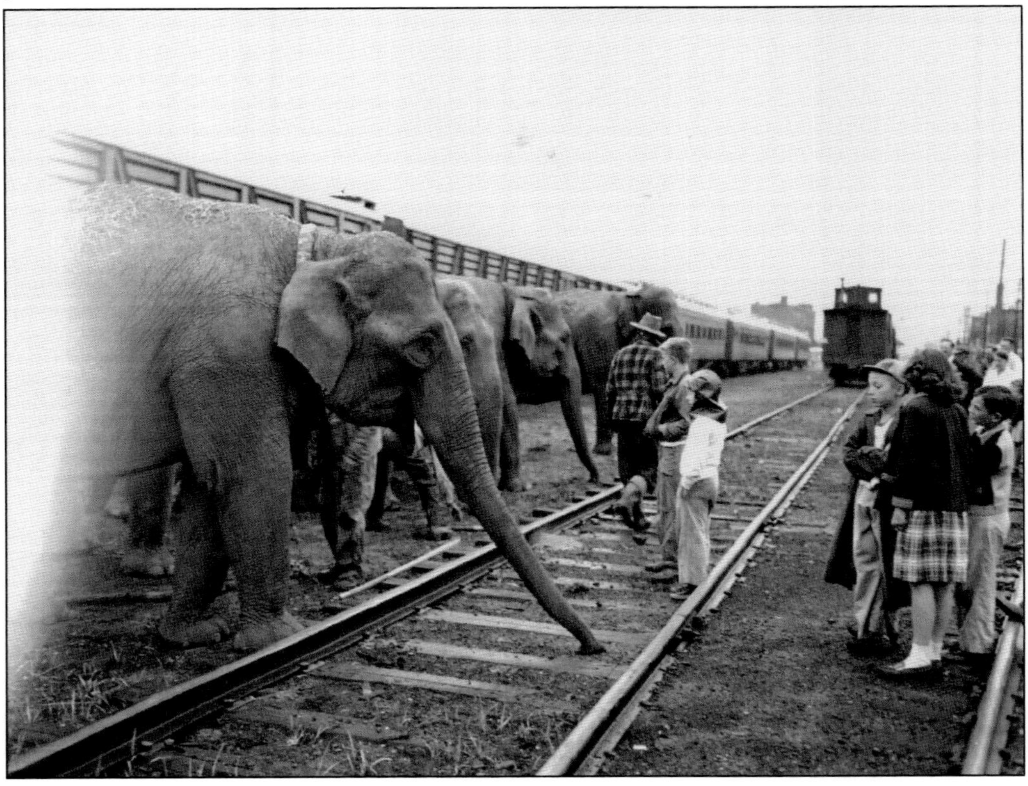

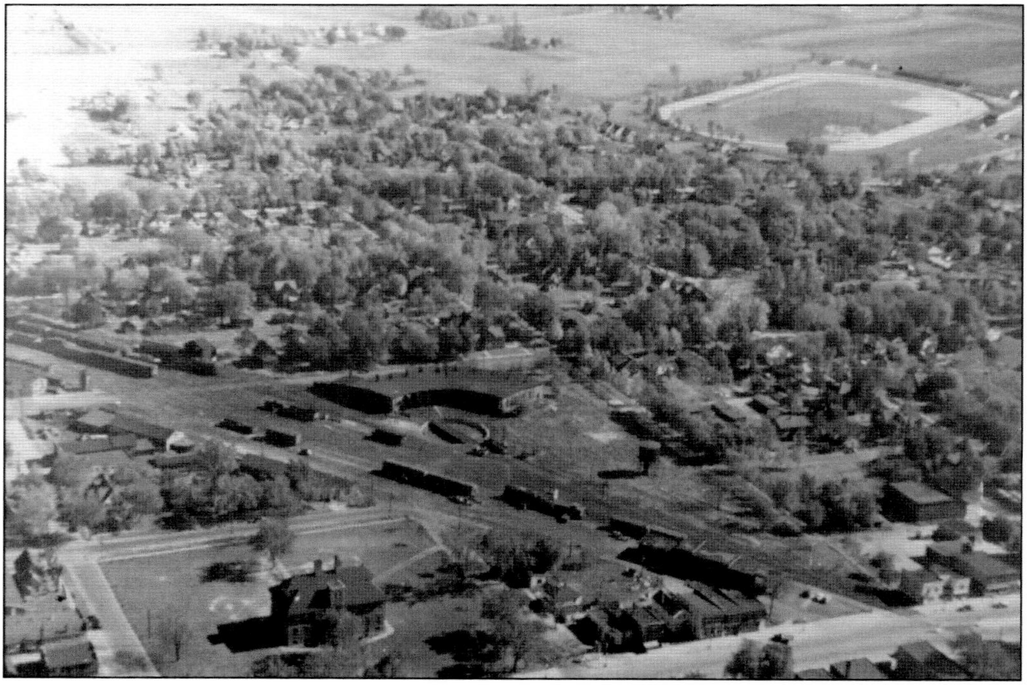

This aerial view, looking to the southeast, shows the large rail yard of the Chicago and North Western system. The roundhouse can be seen at the center. In the upper right are the fairgrounds. The building at lower left in the center of the block known as Washington Square is Washington Elementary School.

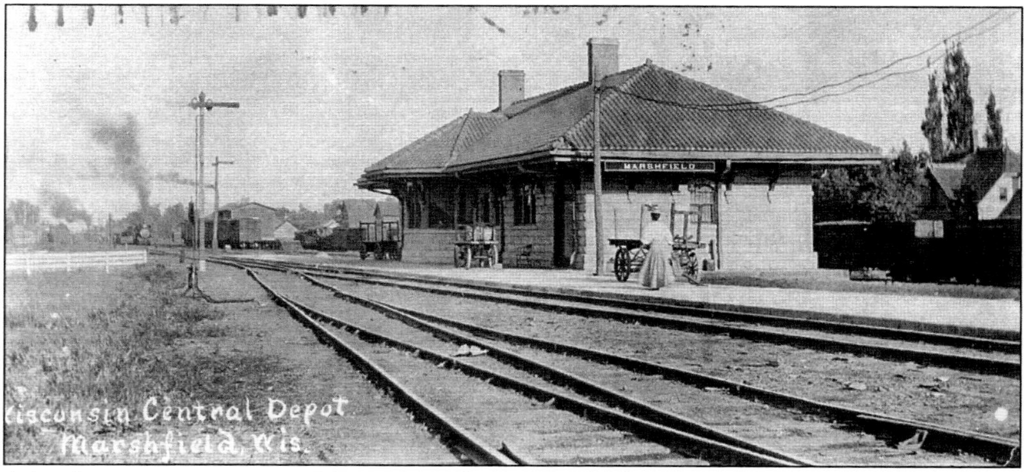

A lonely passenger, in turn-of-the-century dress, waits for the train at the Soo Line depot on the north side of Marshfield. About 60 years later, as passenger service declined, passenger trains no longer stopped in town. Today, the closest passenger service is the Amtrak station in Tomah, some 60 miles to the south.

Two

Logging

Marshfield was located in the center of thousands of acres of virgin timber. The area lacked rivers deep enough to float logs to a sawmill. This prevented early logging of the area. The arrival of the railroad changed this and allowed companies to harvest the natural resource.

North of Marshfield, in what is now the town of McMillan, Marathon County, brothers Benjamin F. and Charles V. McMillan built a sawmill in 1875. Using the railroad they built to Mannville, just west of Marshfield, they shipped their lumber via the Wisconsin Central Railroad to help build cities across Wisconsin. William Upham and his brother Charles arrived in Marshfield in 1878 and set about organizing the village as a central processing location for raw materials from the surrounding forests and shipping the finished products to urban areas across the state. He had built a sawmill in the village of Angelica, located west of Green Bay, prior to coming here. In 1878, he built a sawmill, in 1879 a planing mill, in 1882 a furniture factory, and, most farsighted, a flour and feed mill in 1885 called the Banner Mill. He built the Marshfield and Texas Railroad to access the timber south of town. Later, it transported coal to the powerhouse he built in what is now Wildwood Park.

The tracks south of the city were removed in 1900. By 1899, the timber was gone, the sawmill was closed, and farming had begun. The land surrounding the city was covered with stumps and piles of debris. The new farmers cleared and burned the debris. Dynamite and block and tackle were used to remove the stumps. The land was plowed, and barns were built. The area's dairy industry was about to begin.

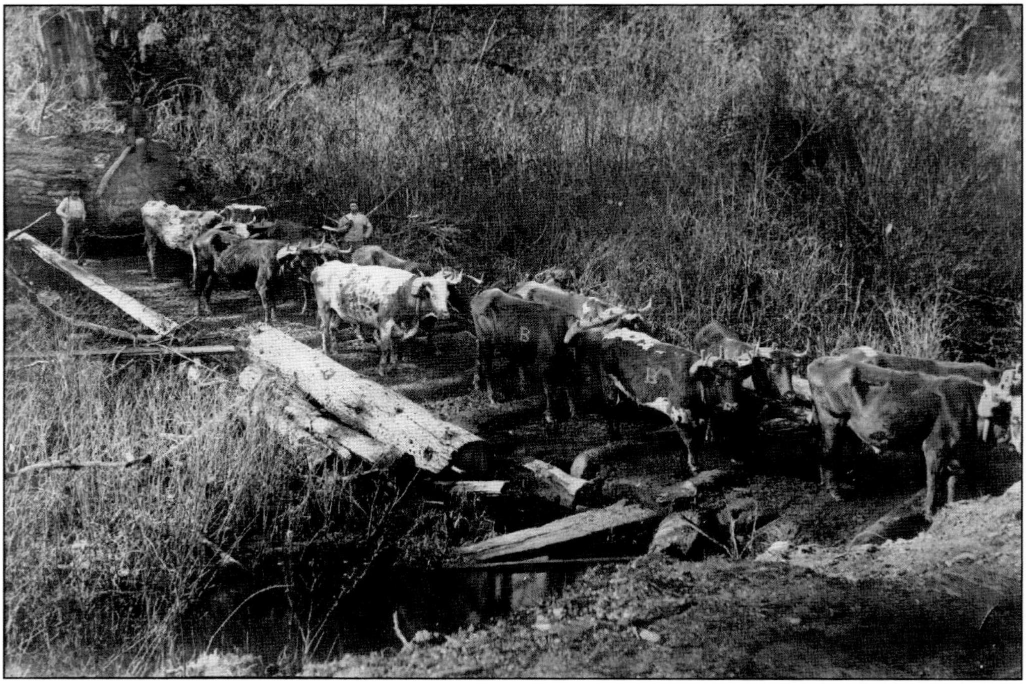

Oxen such as these were a common sight in the lumber camps located throughout Wisconsin, as well as in the Marshfield area. Here, a 12-oxen team drags a 14-foot-diameter tree across a small stream. Trees this size, while not common, were found in the region.

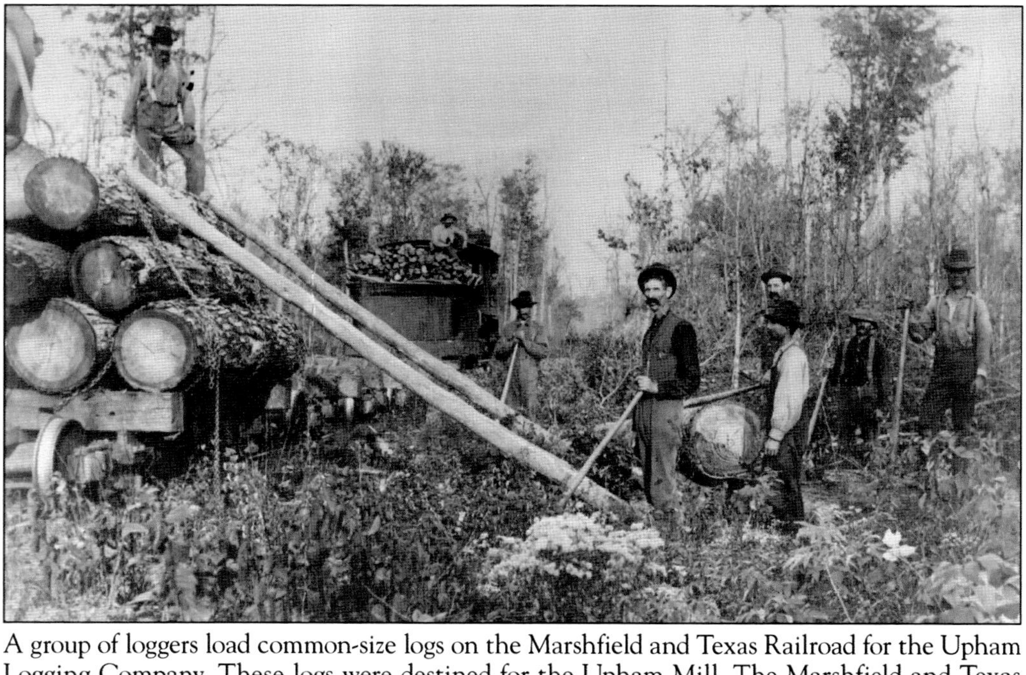

A group of loggers load common-size logs on the Marshfield and Texas Railroad for the Upham Logging Company. These logs were destined for the Upham Mill. The Marshfield and Texas Railroad, a logging railroad, was jointly built by the Upham Manufacturing Company and the Wisconsin Central Railroad. The name came when Upham was asked how far south it would run and said, "Probably to Texas."

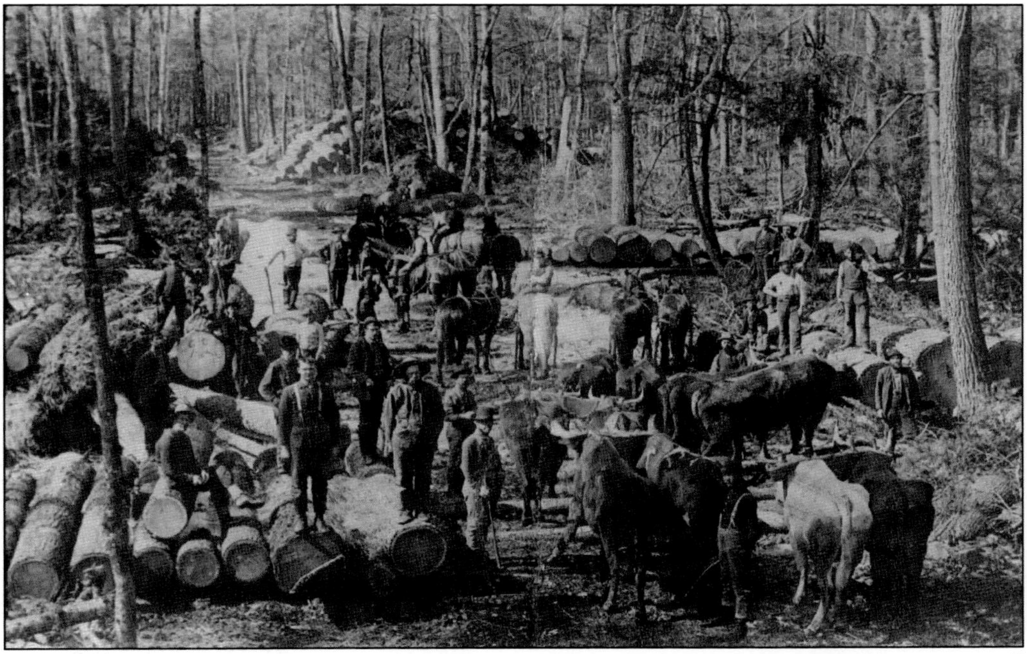

This 1910 logging camp photograph shows little change since the 1880s. Oxen and horses are still the main means of power and logging remains a very labor-intensive activity. It would be several decades before the chainsaw, caterpillar tractor, and the logging truck would replace human and animal power in the forests.

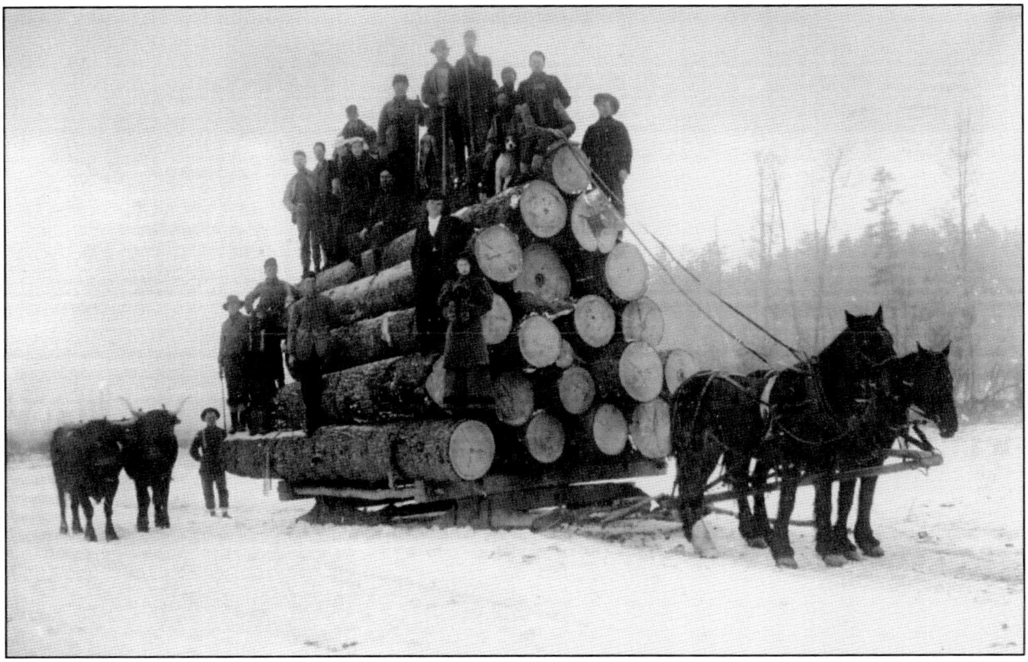

This load belongs to the P. Cramer lumber camp. Each camp competed to deliver the largest load. Next to the oxen at left is Leonard Lang, on top of the load is Carola Wright, seated is Herbert Cramer, the woman is Alice Aliu (Mrs. Hiram Below), Louis Thompson is to the right of the driver, and Frank Herman stands behind him.

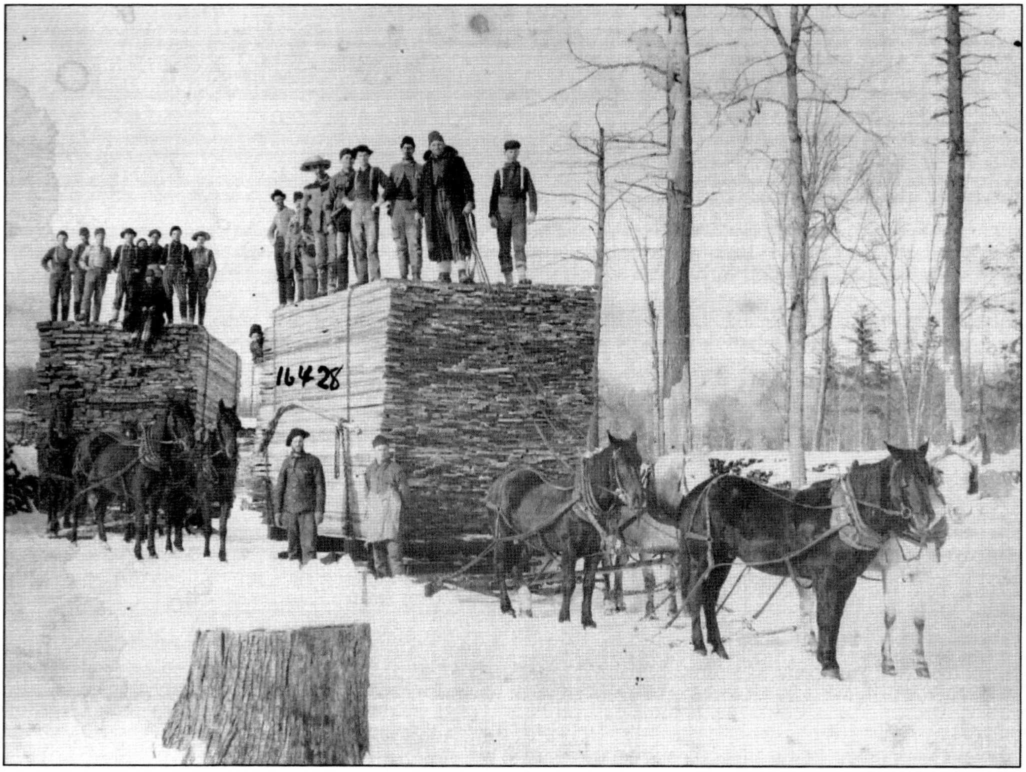

These two sleds of cut lumber belonged to the E.S. Howe Camp. The first sled has 16,428 feet of lumber. Lumber was often stored at the mill site until enough was gathered for an entire trainload for shipment to markets. Most mills had railroad spurs running to them for easier loading and shipment.

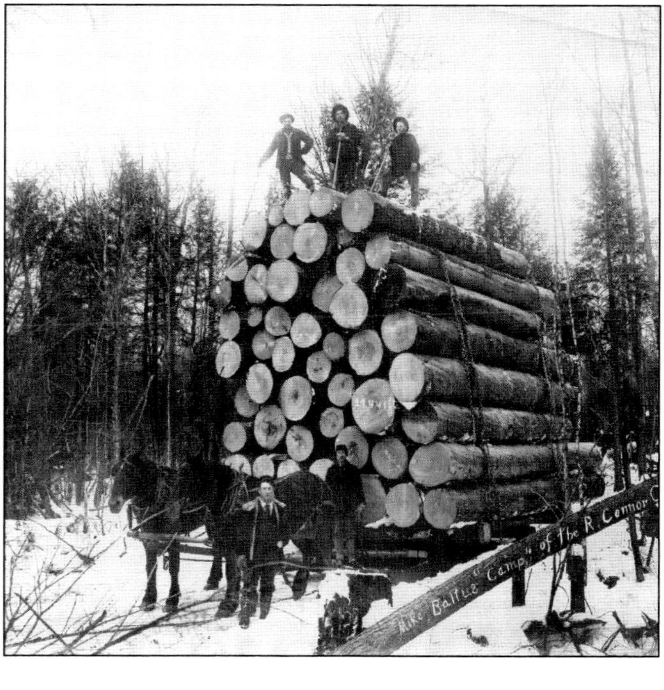

Mike Baltus, in 1910, hauled the largest load of logs in Wisconsin—29,441 feet of hemlock, 18 to 24 feet in length—to R. Connor Camp No. 8, northwest of Rozellville, a small town just northeast of Marshfield. The Connor Company had camps throughout the northeastern area of the state.

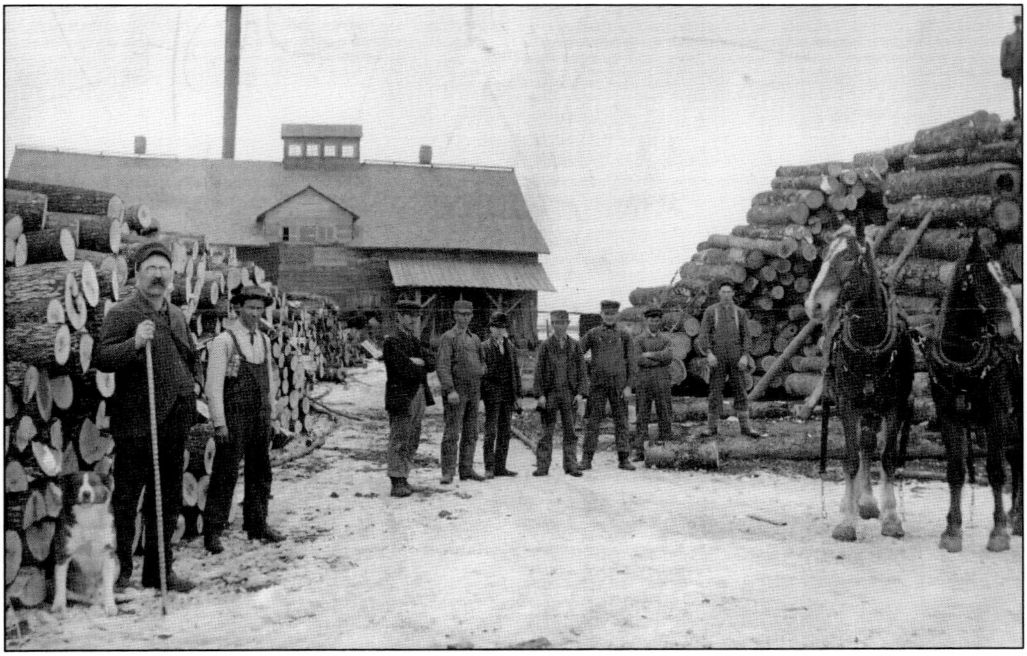

A typical group of men and horses is pictured in the log yard of a sawmill. This scene was echoed at mills throughout the state of Wisconsin. The horses were very well cared for, since they were so valuable and expensive. They often were treated better than the crews who worked with them, as they were harder to replace.

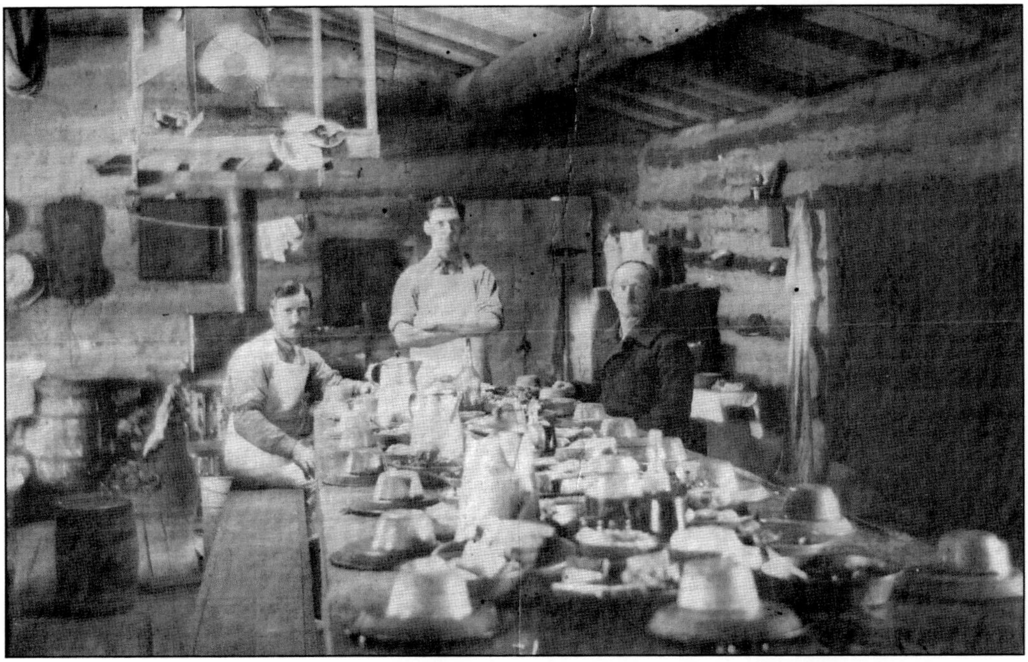

A group of cooks is pictured in a typical logging camp dining hall in 1907. The men were served breakfast at dawn, lunch in the woods (unless they were very close to the camp), and dinner in the evening in the mess hall. Guests could visit but were not allowed to eat at the camp. Complete silence while eating was required.

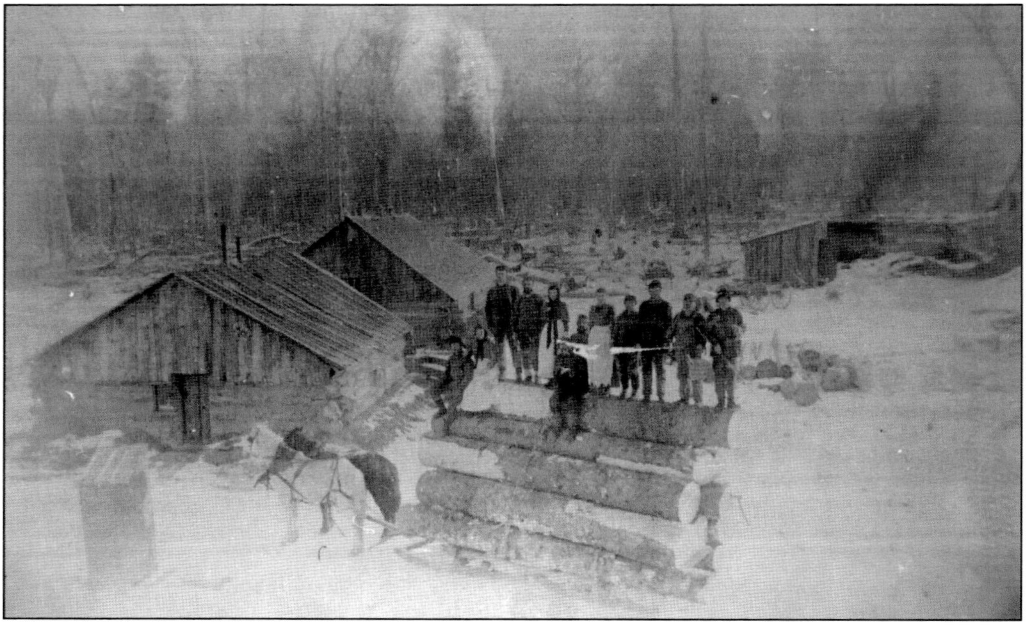

The Hayward logging camp was located just south of Marshfield near the former junction of Highways 10 and 13. The area, locally known as the Teapot Dome corner, was named after a gas station and motel that stood there in the recent past. This area in the town of Richfield had rich stands of timber. The Upham Company's Marshfield and Texas Railroad was built to tap this resource.

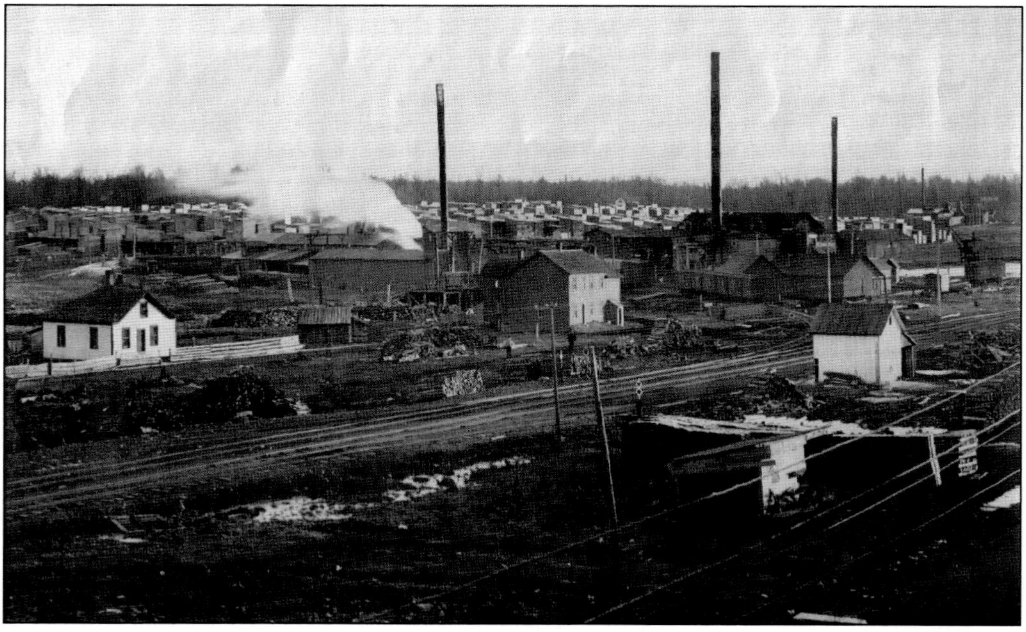

The R. Connor Company mill was built in 1872 in Auburndale, a small town east of Marshfield that was founded by Robert and John Connor. They had immigrated to Canada in 1854 from Scotland. Robert and his brother William came to America to obtain enlistment bounties to fight in the Civil War. They returned to Canada after the war and then migrated to Central Wisconsin in 1872.

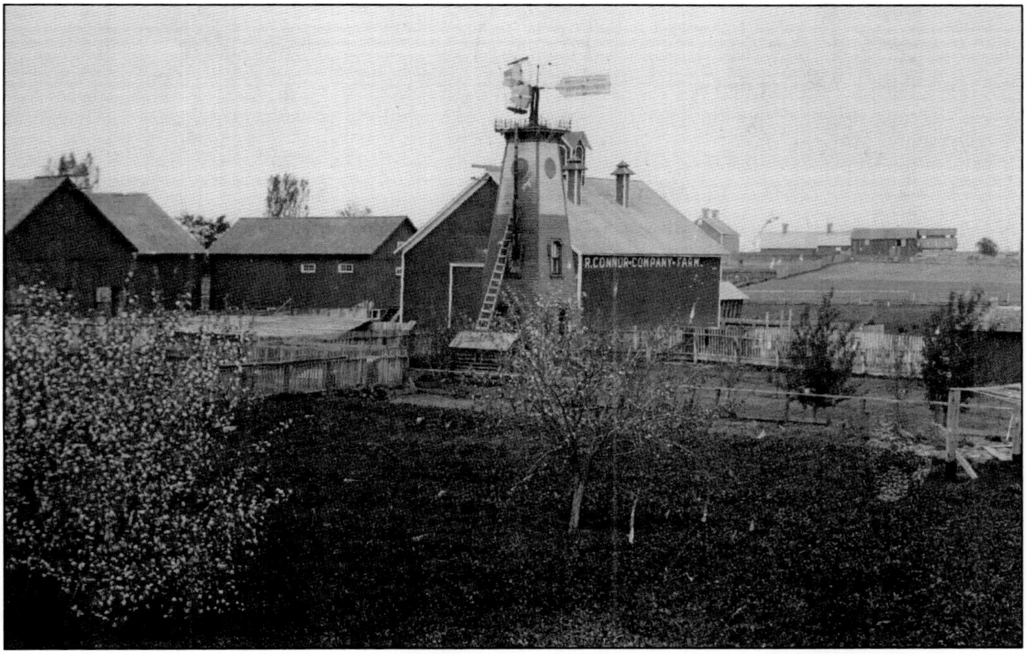

The Connor Company operated its own company farm outside of Auburndale to produce food for its logging camps throughout central and northern Wisconsin. It was a model farm for its era and helped cut the cost of feeding the many logging crews and mill workers in the company's operations.

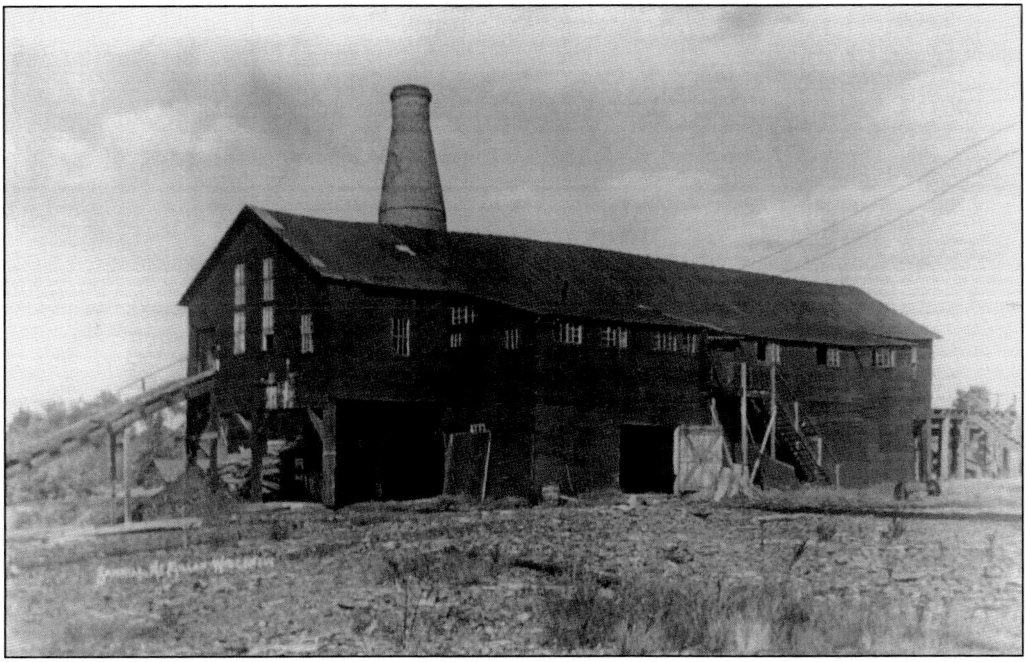
The McMillan Mill was located to the north of Marshfield in what is today the town of McMillan, Marathon County. It was built by Benjamin Franklin (B.F.) and Charles Van Vechten (C.V.) McMillan and operated under the name McMillan Brothers. Construction of the mill was begun in March 1874, and it opened the following year.

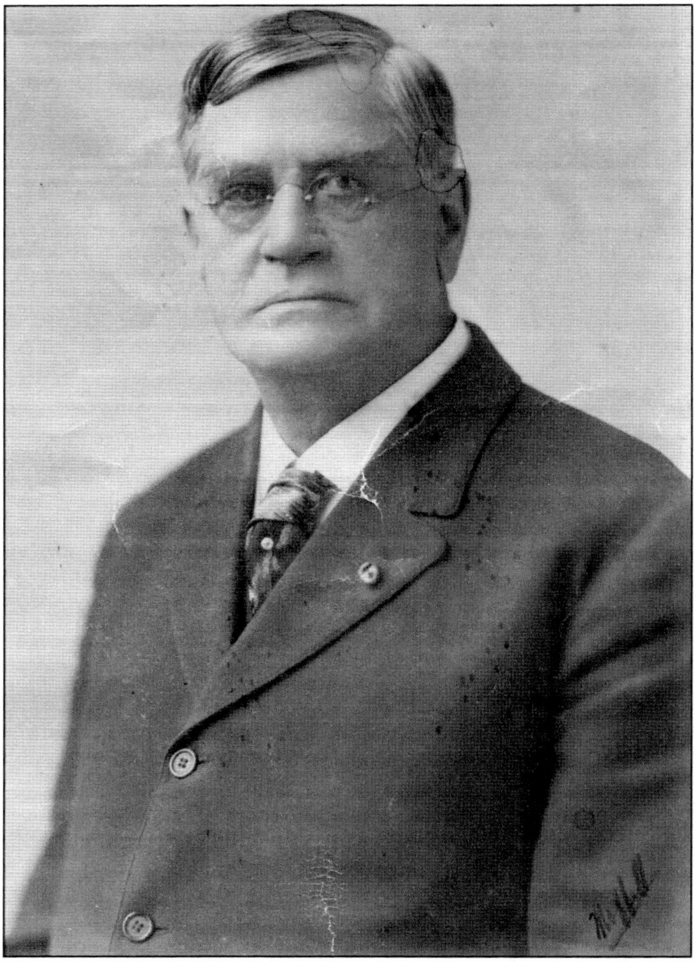

William Upham was a Civil War veteran. He was born in Massachusetts and was a graduate of West Point. He and his brother Charles recognized Marshfield as a central location to convert raw materials from the forests into products for sale in the emerging cities of Wisconsin. They had previously operated a sawmill in Angelica, a small town west of Green Bay.

William Upham built the first sawmill in 1878, which closed in 1893 when the timber was gone. He also built a planing mill in 1879, a furniture factory in 1882, and a flour and feed mill in 1885, recognizing a move to a more civilized era. The days of drunken brawls in the streets, gunplay, and murders were over. Marshfield was becoming a city fit for families.

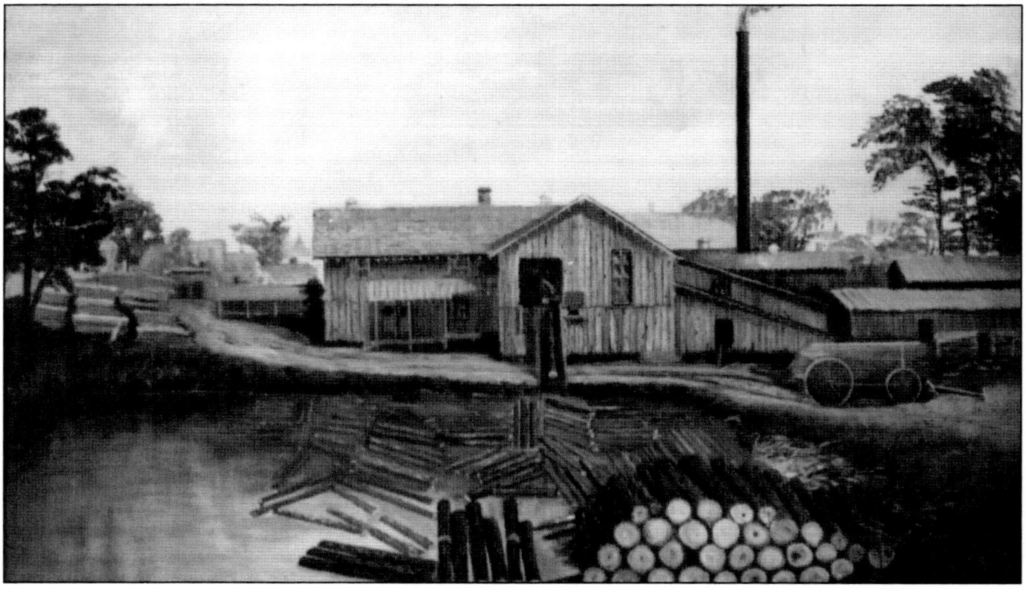

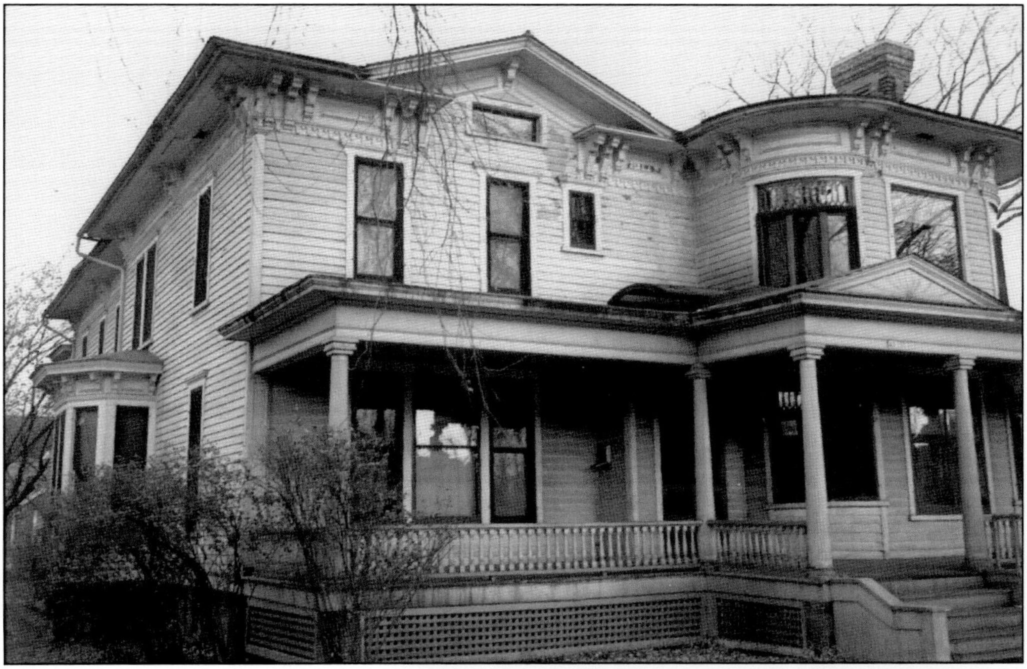

From this home on the corner of West Third Street and South Walnut Avenue, William Upham not only ran his businesses but also entered politics. He served in various local offices including mayor, and in 1895 was elected governor of Wisconsin, serving a single two-year term. It was on this lawn that, after the Great Fire, he symbolically announced that the mill would be rebuilt and the city was saved by raising the American flag.

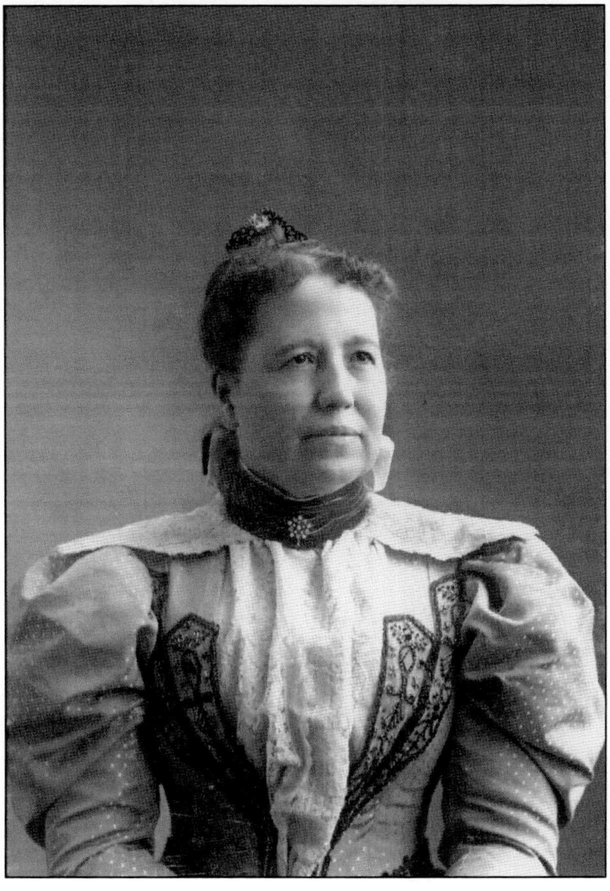

William Upham was married twice. His first wife was Mary Kelly (pictured here), with whom he had two adopted daughters. Mary Kelly died in 1912, and Upham married Grace Mason in 1915. He was 73 and she was 29. They had two sons, Frederick and William H. Junior. William H. Jr. died in 2009. William Sr. died July 2, 1924, and is buried in Marshfield.

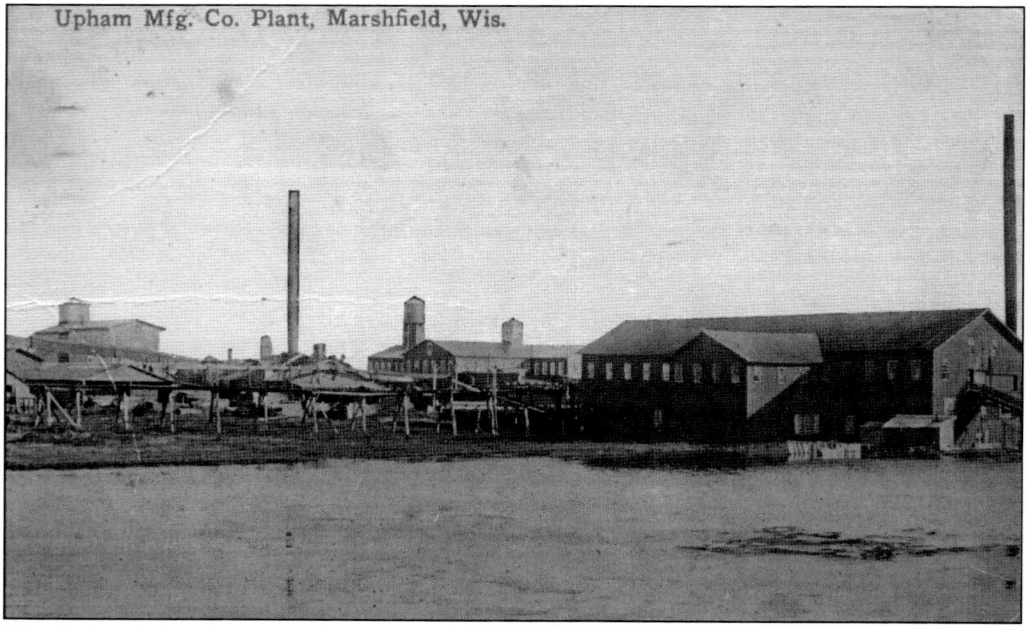

The Upham Manufacturing Company and Saw Mill was located in Marshfield in the area today known as Hackman Athletic Field and the Oak Avenue Community Center, better known locally as the "Old Armory." This plant produced lumber and furniture. The railroad spur ran from the Wisconsin Central main line south to the mill. The spur was later continued south along Oak and Spruce Avenues to the town of Richfield.

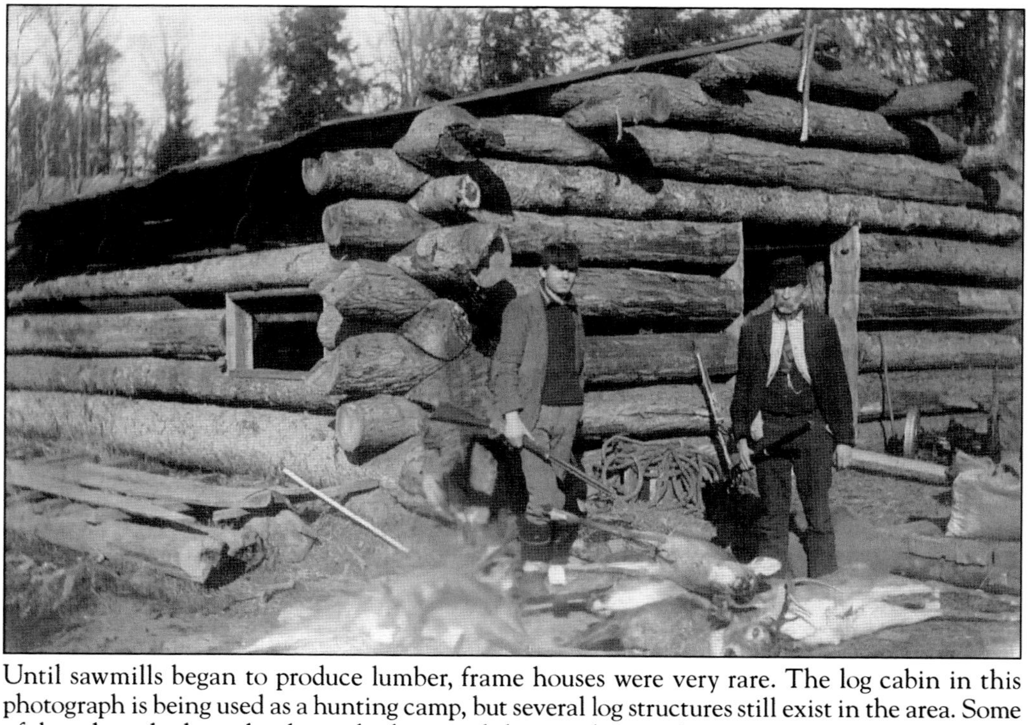

Until sawmills began to produce lumber, frame houses were very rare. The log cabin in this photograph is being used as a hunting camp, but several log structures still exist in the area. Some of them have had another house built around them and are no longer visible. Most disappeared by the first decade of the 20th century.

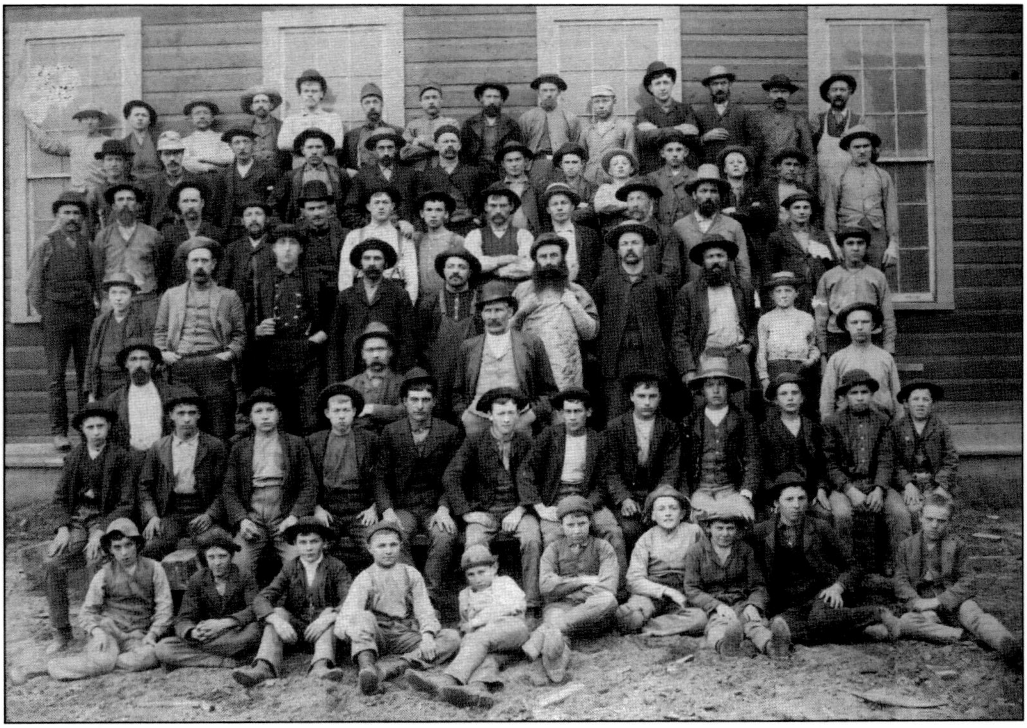

Pictured is a typical plant crew from around the beginning of the 20th century. Note the ages of the workers in the first two rows. Obviously, this was before child labor laws. Since saws and power belts were not required to have safety features, the loss of fingers, toes, arms, and legs, as well as death from the saws was not uncommon. Often, injured workers were fired for being unable to work.

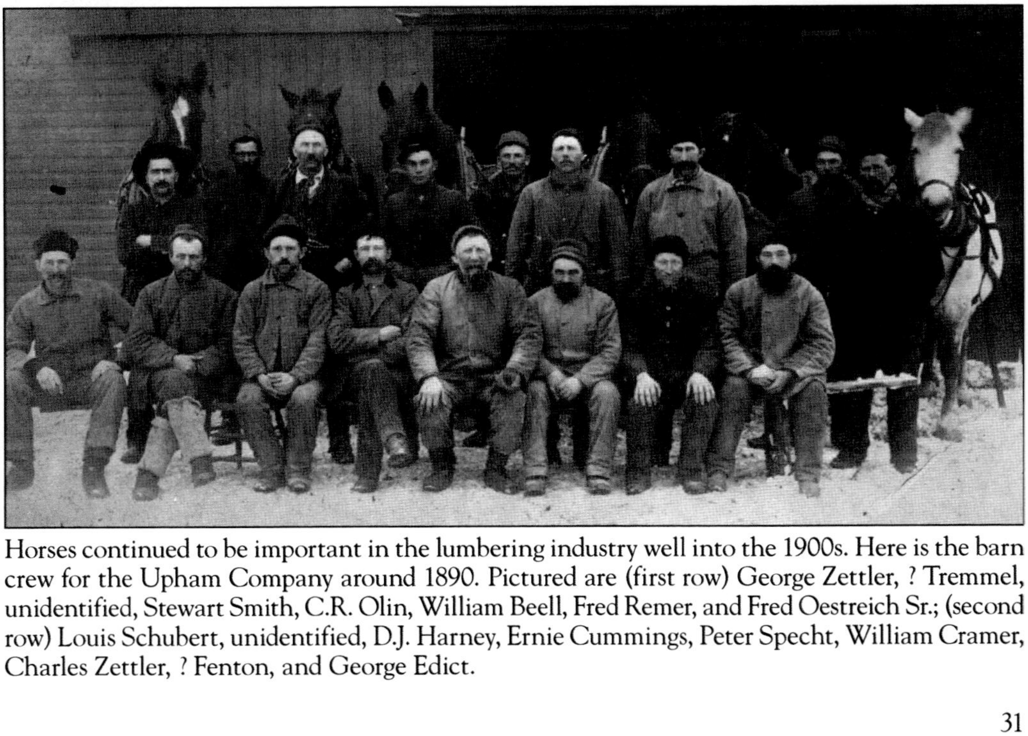

Horses continued to be important in the lumbering industry well into the 1900s. Here is the barn crew for the Upham Company around 1890. Pictured are (first row) George Zettler, ? Tremmel, unidentified, Stewart Smith, C.R. Olin, William Beell, Fred Remer, and Fred Oestreich Sr.; (second row) Louis Schubert, unidentified, D.J. Harney, Ernie Cummings, Peter Specht, William Cramer, Charles Zettler, ? Fenton, and George Edict.

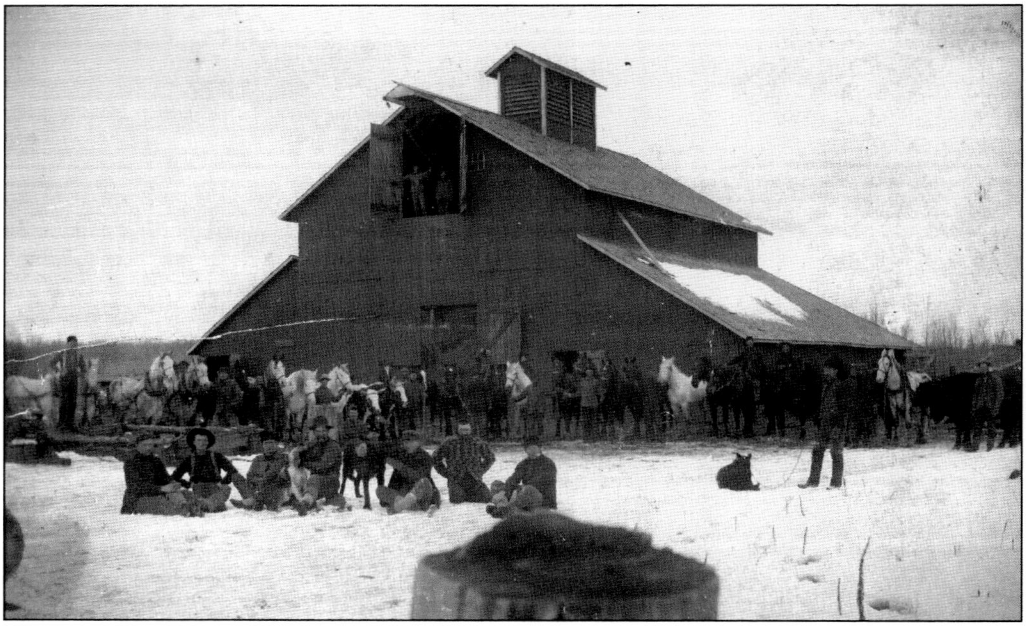

The horse barn for the Upham Mill was located to the east of the Marshfield Milling Company. Note both the number of horses being held by the barn and the size of the structure. Its location near the milling company did help with the procurement of some feed, but other feed had to be grown on local farms.

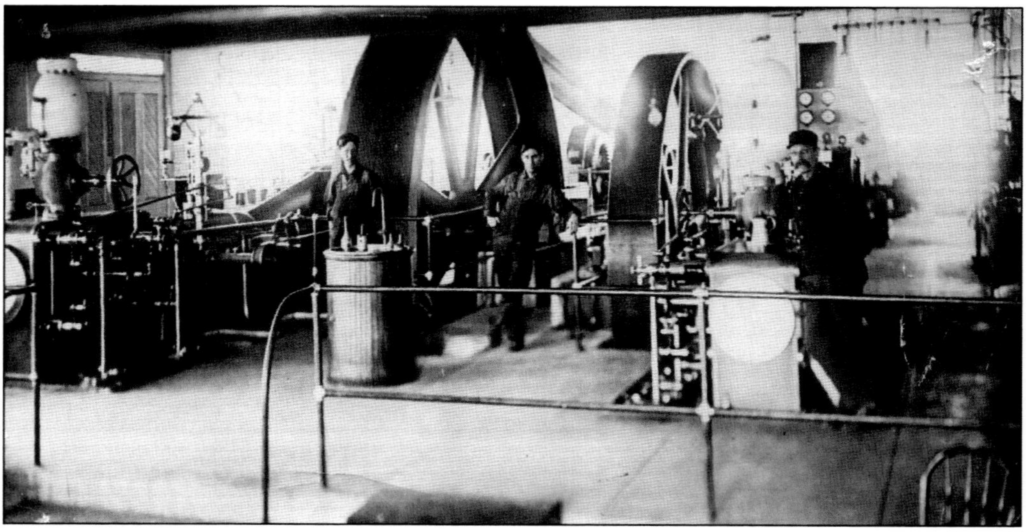

The Upham Manufacturing Company had its own electric power plant. In 1892, a waterworks franchise was awarded to Upham, and the privately owned Marshfield Water, Electric Light & Power Company was born. After a court battle, the city purchased the company from the Upham family in 1904. Eventually, the Department of Public Works was formed to operate it. In 1907, electric service was available throughout the city, but only during daylight hours.

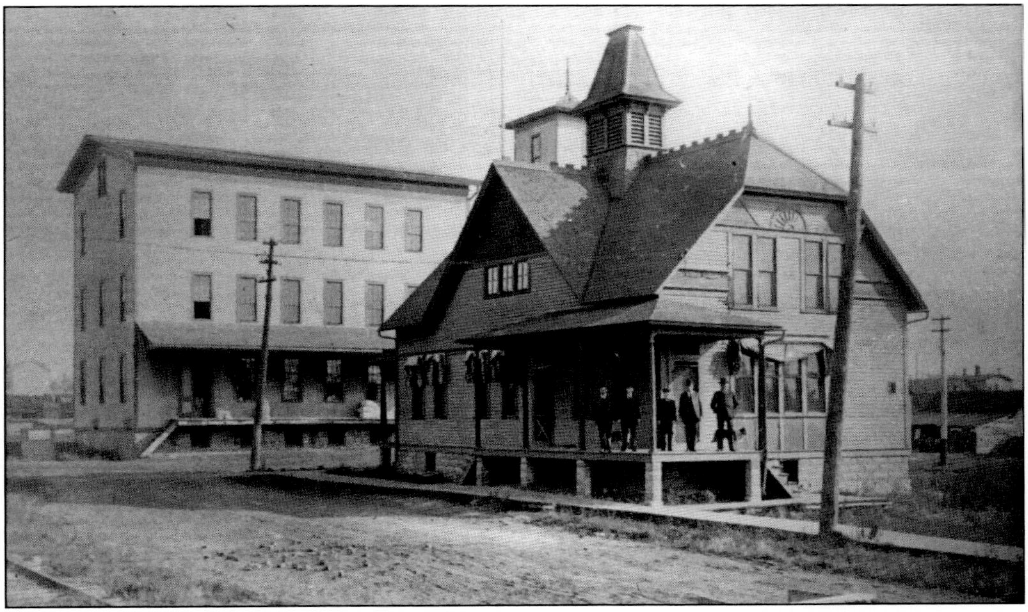

The Upham offices were located near the Banner Mill on West Third Street. The men on the porch are not identified. The office had been a schoolhouse located at the southeastern corner of Arnold and Chestnut Streets, across from today's Columbia Park.

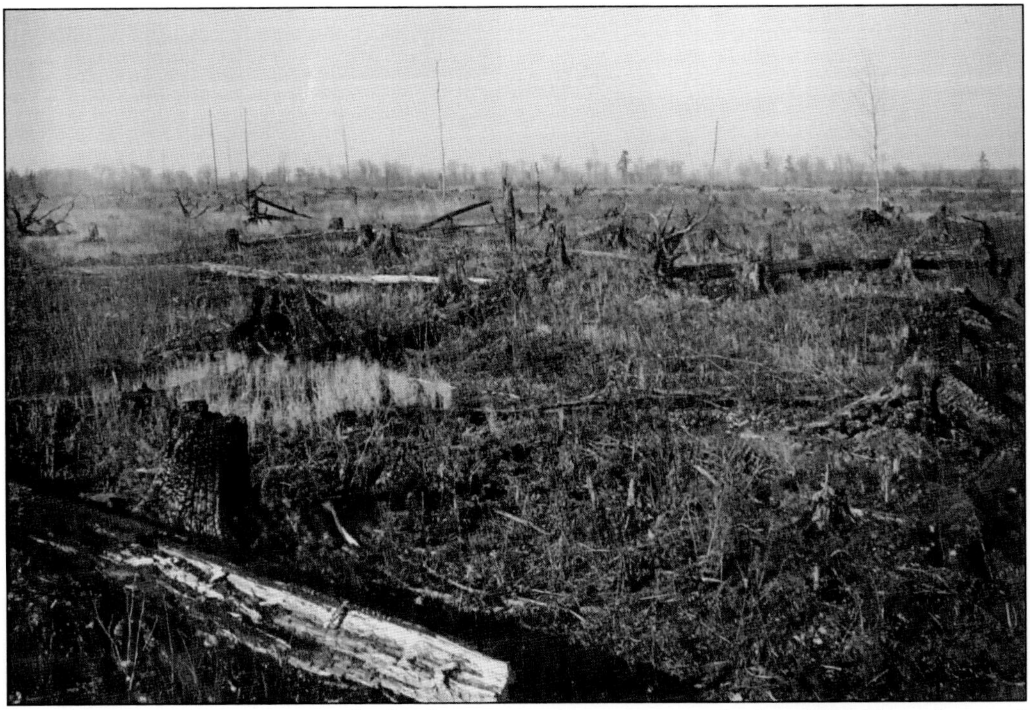

By 1899, the timber was gone. The land was covered in stumps and piles of dead branches, and other waste was left behind by the loggers. The Upham Sawmill in Marshfield closed, and the enterprise turned to the manufacture of finished products, such as furniture, and a feed mill. The logger was soon to be replaced by the farmer. Other agricultural-based businesses began to appear.

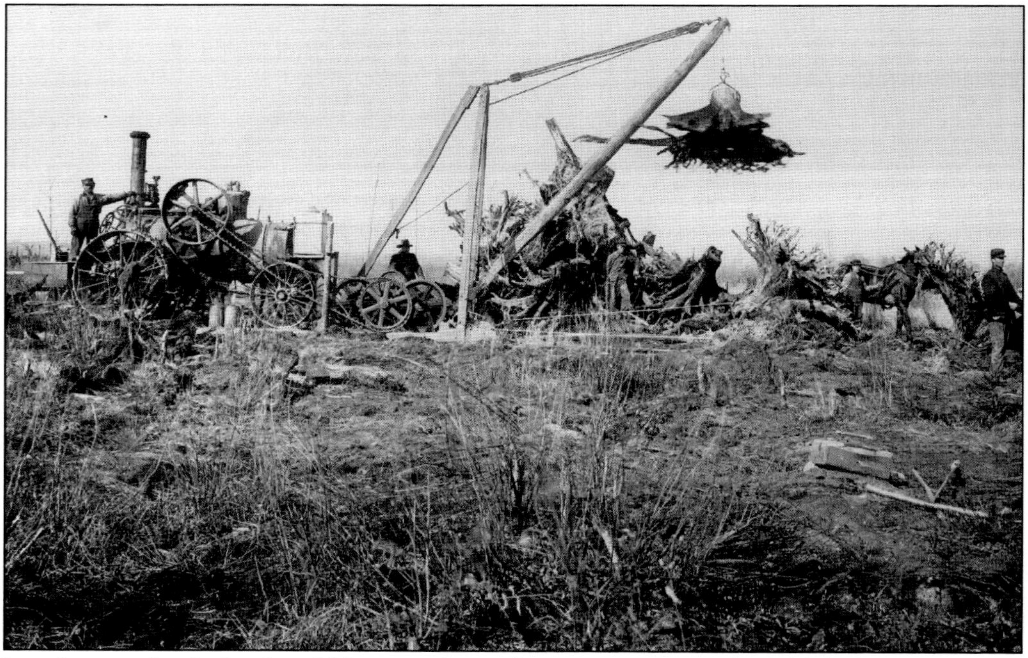

In order to make the land useful for agriculture, the stumps covering the fields had to be removed. This required a great deal of manual labor. Roots would be cut, block and tackle attached to the stump, and a team of horses or oxen would attempt to pull out the stump. Often, dynamite was used. The local papers regularly carried stories of loss of life or limb from the explosions.

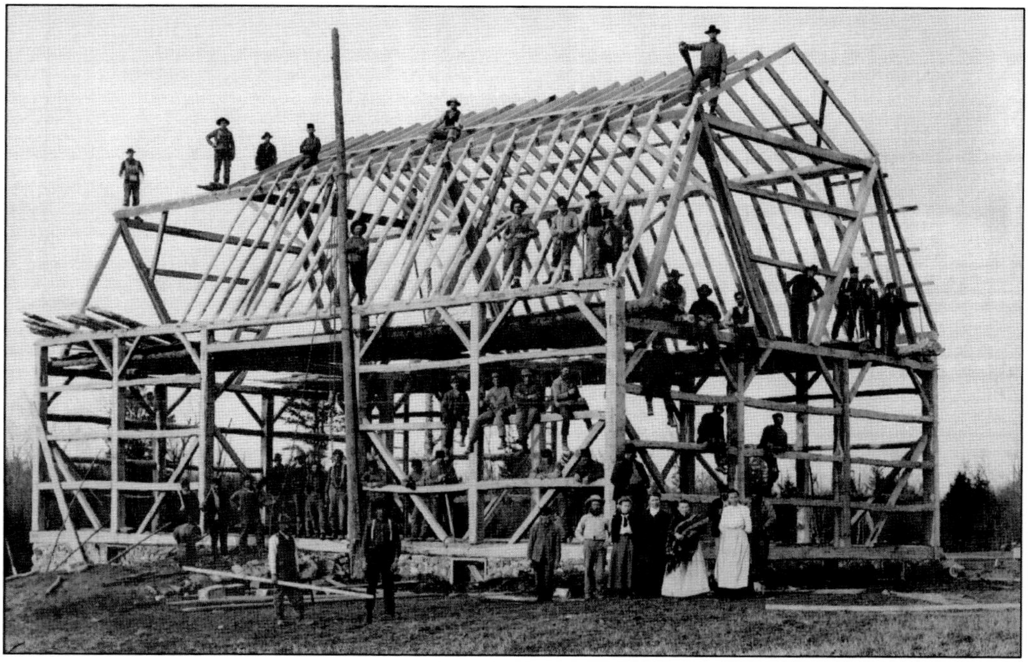

Then came the barn raising, an example of the cooperation between the farmers who moved into an area. All gathered together to help each other out and have fun while doing it. Often a barn dance would be held when the new structure was completed. Today, this activity can still be seen from time to time in the area as the Amish farmers come together to help each other out.

Three

Social Life and Recreation

The city grew from its rough beginnings as a male-dominated lumber town and began to take on a bit most sophistication, but some of the rough-and-tumble fun remained. New cultural groups began to appear throughout the city on all social levels.

The German heritage of the majority of the population was reflected in the men's singing group the Maennerchor, whose members met and performed regularly at the Sanger Hall. The women had several art groups, and the Fortnightly Women's Musical Club put on plays and operettas. There were groups for young women and men as well that celebrated the arts.

Various fraternal organizations for both men and women grew in popularity. There were chapters of the Elks, Eagles, Knights of Columbus, Modern Woodmen of America, and Masons for the men. The women belonged to the Eastern Star, Jobs Daughters, Royal Neighbors of America, and the Daughters of the American Revolution.

The high school offered drama clubs, class plays, band, debate teams, and other forms of activities beyond the school day that would expand the horizon of the students.

The physical aspect of recreation was not overlooked. Various sports teams were created, both in the schools and among the adults. These included baseball, football, and basketball in the high school. Later, hockey entered the picture at the senior high school. Boxing was also a very popular sport, and bouts were regularly held at the armory and in several rings in the basements of taverns along Central Avenue. There was a Golden Gloves competition in town and a boxing club at the high school. Roller-skating and ice-skating were both very popular, and a toboggan run was built in one of the parks for the use of the adults.

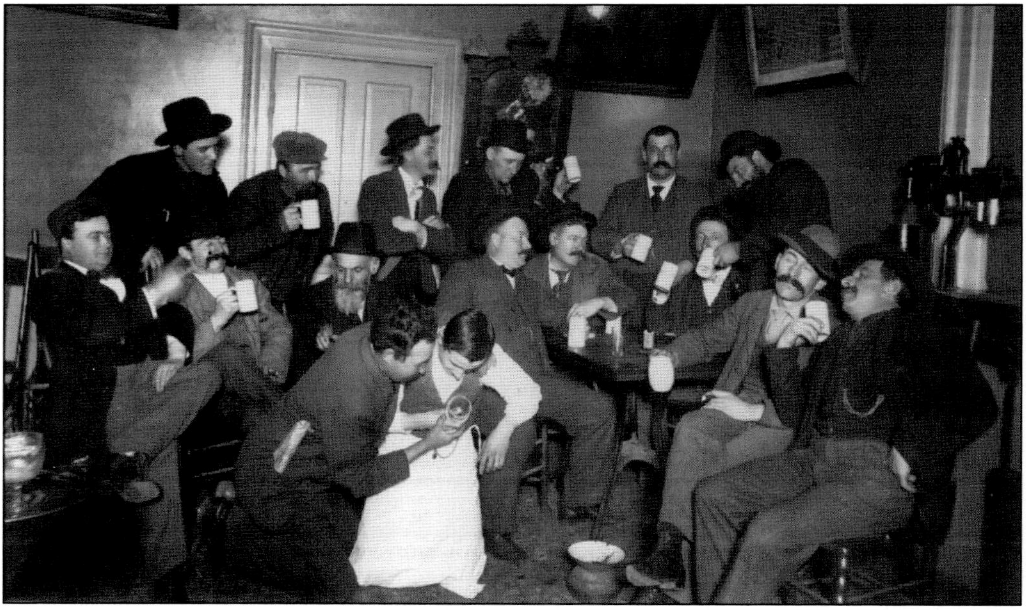

Baumann's was one of the most popular places in town and, as can be seen, it was a place for fun. Pictured in June 1901 are (first row, seated) Joe Morel, Nic Ludovic, Herman Pankow, Emil Scheibe, George Zettler, and Gus Laschinski; (second row) Jake Kuehmichel, John Thereof, Joe Pflum, Lou Baumann, and J. Christ Dorpat.

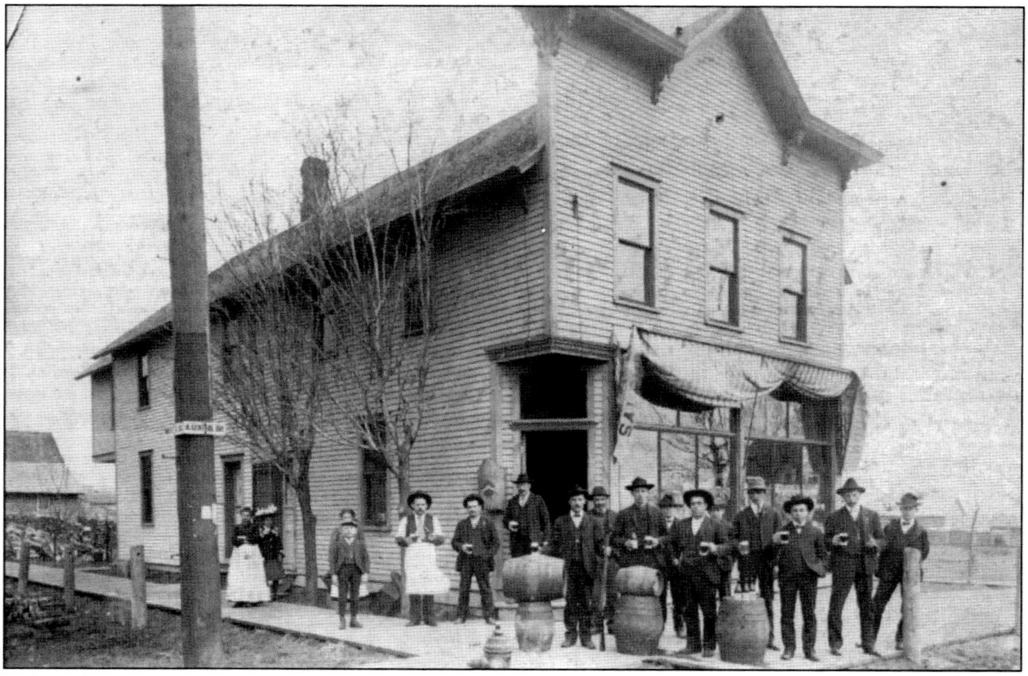

Rebsteck's Saloon was located farther north on Central Avenue. It also drew a large and fun-seeking crowd. Each block of Central Avenue, both north and south, hosted a saloon, and many more were located a block or two off the main business district. There were sample rooms connected with the various hotels. Some of the fraternal groups located their meeting halls on the second floors of the saloon buildings.

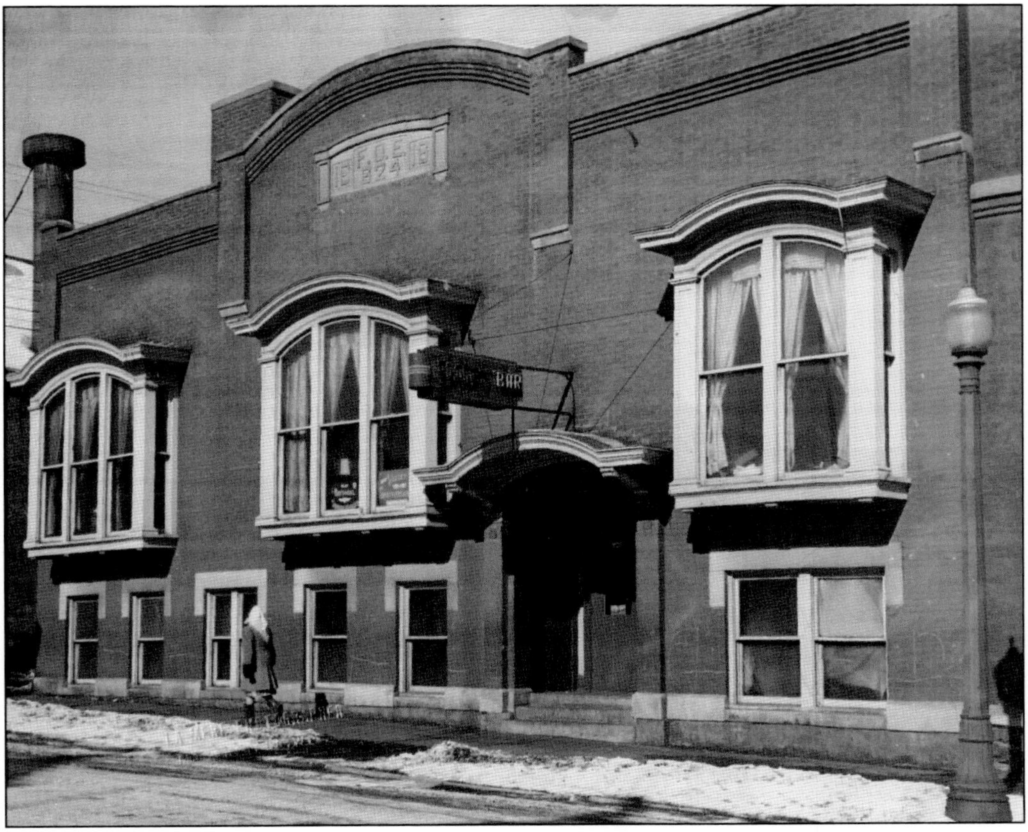

Fraternal organizations for men also began to appear in the late 19th and early 20th centuries. One was the Eagles club, at one time located in this building between the Elks Club and Adler's Opera House on East Second Street. Featuring a hall, bowling alley, and swimming pool, this facility was enjoyed over the years by many other groups, including square dance clubs, for their activities.

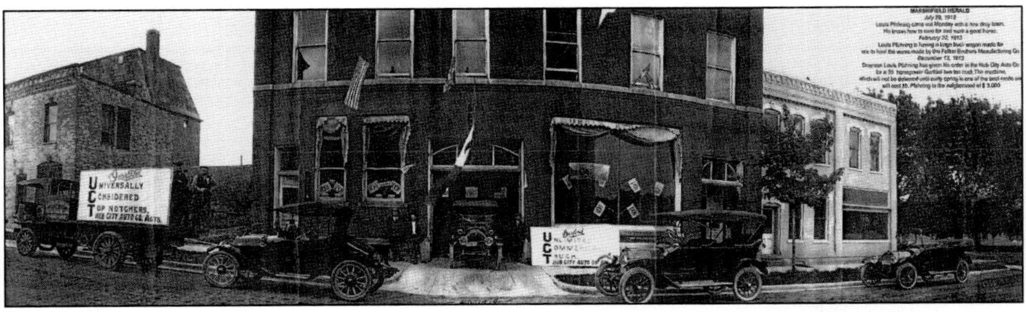

This 1919 photograph shows two fraternal groups, the Elks and the Eagles, separated by the Louis Pfahning Truck Company. On the floor over the Pfahning Company was a roller-skating rink. The building to the far left is the Adler Opera House, which featured many of the big names in vaudeville who frequently passed through town on one of the many passenger trains.

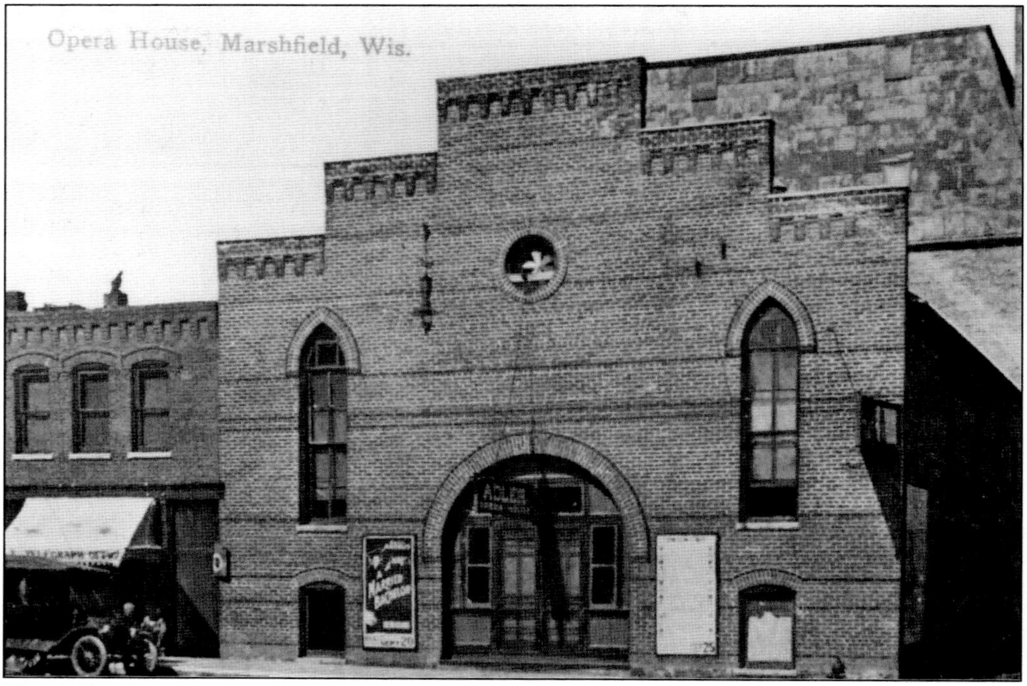

The Adler Opera House was built in 1896–1897 by Philip Adler. An organ was installed in 1922 to accompany silent movies. Among the young performers traveling in road shows appearing there were John Barrymore, Boris Karloff, Frank McHugh, William Desmond, Charles Winninger (a local boy from Athens, Wisconsin), and Mary Robson. Movies were no longer shown there after 1955, and the opera house was razed in 1964.

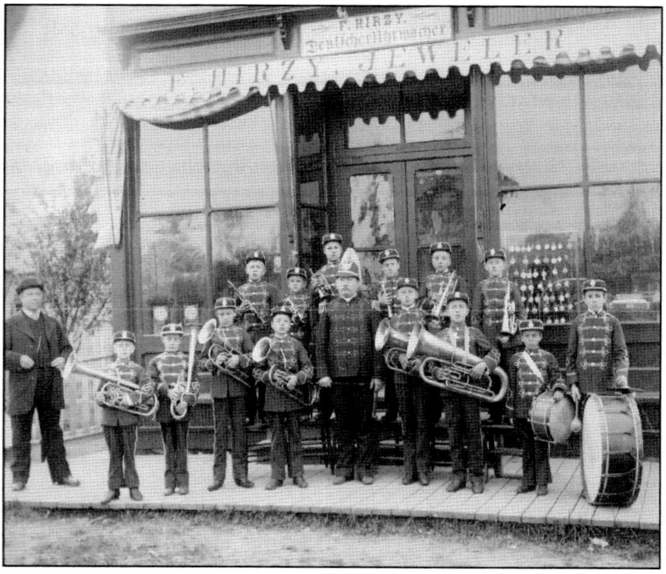

Ferdinand Hirzy was an experienced watchmaker and music master who came to Marshfield from Hungary in 1886. He opened a watch and musical instrument shop. In 1891, he organized a "juvenile band." Pictured from left to right are (first row) Joseph Mettelka, Arthur Warnecke, Otto Warnecke, John Jaeckel, Frank Mettelka, Ferdinand Hirzy, unidentified, Robert Krohn, Eddie Eckhoff, and Frank Schuh; (second row) Alex Krohn, Theodore Steinmetz, Tony Mettelka, Otto Eckhoff, Henry Brockman, and Wendel Krohn.

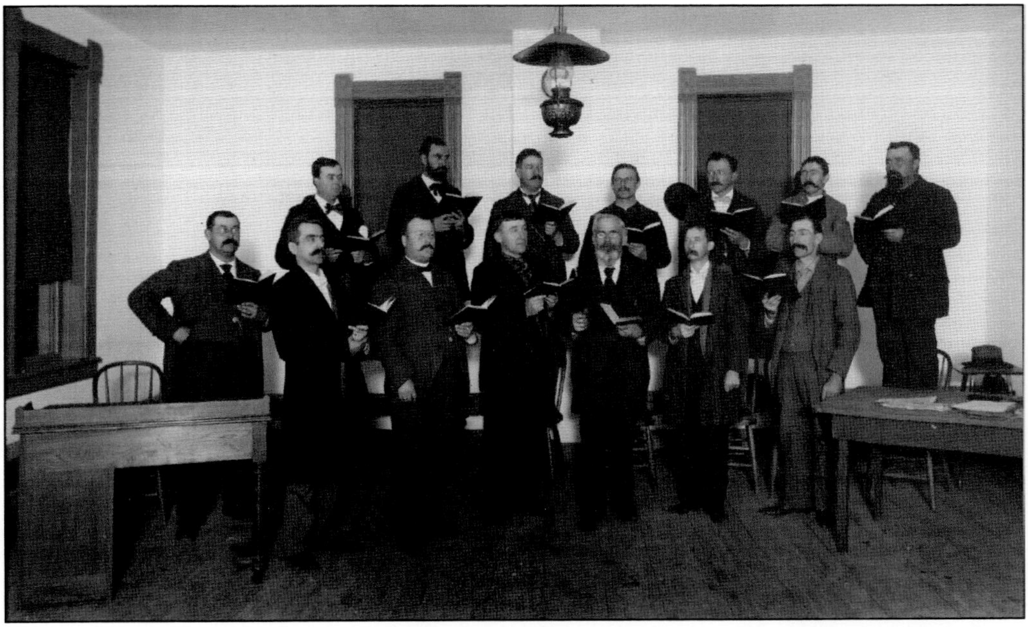

The Marshfield Maennerchor was organized in 1896 and met upstairs at Baumann's Hall, above the tavern, which became known as Sanger-Halle. The members pictured here include, from left to right, (first row) Louis Baumann, M.J. Kraus, Ferdinand Hirzy, Joseph Pflum, H.J. Pankow (director), John Therolf, and George Zettler; (second row) J.H. Morel, J.C. Dorpat, A.G. Pankow, Gus Laschinski, Emil P. Scheibe, Nic Ludovic, and Jacob Kuehmichel.

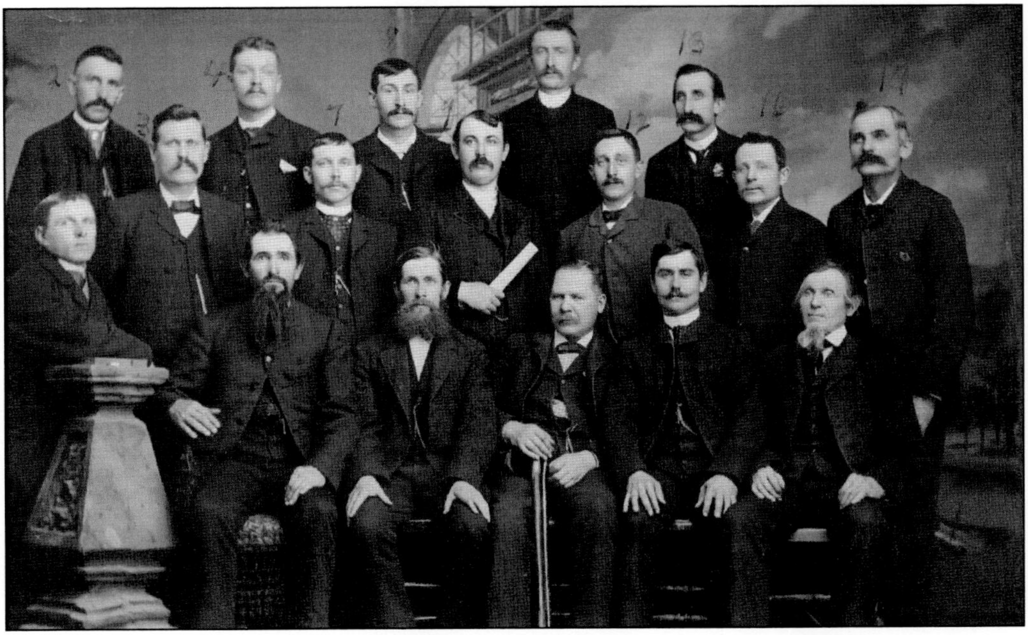

According to the caption, this photograph of the Maennerchor was taken in 1889. The members are listed from left to right as (first row) Albert Radloff, August Berlin, John Schauer, Carl Marquardt, and Carl Thom; (second row) Gust Luschinski, Albert Gerwing, Albert Kisten, Reverend Thom, August Schauer, Herman Kekrberg, and H.J. Pankow; (third row) John Eckhof, A.G. Pankow, George Zeutler, Gust Karow, and F.L. Luerders.

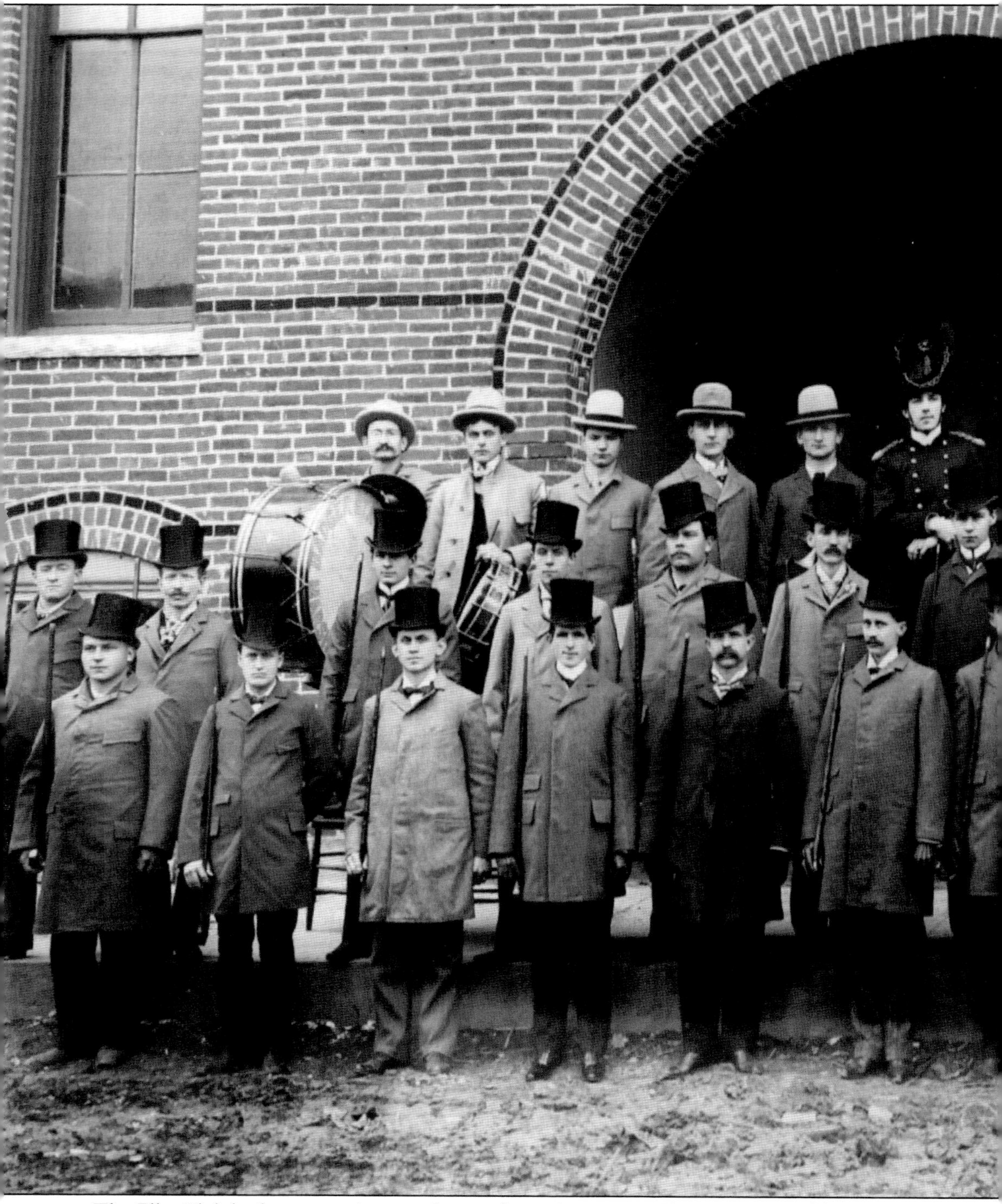

The Elks Club had a minstrel group that performed on stage. They are pictured here in front of the Adler Opera House on East Second Street in 1898. From left to right are (first row) Fred Beell, Lacy Gwin, John Hartl, Frank Sinclair, Will Kamps, Charles Benlick, Andrew Nelson, Arnold Voelker, Dr. H.A. Lathrop, John P. Hume, Edward F. McIntyre, and Prof. A.D. Adams; (second row) Cully Mess, Fred Kamps, Willard White, Dan White, Archibald Bouldrie, unidentified, Will

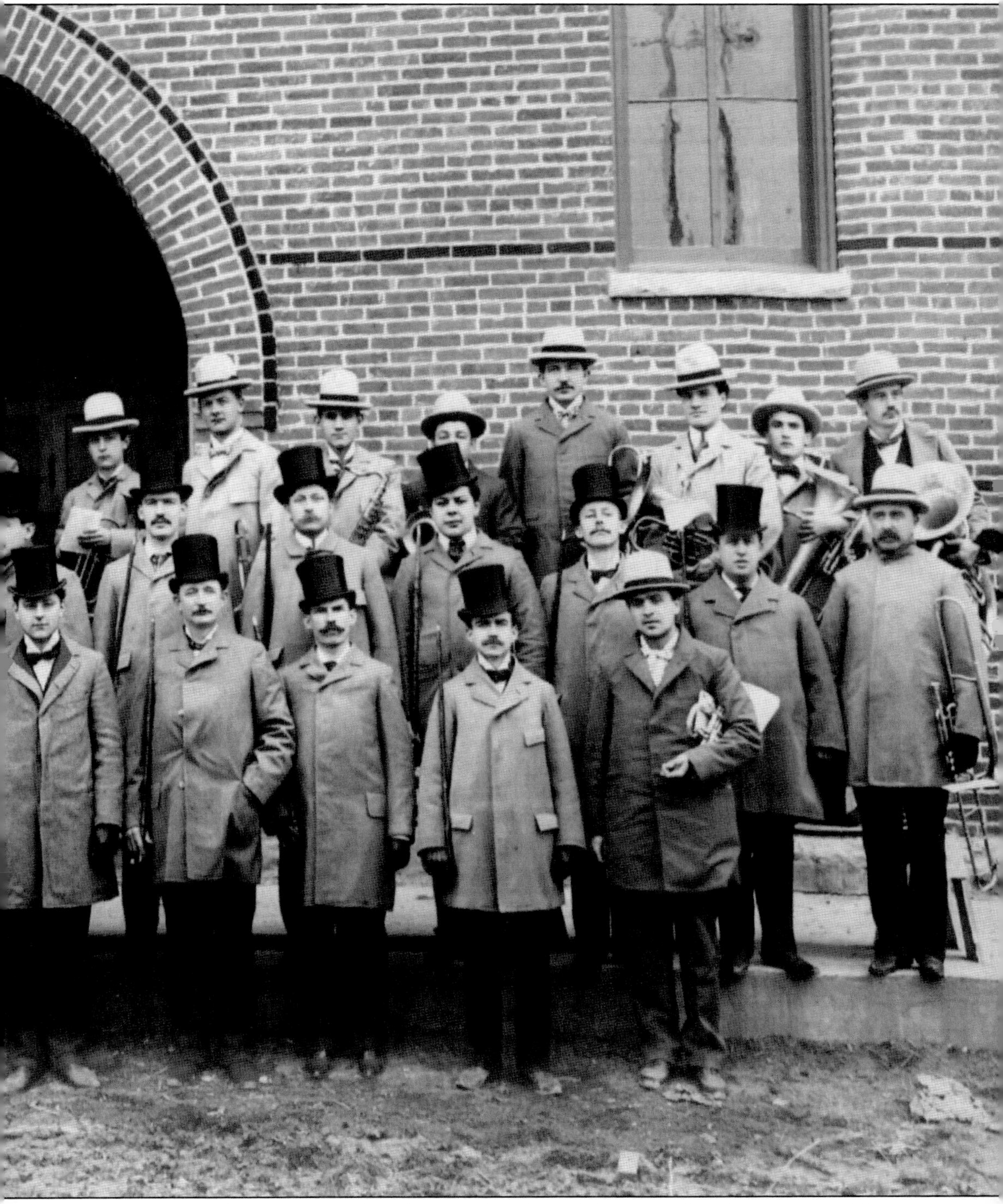

Wheeler, Adam Paulus, Angus Udell, Ed Finney, Joe Hafer, John L. Voelker, Ed Reese, and Harry Ferguson; (third row) Claude Semmes, Bob Degroff, unidentified, Jim Vaughn, Frank Zweck, John Stierle, Peter Hanson, unidentified, John L. Nelson, Andrew Rumenopp, Mose Lupient, Herman Bartell, Fred Kohl, Frank Pflum, and W.A. Drumb.

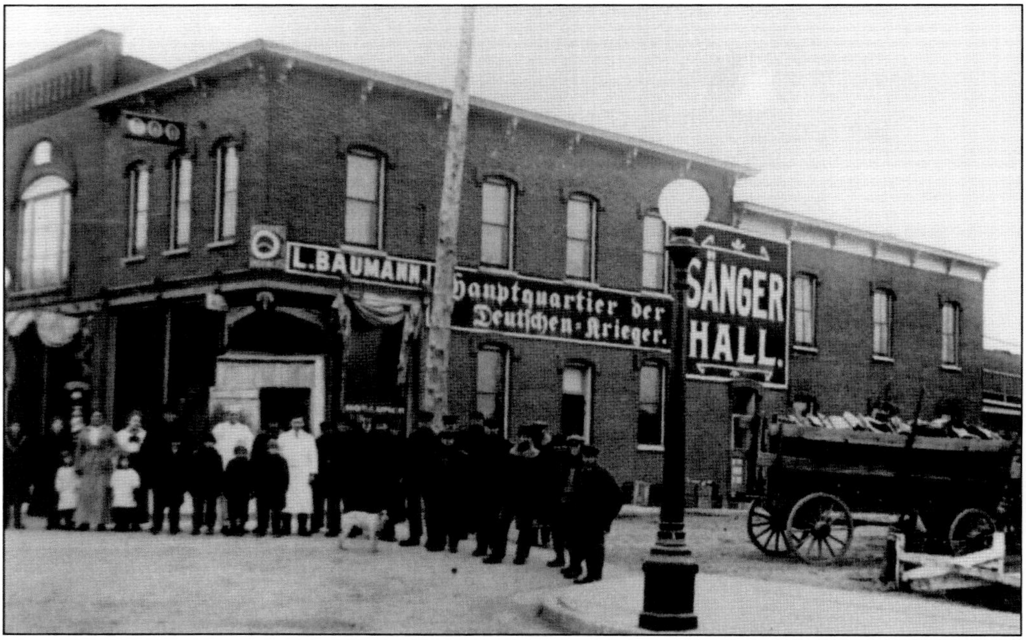

Baumann's Tavern and Sanger Hall stood on the northeast corner of North Central Avenue and East Depot Street, now occupied by the Kwick Trip Service Station. As Marshfield grew and became a bit more refined, social interests moved from the lumberjack's saloons to social organizations, music, the arts, and other cultural activities. This did not mean the end of the saloon. Today, Marshfield boasts more than 20 bars.

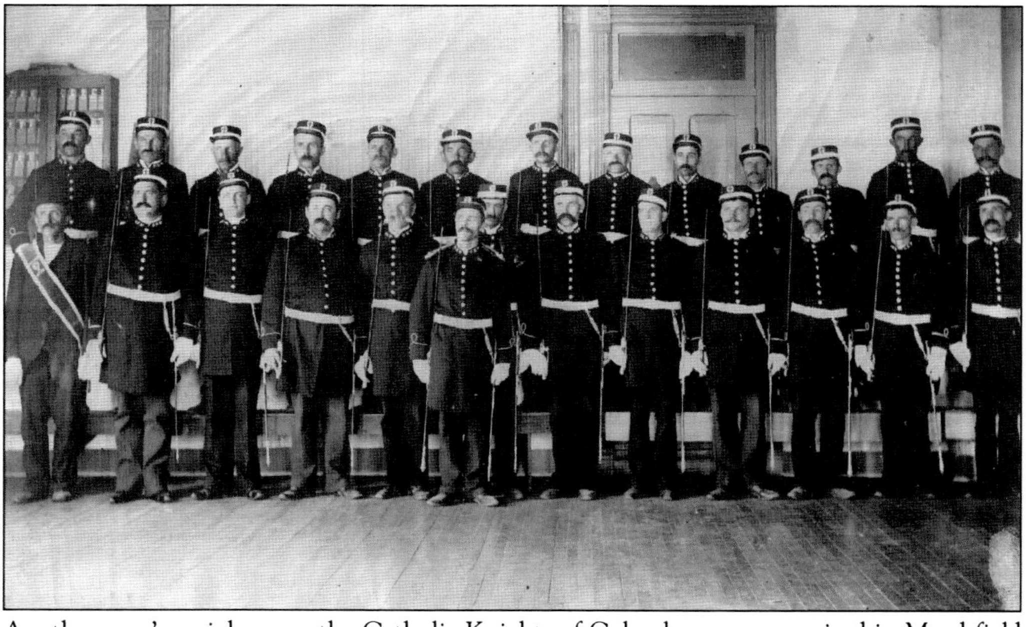

Another men's social group, the Catholic Knights of Columbus, was organized in Marshfield in 1915 and named after Fr. John Eisen, who built St. John the Baptist Catholic Church in the 1890s. He served as its pastor until his death in 1907. The group met above what is today Crabby Dave's Tavern on South Central Avenue. In this photograph, John K. Stauber is at front center and the other men are unidentified.

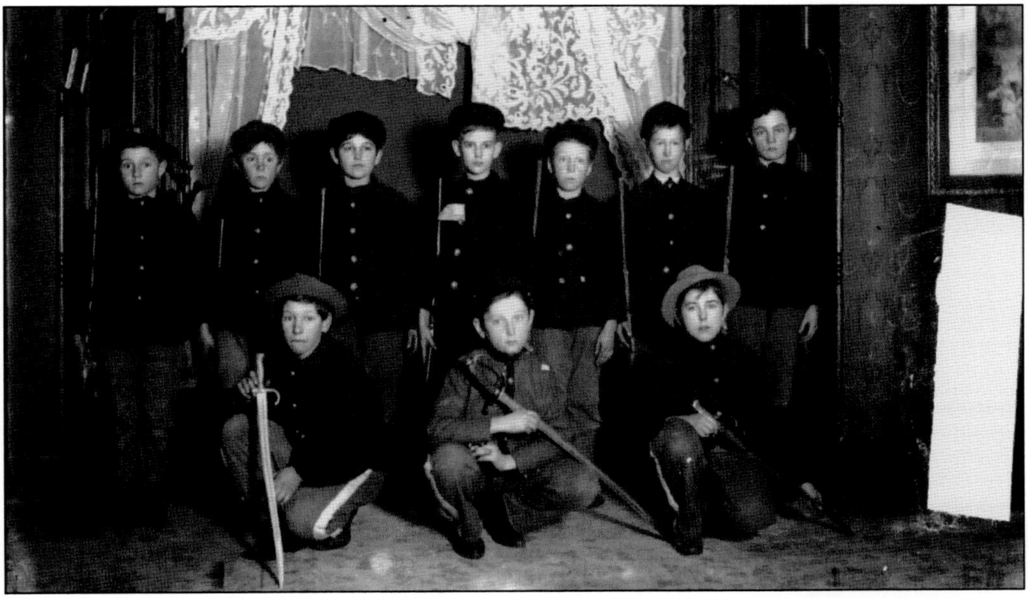

After the sinking of the battleship *Maine* in the harbor of Havana, Cuba, patriotic feelings ran high toward an invasion of the island. This group of young boys was organized in 1898 and was called Cole's Cuban Cadets. There are four names written on the back of the photograph: Charlie Cole, Ray and Clyde Tearman, and Lucious Foster. The others are unidentified, and the order is not specified.

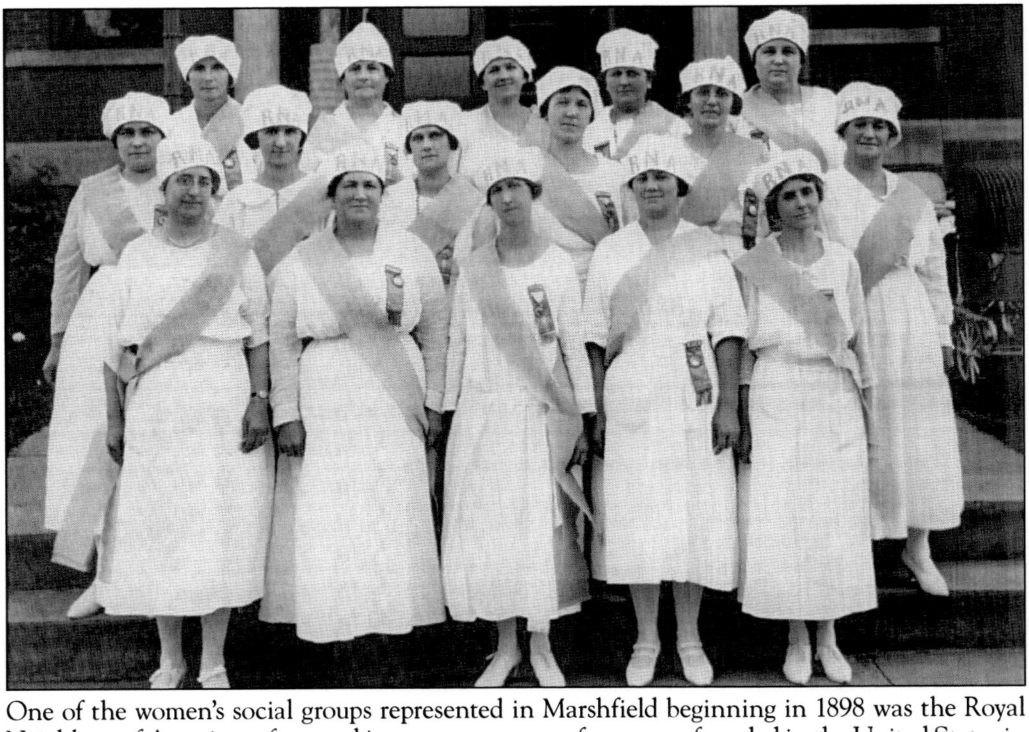

One of the women's social groups represented in Marshfield beginning in 1898 was the Royal Neighbors of America, a fraternal insurance company for women founded in the United States in 1895 and open to women ages 18 to 45. It was affiliated with the Modern Woodmen of America, a men's insurance and fraternal group. Both still exist.

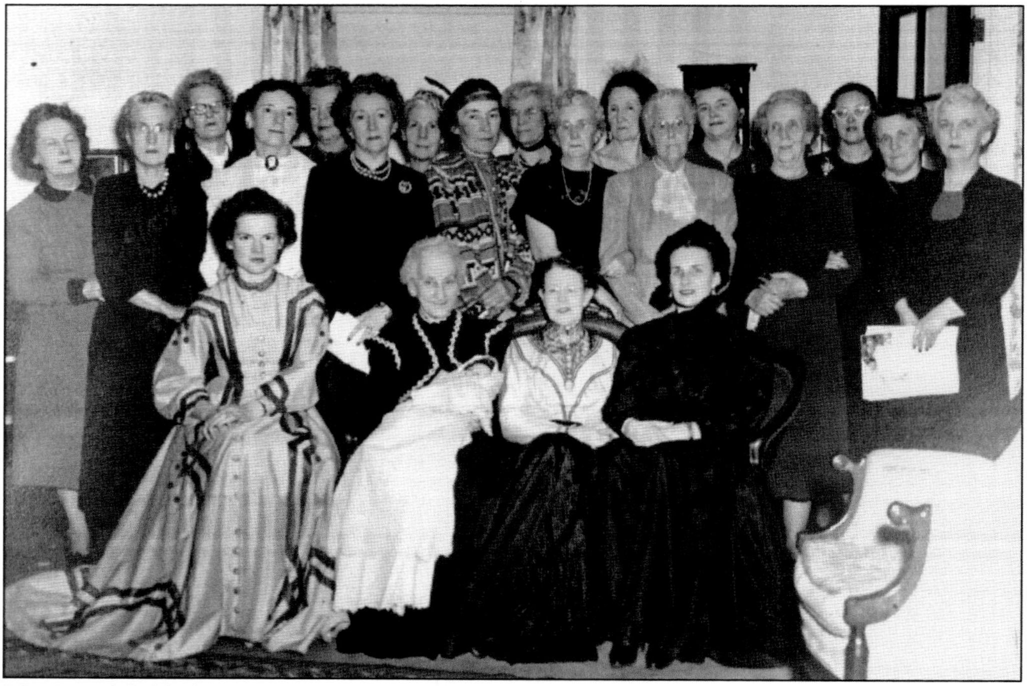

The Marshfield chapter of the Daughters of the American Revolution began in Marshfield in 1908. These members, photographed sometime between 1947 and 1949, included (seated) Augusta Roddis, Nellie G. Kamps, Mrs. Howard LaPere, and Marg Corneveaux; (standing) Ann Salter, Lorene L. Vedder, Helen S. Glassner, Fanny Cole Purdy, Catherine Roddis Beggo, Lois D. Graham, Catherine P. Roddis, Lorra Dresendoe, Ida Saxon Krause, Margaret McCorison, Jessica L. Williams, unidentified, Eleanor Winch, unidentified, Helen C. Laird, and Eunice Scheiber.

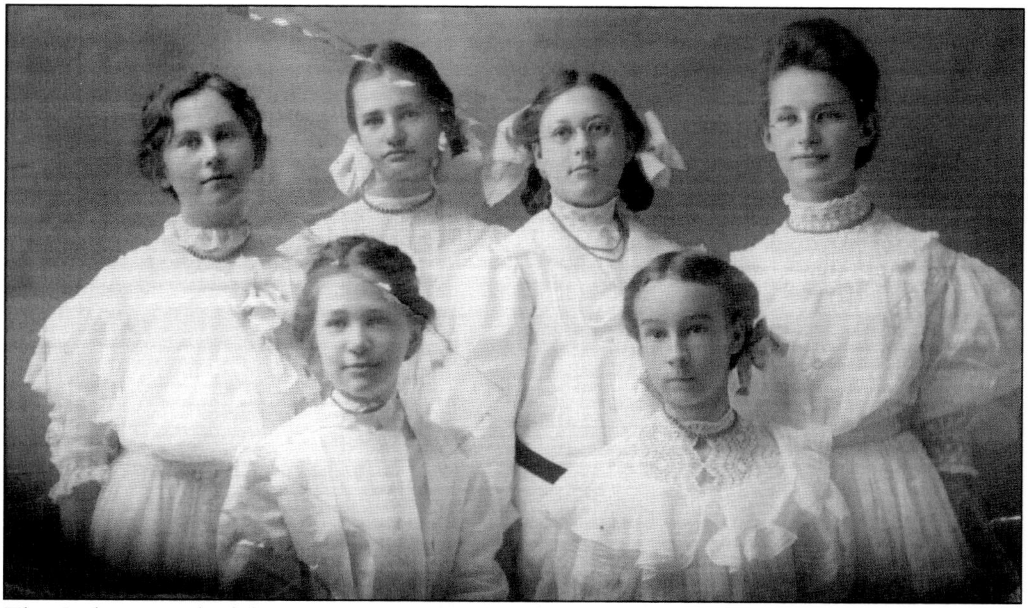

The Girl's Musical Club existed in Marshfield in the early 1900s. This group of young ladies is only partially identified on the back of the photograph. Included are Billie ?, Dorothy Finney, ? Sexton, Marion Connor, and Pauline Blodgett.

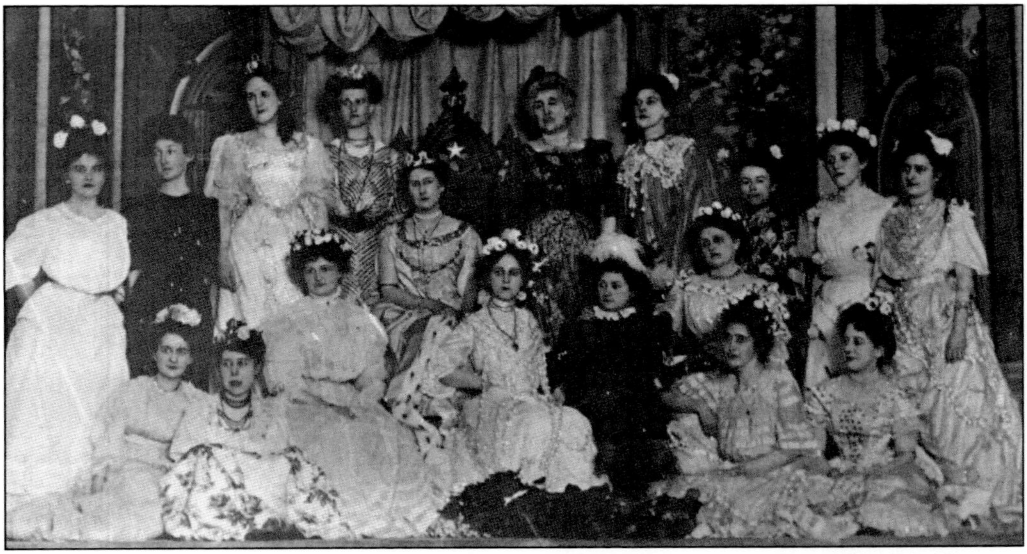

The Women's Fortnightly Musical Club presented *The Dancing Princess* on May 28, 1907. The cast included (seated) Carrie Louise Reynolds, Clara Mason, Carola Forrest, Alice Below, Florence Connor, Minnie Glassner, Eva F. Bailey, and Frida Doege; (standing) Gertrude Winch, Jessica Williams, Mrs. Harry Bly, Mrs. Wilson Rector, Mrs. Royal Dale, Emma Pulling, Jennie Dorschel, Vera Vollmar, and Alice Vaughn.

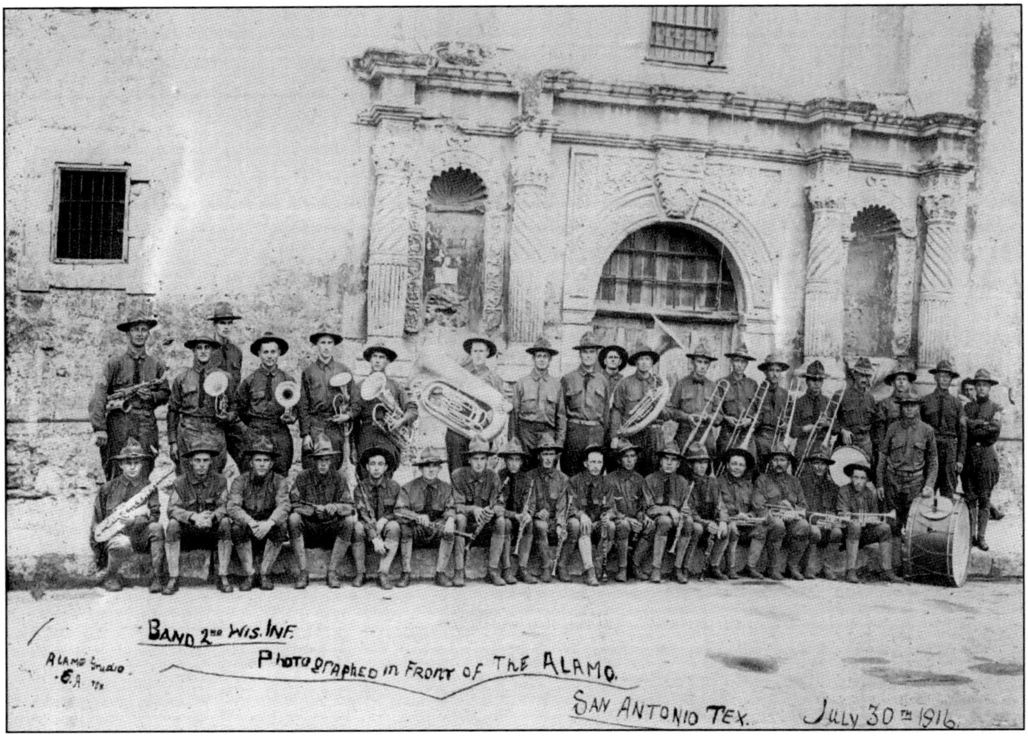

During their service on the Mexican border in 1916, this band found time to visit the Alamo and have this photograph taken. Marshfield's musicians had been selected in 1899, through a strong competition among various state bands, as the 2nd Regiment Band. They were sent to Waco, Texas, for training.

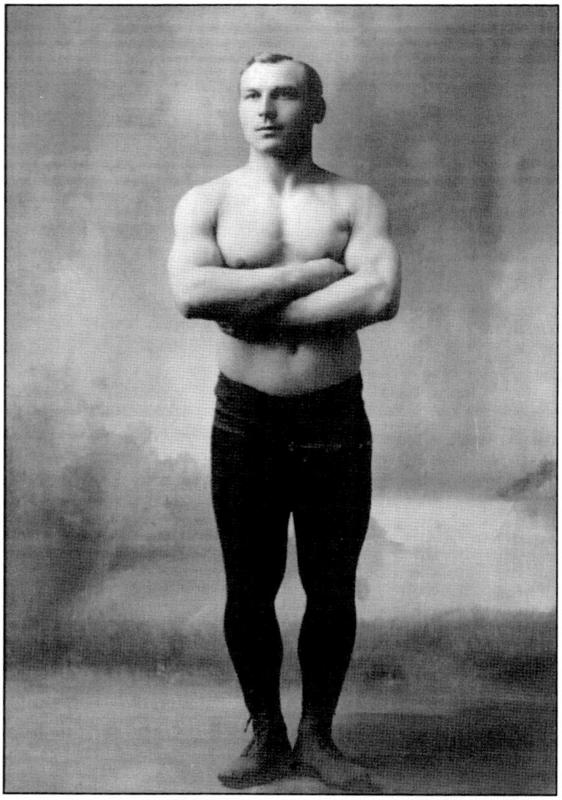

Fred Beell was one of the best-known men in the city, a professional wrestler and later a policeman. Though qualifying as a lightweight, he fought and defeated the champions in the middleweight and heavyweight divisions, reigning as the undefeated champion in all weight classes. He fought all over the United States. As a part-time policeman, he was killed in August 1933 while attempting to thwart a robbery at the Marshfield Brewery. The thieves were looking for federal revenue stamps held in the vault.

Baseball has always been a popular pastime in Marshfield. One of the first fields was at City Park, which is known today as Columbia Park and contains many trees and a band shell. Pictured are unidentified members of the city team from 1931.

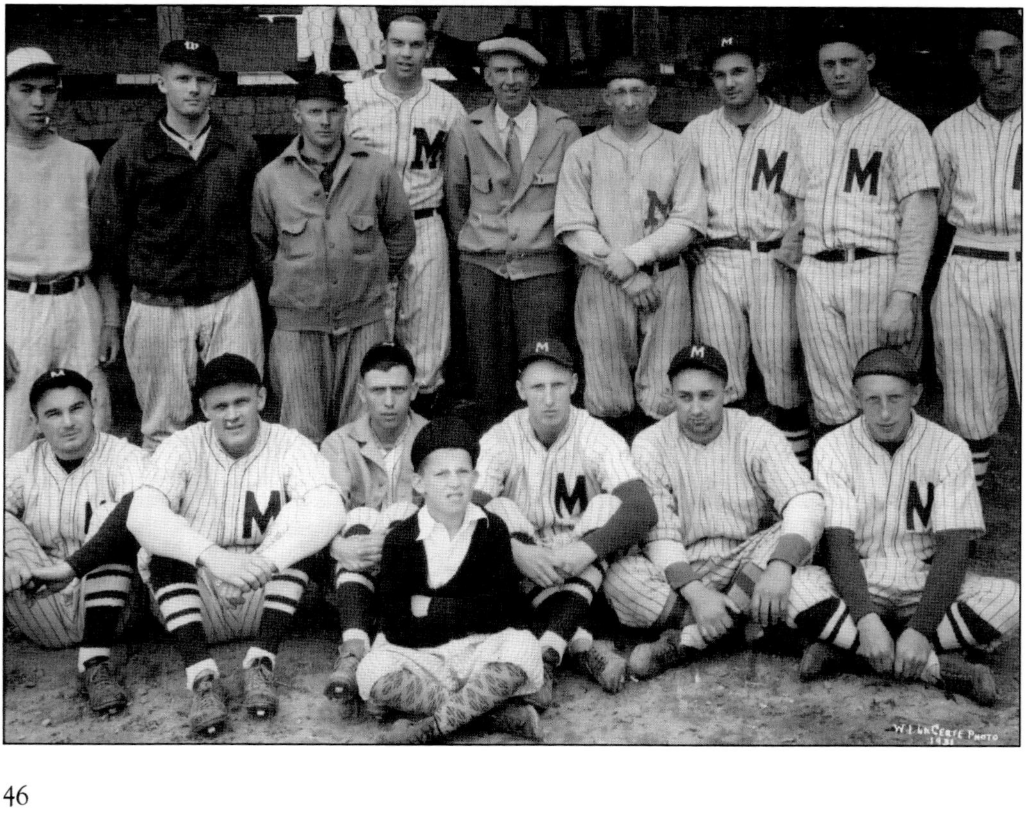

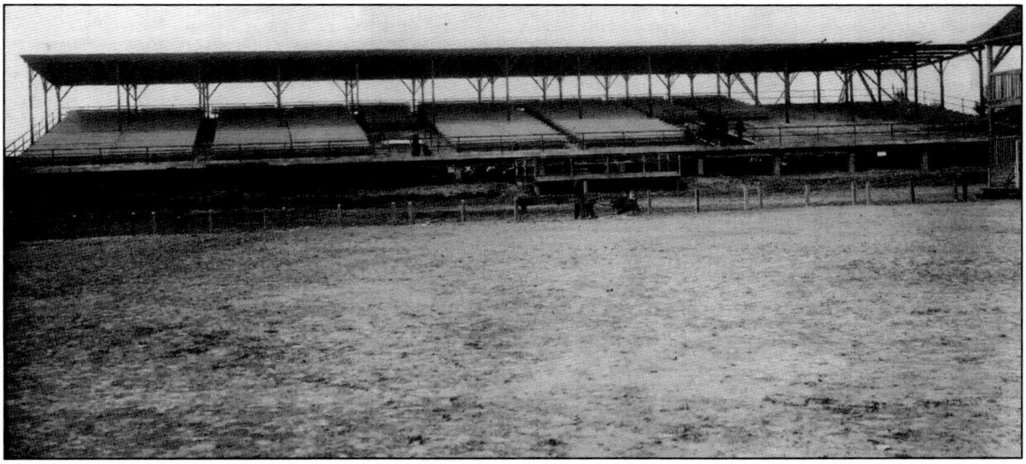

Another baseball field was located at the fairgrounds since 1930. The fairgrounds were a multiuse facility. A racetrack for horses and, later, cars ran around the baseball field. A grandstand was located along part of the track. It was also the location of the Central Wisconsin State Fair, held each fall. The grounds continue as the location of both the fair and softball games.

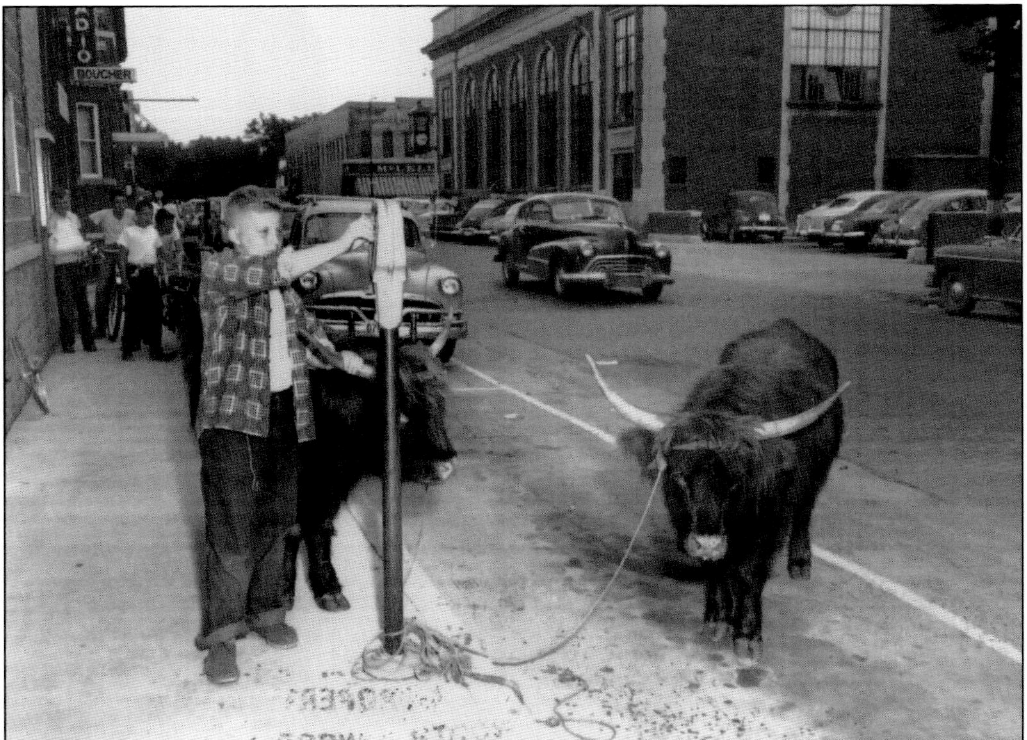

As a group of his friends looks on, this young exhibitor has decided to make use of the modern hitching post. He has dropped a few nickels in the meter so the police do not ticket his charges, which probably were to be exhibited at the Central Wisconsin State Fair. The image shows the area just west of the Central Avenue business district on Third Street.

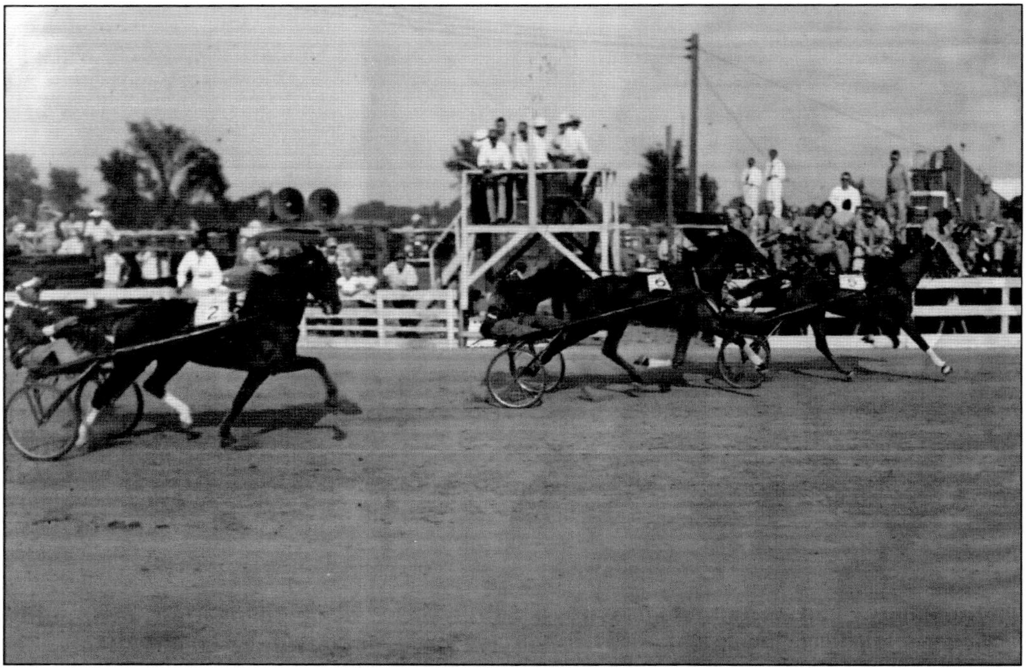

Harness racing was very popular at the fair. Many of the prominent men in the community had horses bred for the trotting races. The competition was fierce, but friendly. Races were held in several Central Wisconsin locations in the early 20th century. Trotters were trained to maintain a special stride and pull a driver in a two-wheeled sulky.

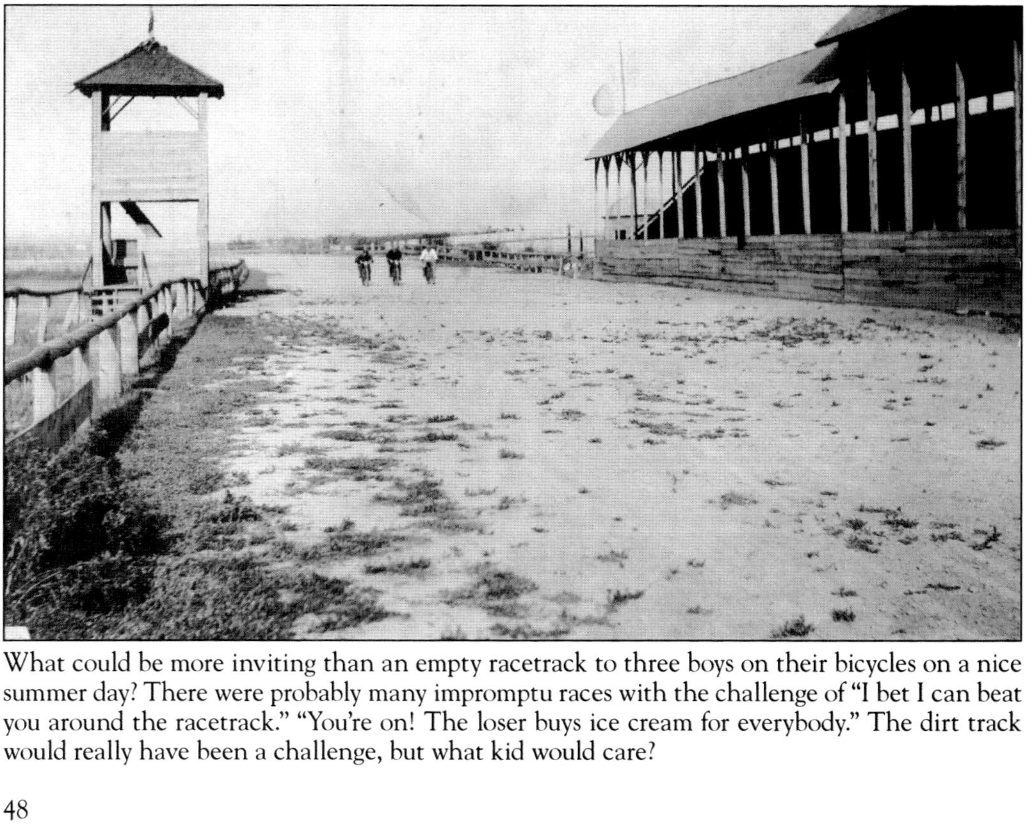

What could be more inviting than an empty racetrack to three boys on their bicycles on a nice summer day? There were probably many impromptu races with the challenge of "I bet I can beat you around the racetrack." "You're on! The loser buys ice cream for everybody." The dirt track would really have been a challenge, but what kid would care?

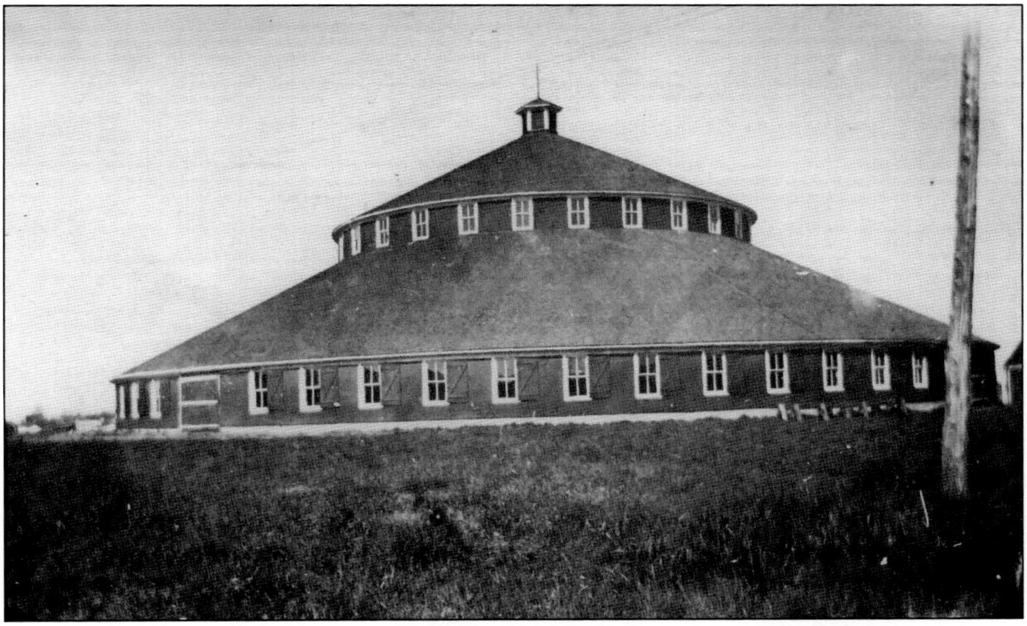

Also located at the fairgrounds is the "World's Largest Round Barn." The barn is 150 feet in diameter and was designed and built in 1915 by Frank A. Felhofer, a local builder. It was designed specifically as a show and sales barn and has no apparent interior support beams. It is still used annually for the fair to house the larger animals during the various competitions.

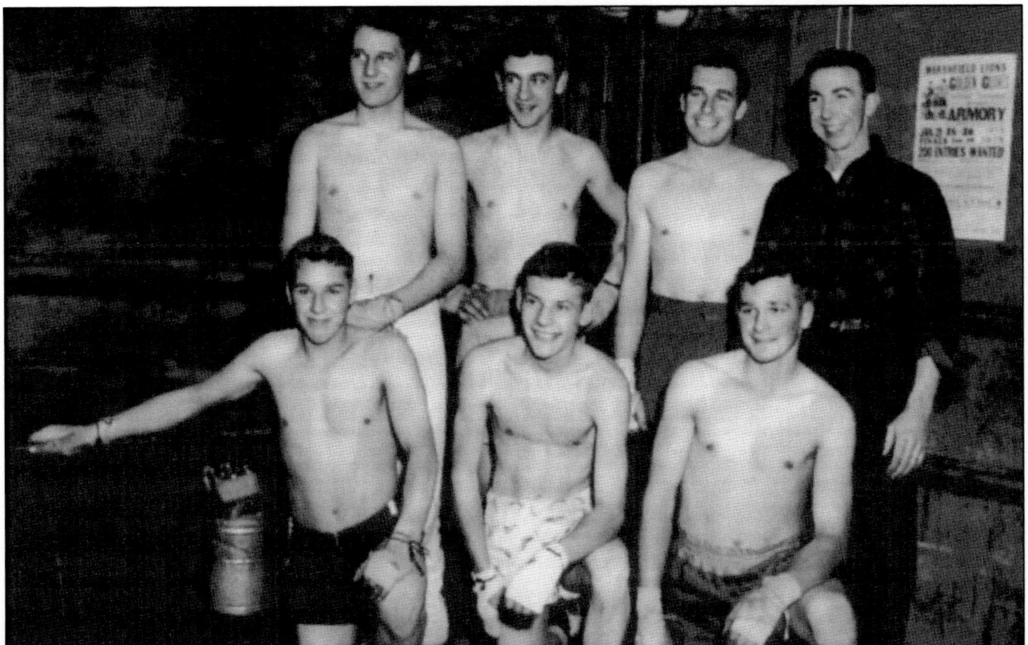

Boxing was also a major sporting event in the city. This group of boxers is pictured in January 1950. From left to right are (kneeling) Dick Schalow, Leon Zuehlke, and Jerry Schalow; (standing) Jack Foster, Don Heintz, Ed Kremin, and coach Flossie Gust. Golden Gloves events were held in Marshfield at the Oak Avenue Armory, now known as the Oak Avenue Community Center.

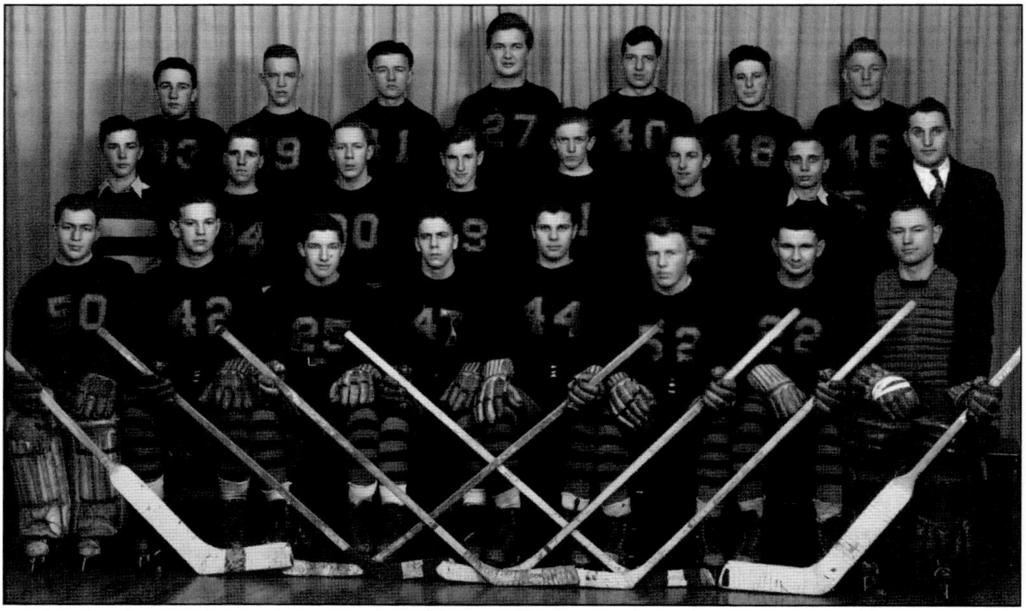

High school sports have always been popular. This is the 1940 high school hockey team. Pictured from left to right are (first row) Robert Heiting, D. Van Epps, L. Bey, R. Stauber, H. Metz, C. Billings, and R. Schunk; (second row) E. Diem, K. Becker, Richard Heiting, V. Luedtke, D. Hoag, W. Scheller, E. Harsch, and Mr. Burnkrant; (third row) J. Conlon, R. Birge, W. Felhofer, W. Chapel, J. MacDonald, R. Lauby, and M. Reinwand.

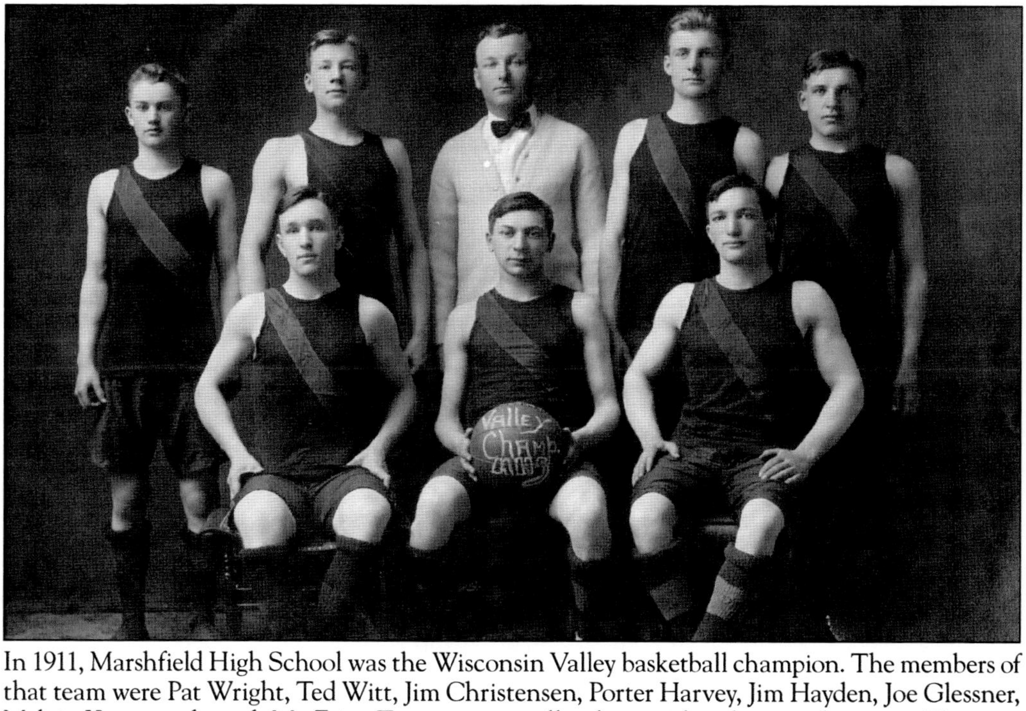

In 1911, Marshfield High School was the Wisconsin Valley basketball champion. The members of that team were Pat Wright, Ted Witt, Jim Christensen, Porter Harvey, Jim Hayden, Joe Glessner, Melvin Kraus, and coach Mr. Fries. Teams were smaller then, with only two substitutes. The pace of the game was slower, few fouls were committed, and fewer shots were taken. Scores were low by today's standards.

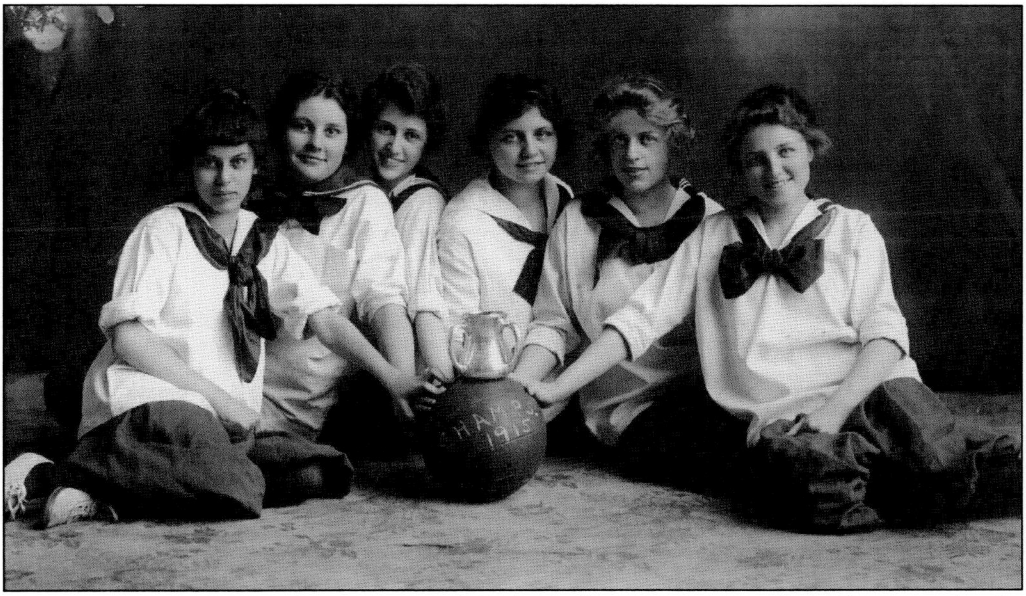

In 1915, it was the high school senior girls basketball team's turn to take a championship by defeating the junior team in overtime for the Marshfield High School girls basketball championship. Competition between schools was not yet a common thing for the women athletes. The members of the team included Clara Williams, Grace Vollmer, Marguerite McDonald, Lorene Noll, Grace Lupient, and Elsaba Hipke.

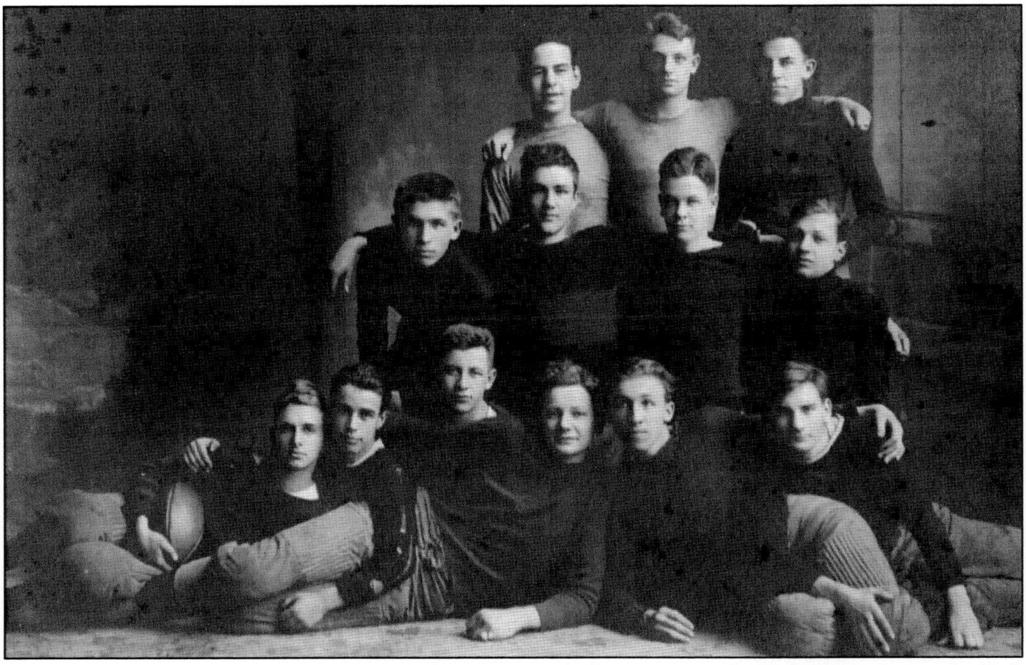

The 1913 Marshfield High School football team, caught here in an informal pose, consisted of left end Whitney, left tackle Pflum, left guard Jenkins, right guard Richard Connor, center White, right end Thom, right tackle Welch, right guard Sweeting, quarterback Anderson, right halfback Reynolds, left halfback Delmore, and substitutes Eckel and William Connor. The coach was Mr. Isley. With the exception of the Connor brothers, no first names were noted on this image.

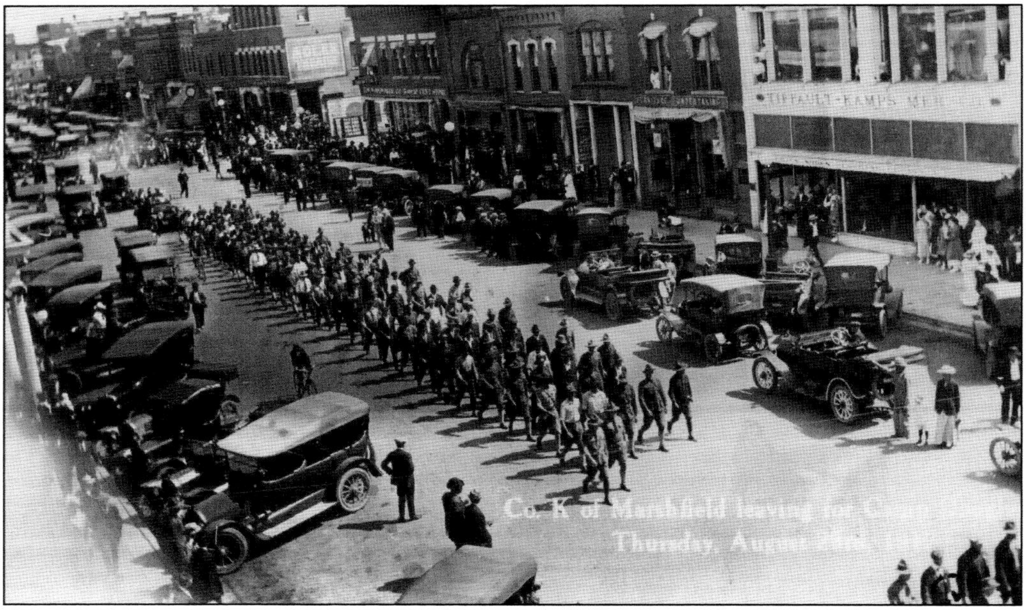

Marshfield also was a city of parades. This parade was a sendoff of Company K of the 6th Regiment of the National Guard of Marshfield to Camp Douglas for training on August 23, 1917. It had been formed out of the surplus of enlistments for Company A, which had been 70 percent higher than the 150 men requirement. It was placed under the command of Capt. William Mittelsteadt, former first lieutenant.

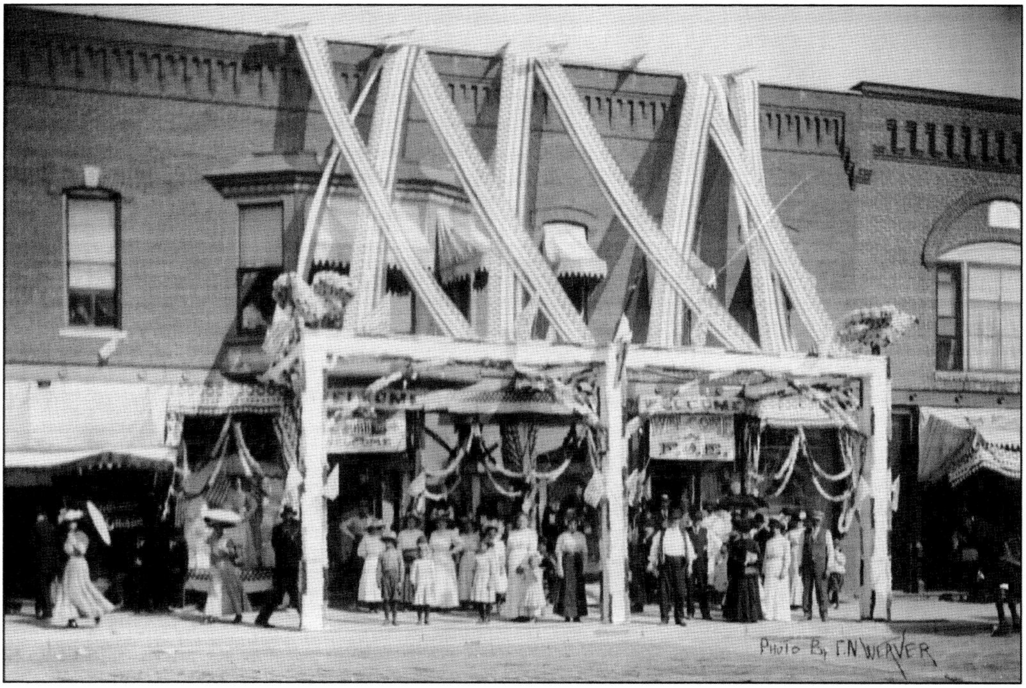

Beautiful decorations welcomed the Eagles convention of 1913 to Marshfield. Located at the hub of many railroads, the city was easily accessible from all parts of the state. Because of this, Marshfield was often the site of state conventions of the various fraternal organizations in the area.

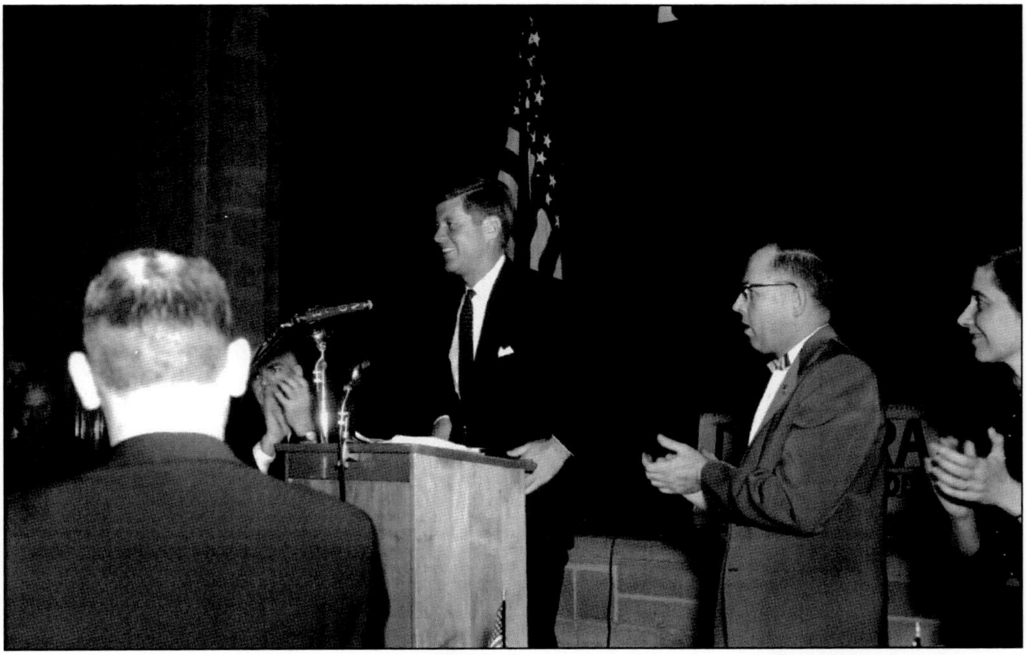

This fact of location also resulted in Marshfield being a stop for the presidential campaign trains of the past. Such people as Secretary of State William Jennings Bryan stopped in 1914 to deliver a speech in favor of Woodrow Wilson, Dwight Eisenhower visited in the 1950s, and John F. Kennedy campaigned here in 1959.

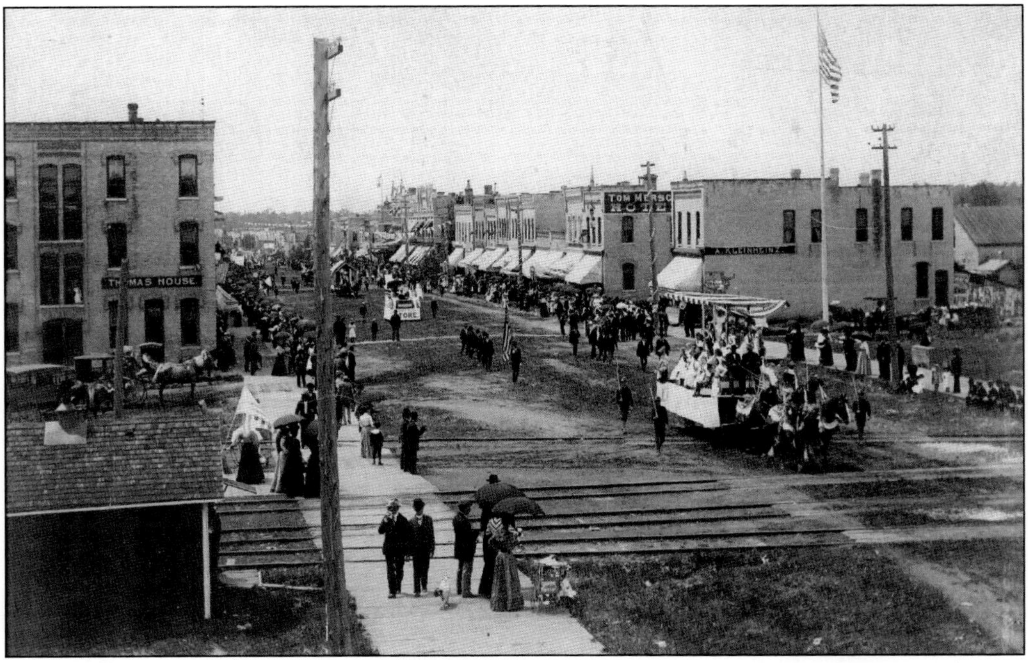

This parade heading north prior to the paving of Central Avenue in 1916 is about to cross the Soo Line tracks. The Thomas House Hotel, one of the finest in the city, is to the left. The Thomas House today contains a fine dining restaurant and various small businesses. The Thomas House History Center, directed by Shirley Mook, is located in the lower level.

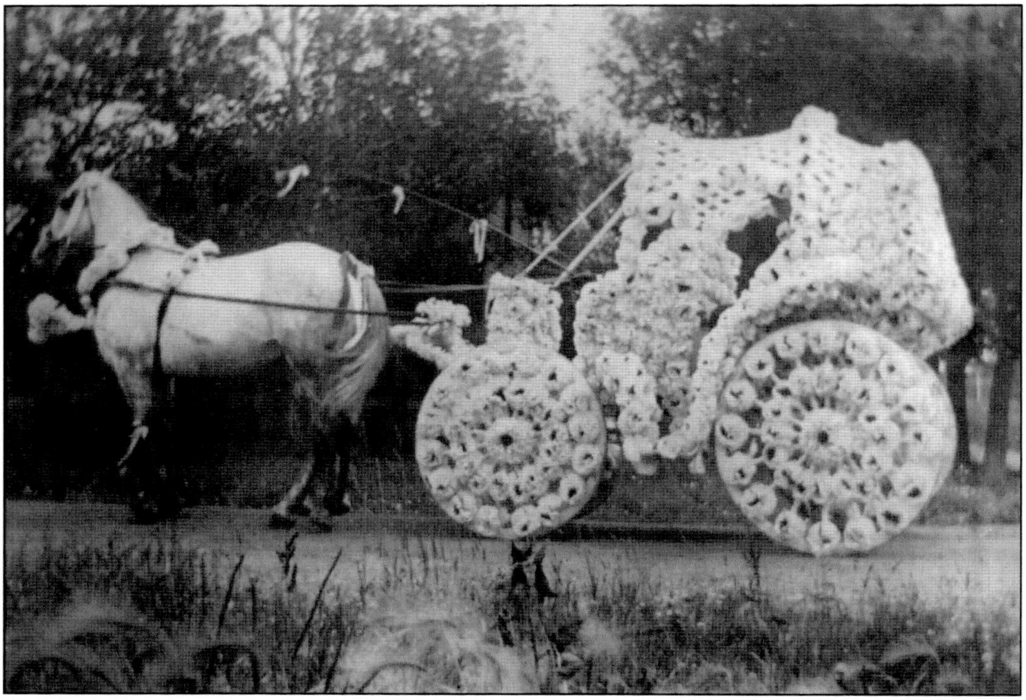

This is an excellent example of the elaborate decorations used in the early parades. This horse cart appeared in the 1913 Eagles convention parade. Many hours were put in preparing for each of the events through downtown Marshfield. Large crowds lined the streets to show their appreciation and enjoy the spectacle. Turnout for today's parades is still as large and appreciative.

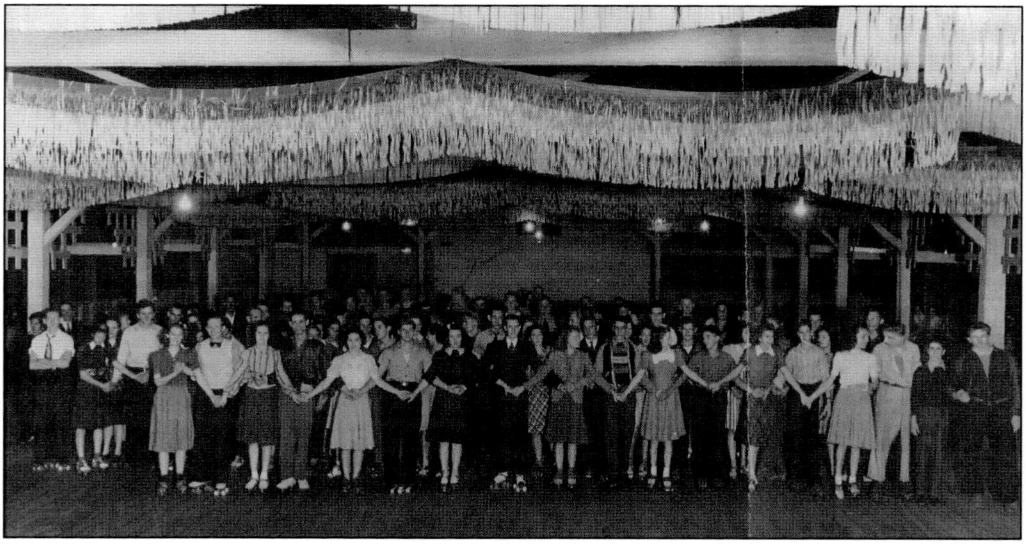

Roller-skating has been a very popular activity in Marshfield since the early 1900s. There have been at least six publicly and privately owned skating rinks in the area. This scene is in the old pavilion at Wildwood Park, which was replaced in the 1990s. Other locations were in the various armories, above a truck dealership on East Second Street, and now at Melody Gardens, a skating rink on South Park Street.

Four

Businesses

Marshfield was a typical city at the dawning of the 20th century. Its main street was lined with buildings containing small shops, general stores, restaurants, saloons, hotels, and various other private businesses. These served the farmers as well as the factory workers. Away from the residential and business areas were the industries. These changed a bit as the years passed, and as old ones closed, often new ones opened. Two companies dominated the late-1800s landscape: the Upham holdings and the Roddis Veneer Company. Upham operated a lumber mill, furniture factory, feed and flour mill, and a company store. Roddis, located on the opposite side of the city, produced high-quality veneers.

On the south end of the city was the Hans Billie factory, which produced sashes and doors for the fine homes that Billie also built around the city. Earlier, he had operated a fixture factory that produced counters for stores and back bars for taverns. Also on the south side was the Blum Brothers Cheese Box factory, begun in 1910. The business closed in 1972. The company held many patents for the process used in creating the wooden boxes.

Other businesses included beekeeping supplies, feed mills, foundry and machine shops, Felker Brother's metal factory (producing pipes of various sizes), a catalogue cheese sales company, a mobile home manufacturer that later turned to modular homes, a brewery, several bakeries, hotels, and many neighborhood grocery stores, one of which is still in operation. The largest employer in town today, the Marshfield Clinic, got its start on the second floor of a downtown store building and went on to become one of the top medical complexes in the nation.

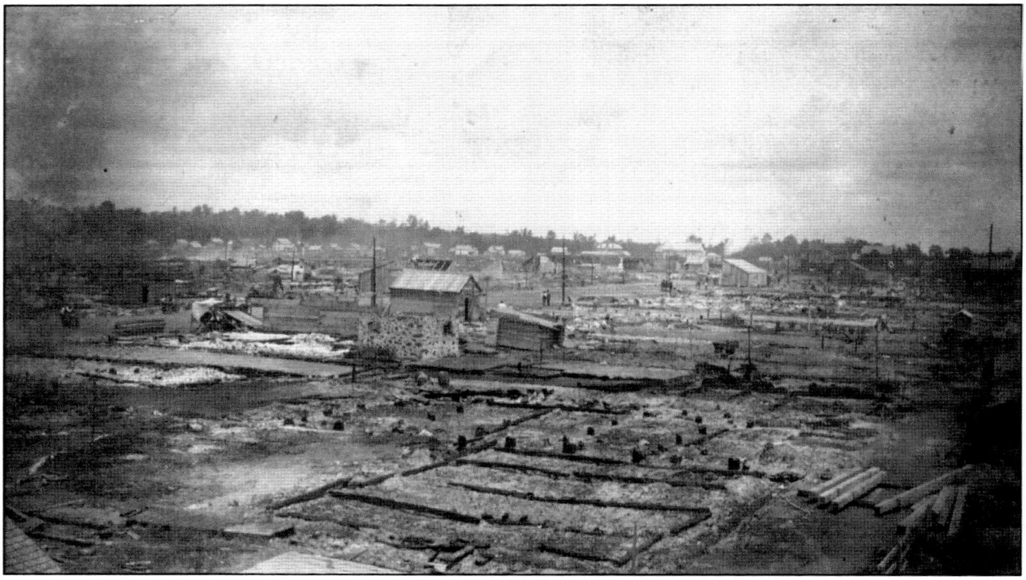

On June 27, 1887, a fire, started by a spark from a train, began at the Upham Mill and swiftly spread through the residential district near the plant and through the business district, destroying everything in its path. Despite all efforts to create a fire break, the flames consumed the heart of the city. After five hours, this was what remained of the area. This photograph looks northwest from the corner of East Third Street and Maple Avenue.

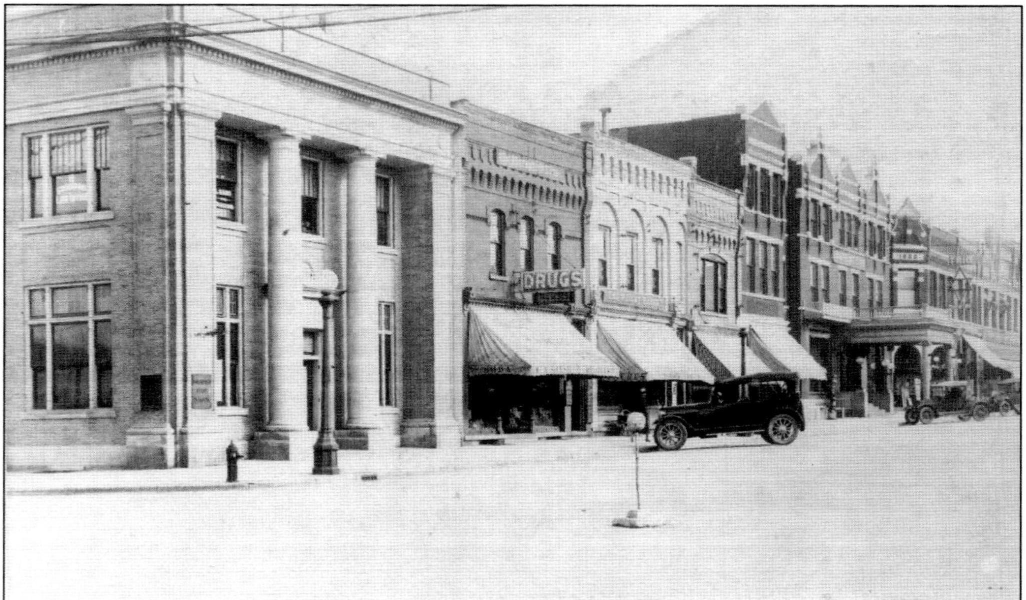

After the Great Fire, all buildings in the business district had to be, by ordinance, constructed of brick. Temporary stores were erected as new buildings were constructed, usually behind them. When the temporary structures were removed, the result was a very wide main street, four traffic lanes, parking, and a small boulevard down the center. Most of the buildings erected at this time are still in use, many with the original facades.

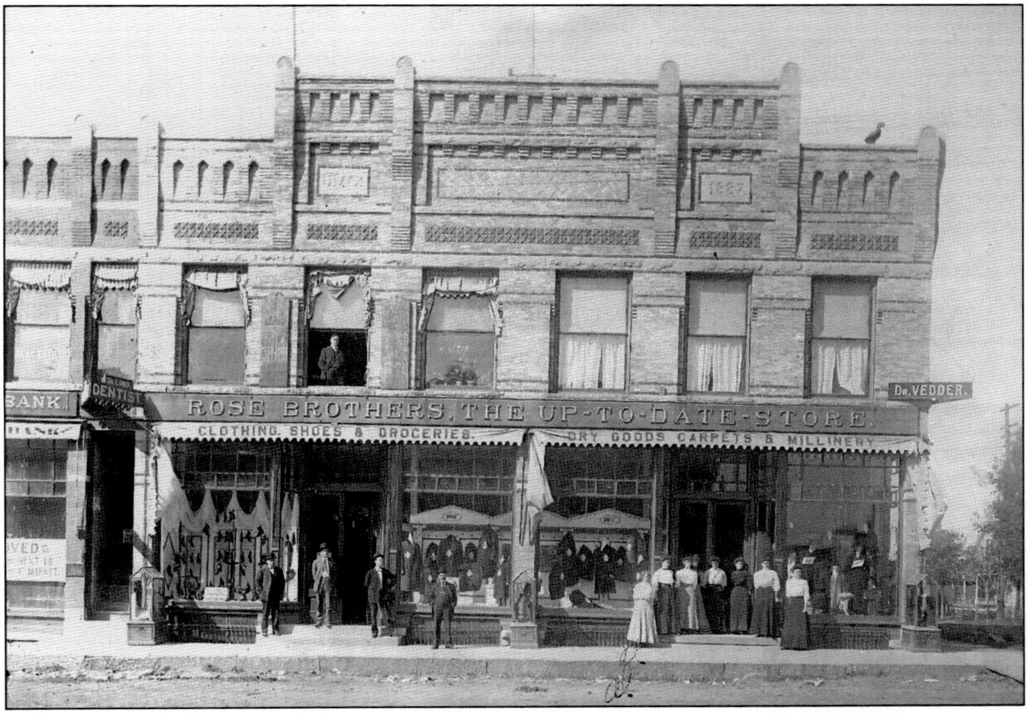

Rose Brothers was a general store started in 1898. It had been the Upham Manufacturing Company's store, located on the southwest corner of South Central Avenue and Second Street. In 1920, it was incorporated with Leo Rose, Mrs. Leo Rose, and Harry Rose, among others, as incorporators. In 1921, it was purchased by C.E. Blodgett, given to his sons-in-law to run, and renamed McCain-Johnson.

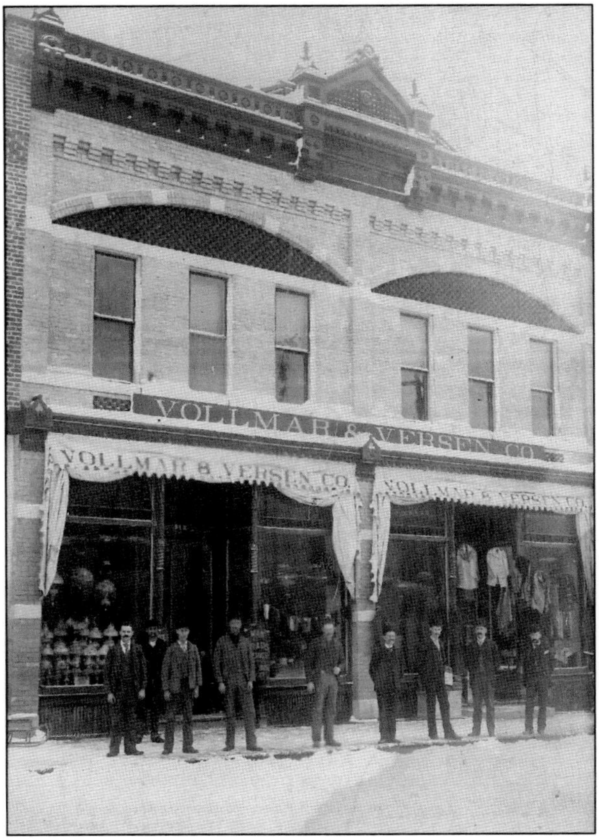

Volmar and Kraus operated a general store on the corner of Second Street and South Central Avenue that later became Tiffault-Kamps Mercantile Company. "Buy at Home" was a slogan started by Fred Kamps and James Van Rooy. A large display showcased companies and their products made in town. These included three cigar factories, Upham furniture, Marshfield Milling flour, Felker Brothers' culverts, J. Mettelka milk cans, and many more.

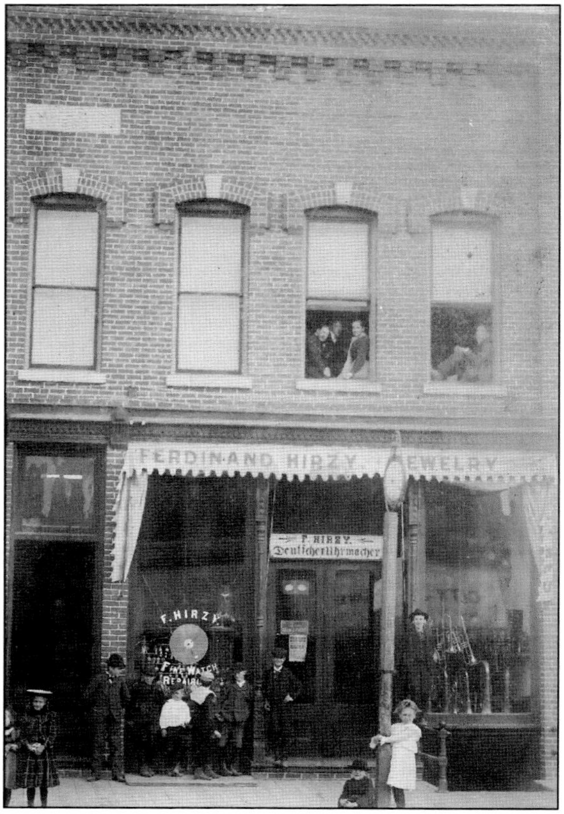

Ferdinand Herzy, organizer of the Marshfield Juvenile Band in 1891, had opened a shop dealing in watches, clocks, jewelry, and musical instruments in 1886. He operated the store until 1892, when he returned to Hungary for a visit. He reopened his shop in 1893 and continued business until 1901, when he returned to Hungary to settle his father's estate. He never returned to Marshfield. He died while visiting Hungary in 1922.

This block of businesses included a variety of stores. Vedder's was a general store, Sexton Brothers was a drugstore and bookstore, while Headstream was a jewelry store, grocery store, and barbershop combined. It was not unusual to combine several types of businesses or products into one store.

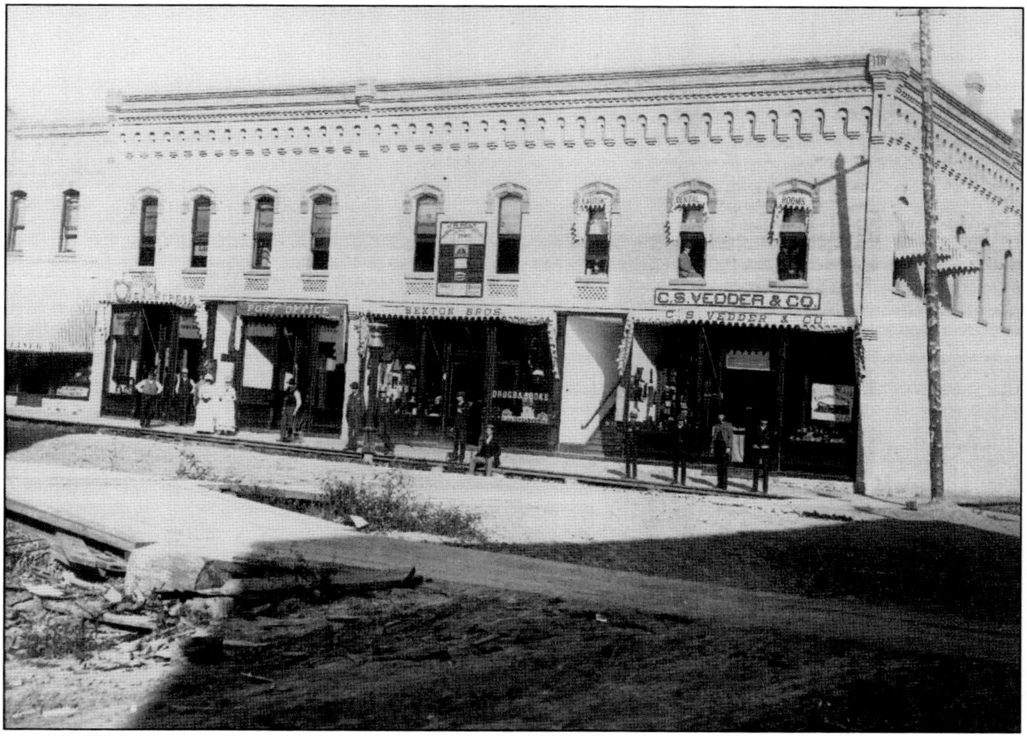

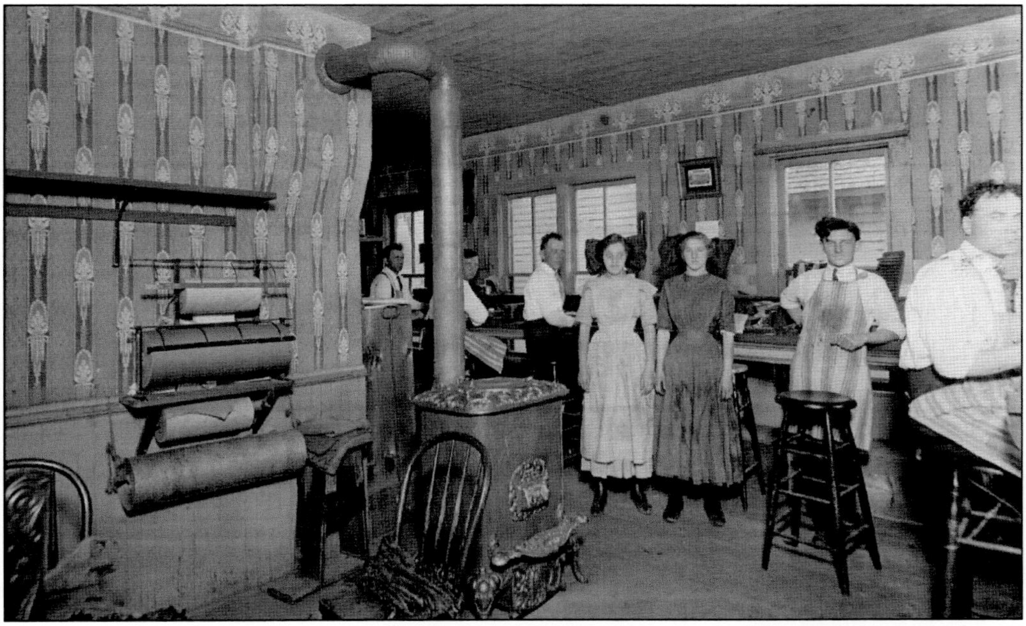

There were several cigar factories in the city. In 1920, Wood County had 48 acres growing tobacco and produced 56,082 pounds, mostly in the Pittsville area. These factories employed young men and women to roll the cigars in small buildings located mainly on the side streets off Central Avenue. Cigar Makers Union No. 72 was active among the young workers.

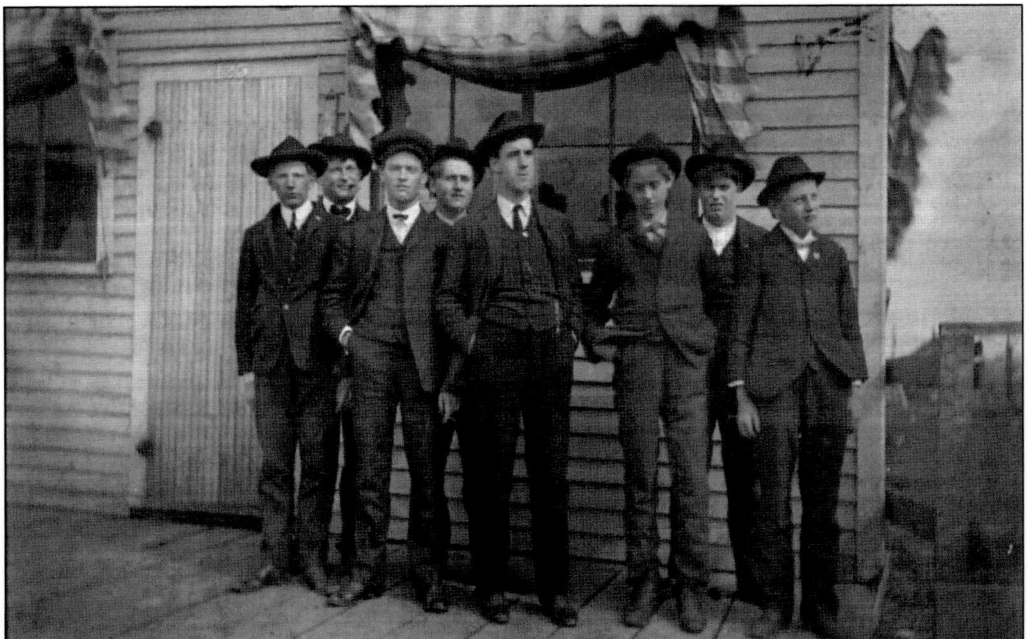

One of the better-known cigar factories was the Bever Cigar Factory at 605 North Central Avenue. It was owned and operated by Arthur Bever. Two of his brothers, Jacob and John, later operated the Bever Brothers Cigar Factory in Grand Rapids, now Wisconsin Rapids. Pictured from left to right are ? Weise, William Herman, Tony Hager, John Bever, Andy Marks, Henry Beine, Arnold Bever, and John Beine.

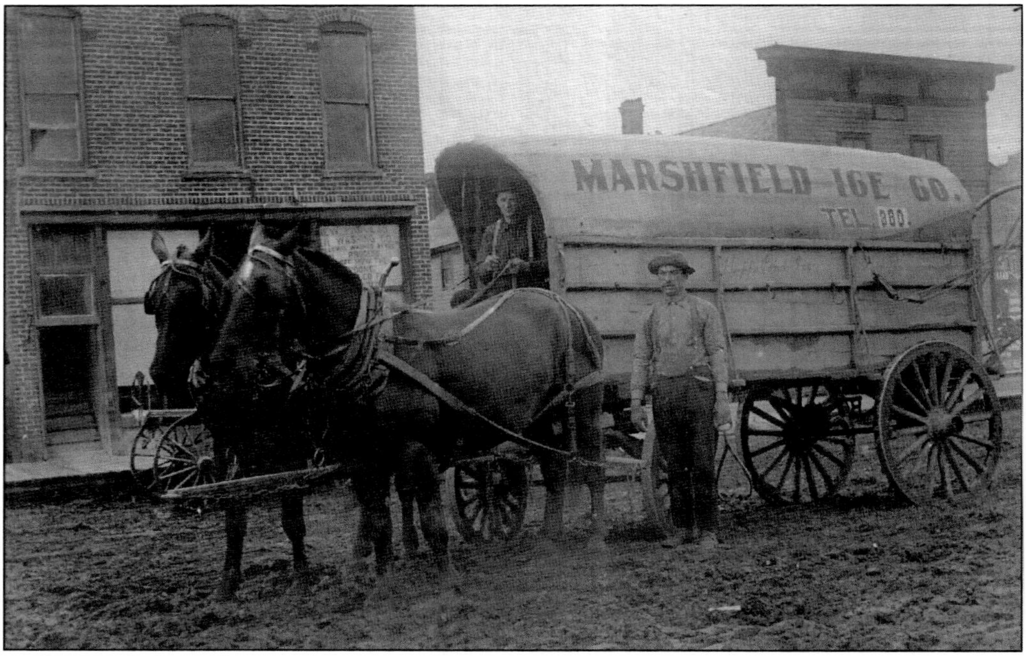

In the days before refrigeration, the iceman was a familiar sight on city streets. The McCrillis Ice Company cut 14,000 tons of ice each winter from the Upham and Hop ponds in the city. They not only sold to homes and businesses in the city but also had contracts to deliver ice to both the North Western and Soo Line Railroad companies for their refrigerated cars.

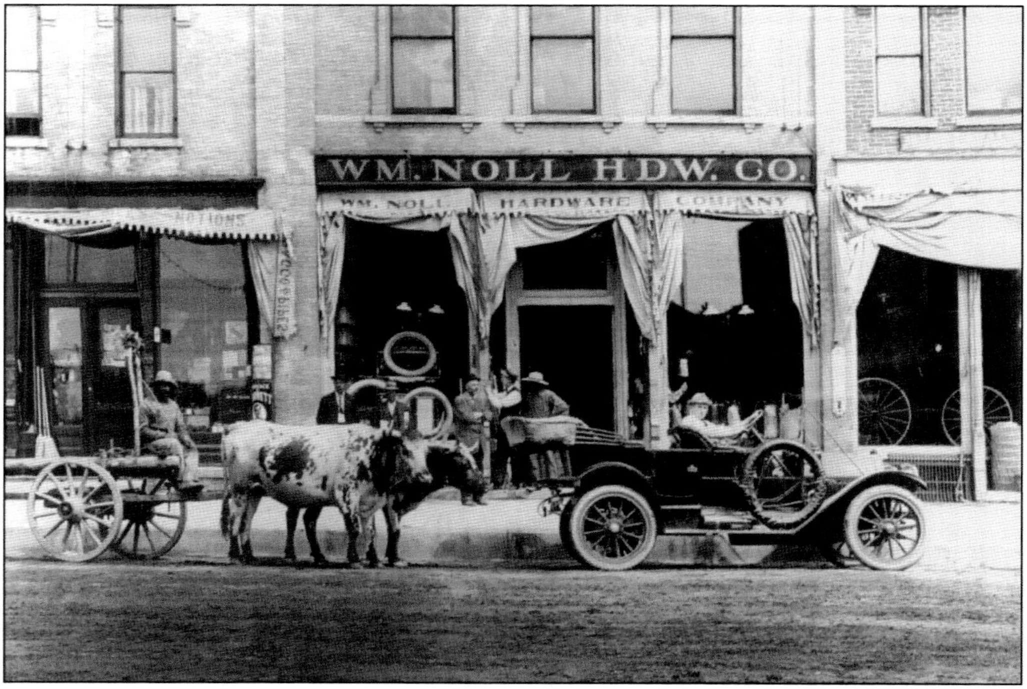

Noll Hardware was rebuilt immediately after the fire. The day after the fire, a temporary wooden shed was erected to do business. This image shows the contact of the past and future of transportation in the area. Horses and (less often) oxen were still found side by side with automobiles into the 1920s.

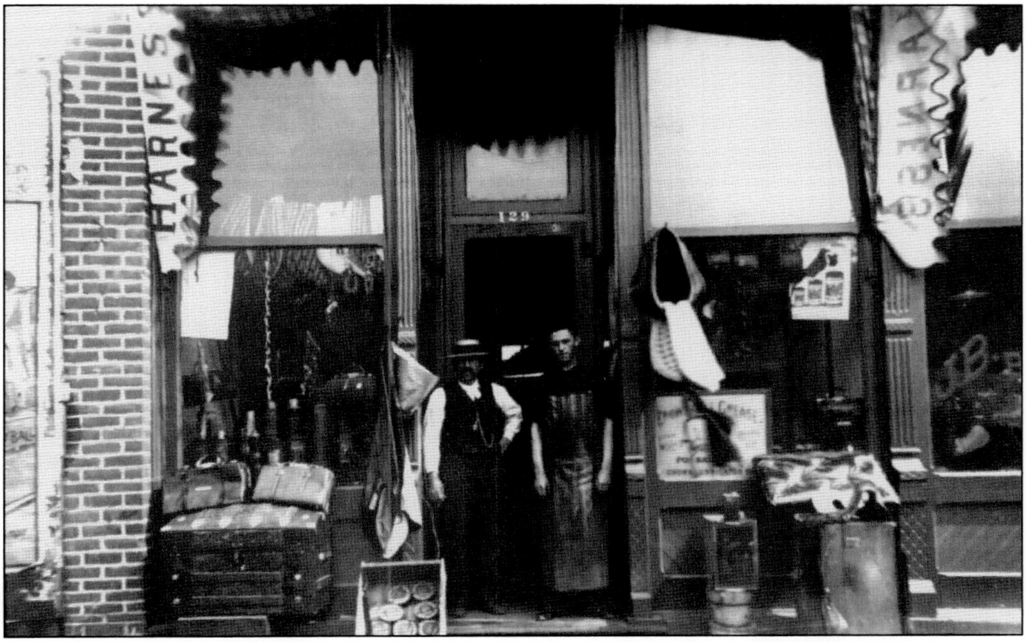

There were several harness shops located along Central Avenue. Simon Pflum operated his harness shop at 120 South Central Avenue until at least 1939. Another shop, also on Central Avenue, was operated at 309–311 by Wasserberger Dickoff into the 1920s.

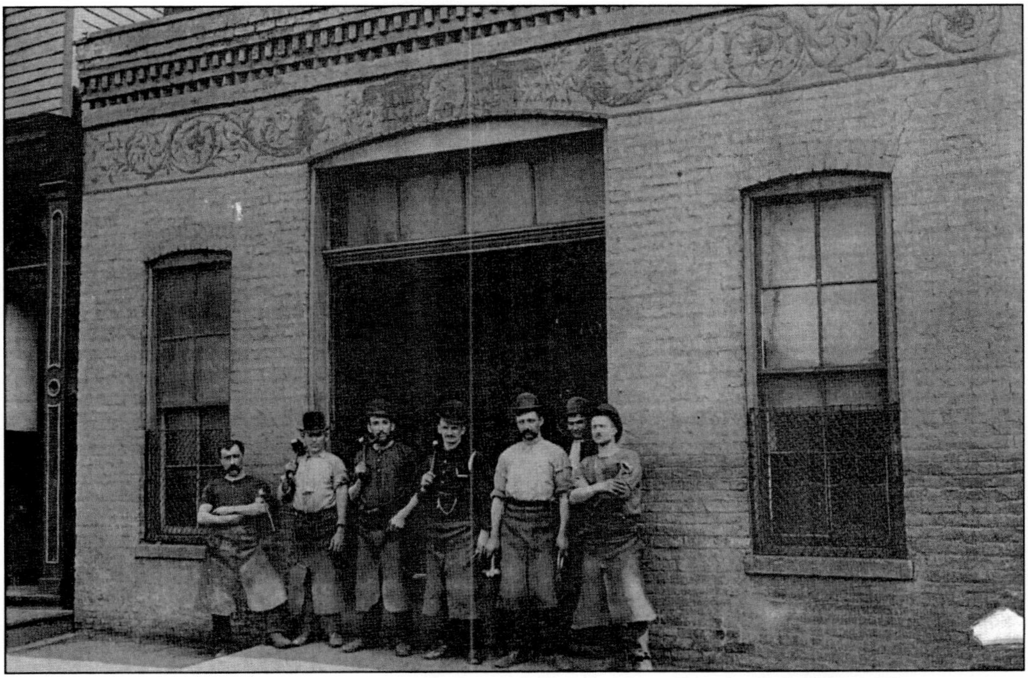

Also found along Central Avenue, as well as on side streets, were blacksmith shops. This imposing structure was the G.D. Geyer Blacksmith Shop, also known as the Joseph Goldbach Blacksmith Shop. Ray Jirschle, the nephew of Louis Jirschle, took over the Jones Blacksmith shop his uncle had purchased, and then purchased the Goldbach Shop in 1940. He operated it until 1946, when the last shop in town closed.

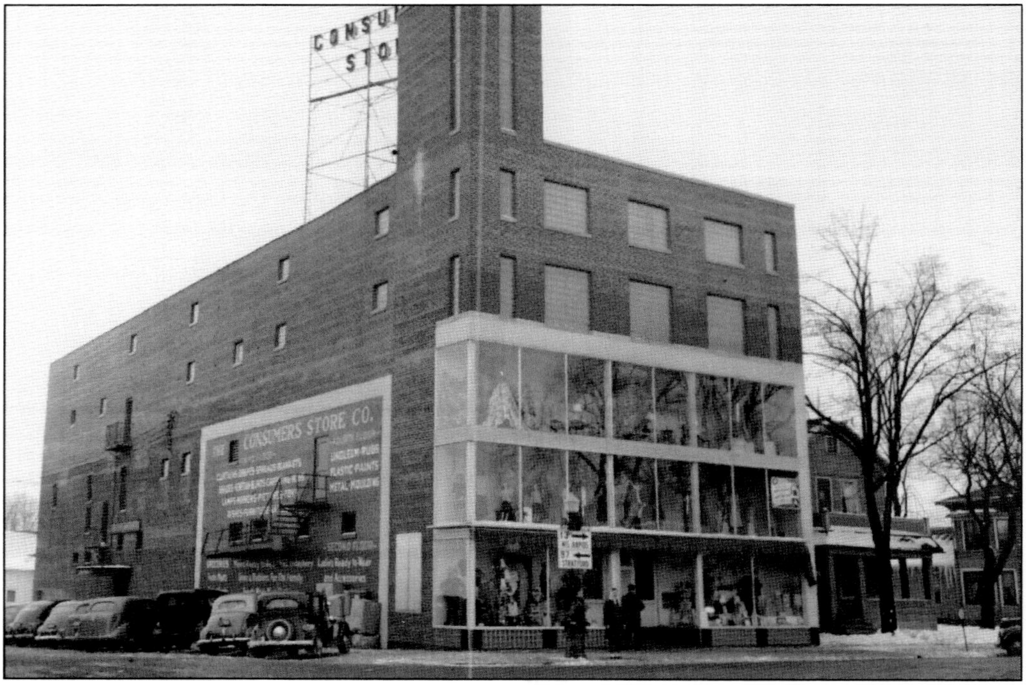

The Consumer Store was located at the corner of North Central Avenue and Arnold Street. Prior to being the Consumer Store in 1925, it was the location of Kestel Brothers Co., The Spot Cash Store. Today, it is the location of the St. Vincent de Paul store. The front has been changed considerably, and the house to the south has been replaced by St. Vincent's outreach offices.

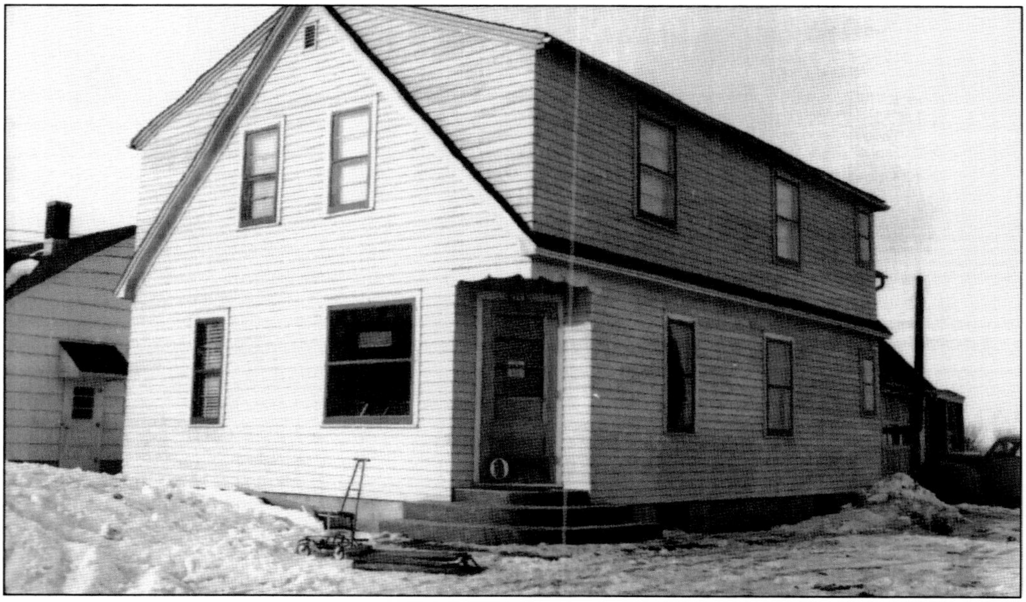

Scattered across the neighborhoods were small grocery stores. Each area had its own store to provide all the necessities within an easy walk of home. Often, they also provided delivery and monthly charge accounts. This store, Wolf's Grocery, has existed through generations of schoolchildren on a mission to acquire candy at noon or after school. The establishment is still in operation today across from Madison Elementary School on East Doege Street.

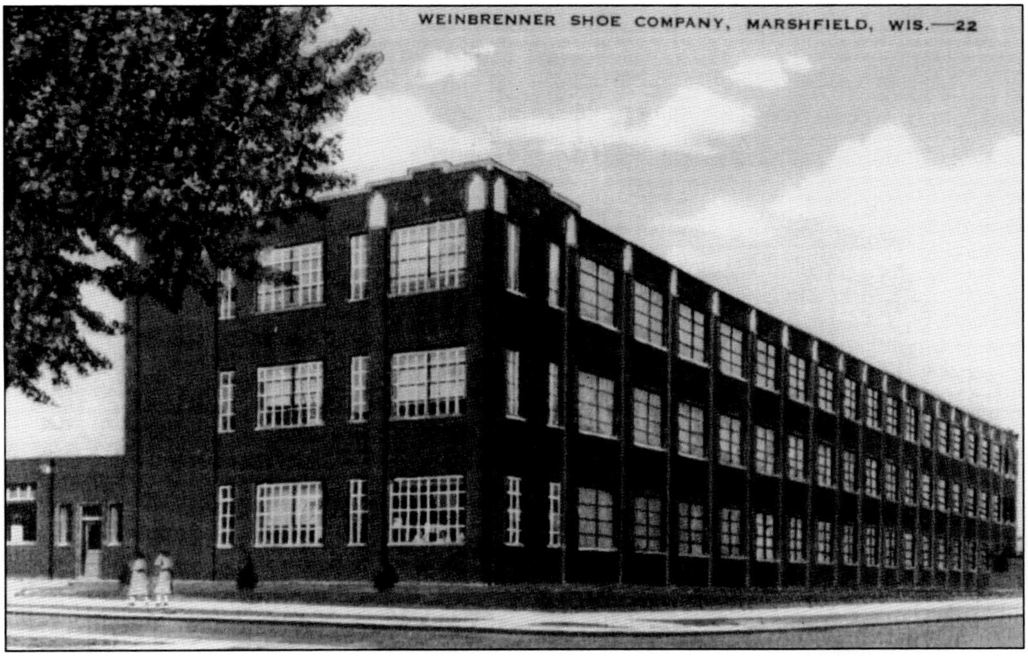

After the Great Depression hit in 1929, jobs were scarce in Marshfield, as elsewhere. In 1935, a building was constructed as a WPA project on the site of the Upham Furniture Company and the Weinbrenner Shoe Company moved there from Milwaukee. The city owned the building and leased it to the Weinbrenner Company for $1 per year, as it continues to do today.

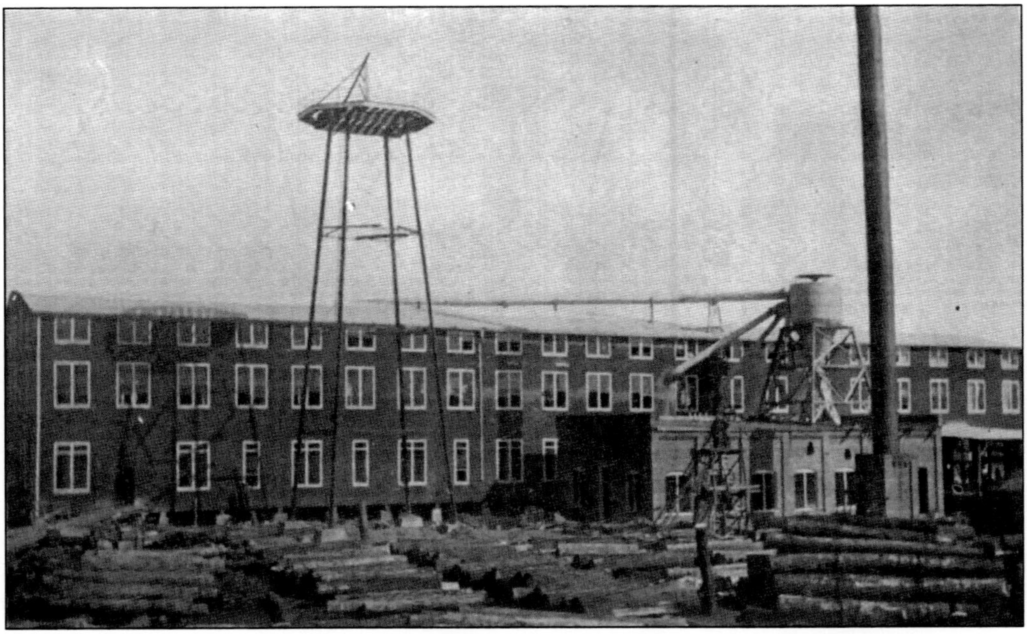

The company that dominated the Marshfield industrial world was the Roddis Corporation. The Hatteberg Veneer Works was established in 1890 with the invention of a new veneer cutter. The plant had financial difficulties until William H. Roddis arrived to take over management in 1894. By 1897, it employed 65 men with monthly income of up to $5,000. Then fire struck. Damage totaled $25,000, and insurance only covered $14,500.

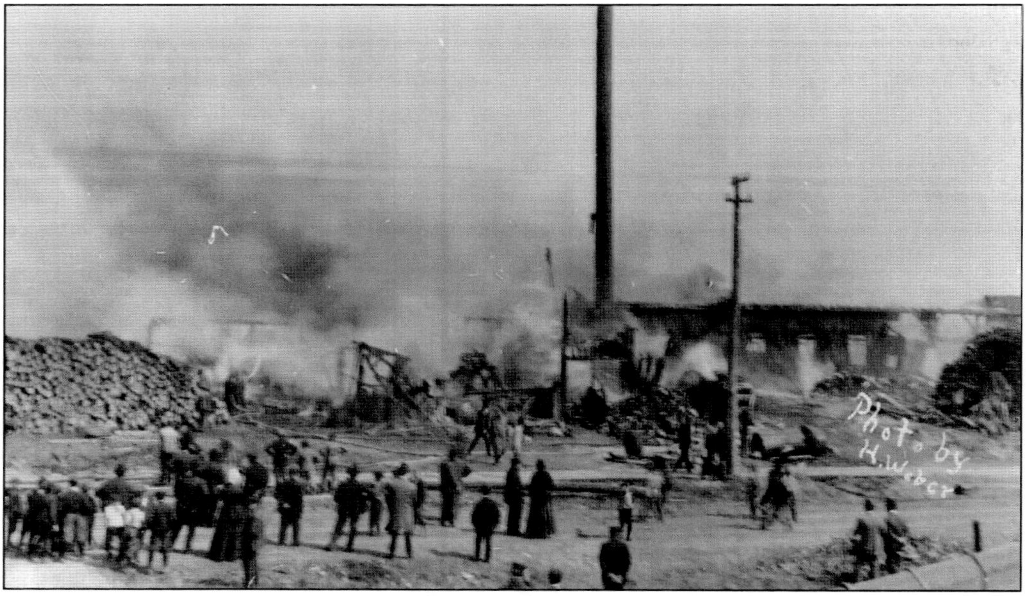

The stockholders met, and rebuilding of the Hatteberg Veneer Works began immediately. Hatteberg decided he would sell out his share, and on July 10, 1897, it became Roddis Veneer. The plant produced panels for folding beds, desks, pianos, and organs. It also manufactured cheese boxes and cheese box stock. In 1899, the company made $30,000, or over $775,000 in today's money. The business was off to great success.

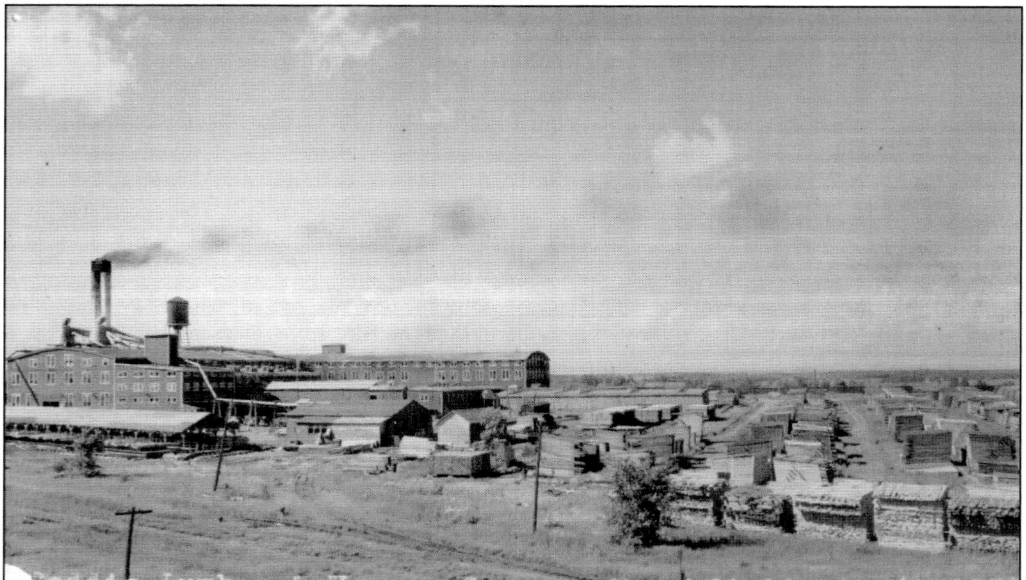

The Roddis Company did not invent flush doors, but it saw their potential and manufactured them on a large scale. A second plant was opened in Park Falls, Wisconsin. Fire struck both plants in a two-week period in 1907. There was a possibility that the entire operation would move to Park Falls, nearer the source of lumber, but Roddis decided to stay in Marshfield. The next year, he was elected mayor.

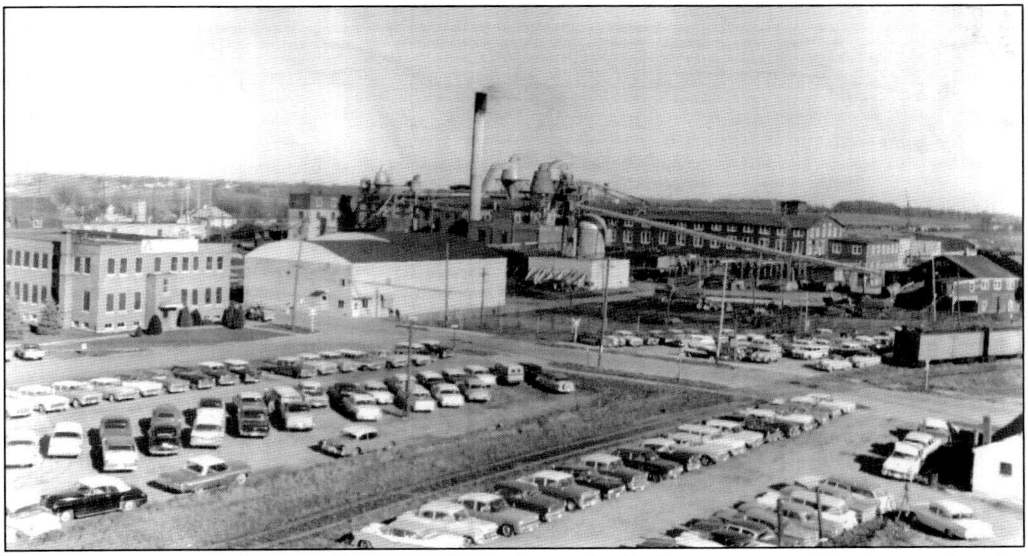

Roddis's grandson William H. Roddis II devised a method of using a steam room to moisturize the hardwood logs. The increased production came just as World War II was beginning, and it allowed the company to furnish the British with aircraft lumber for the Mosquito Bomber and marine interior lumber for Liberty Ships. They also provided the plywood for the US Army gliders. The term "Flying Trees" symbolized the work of the company.

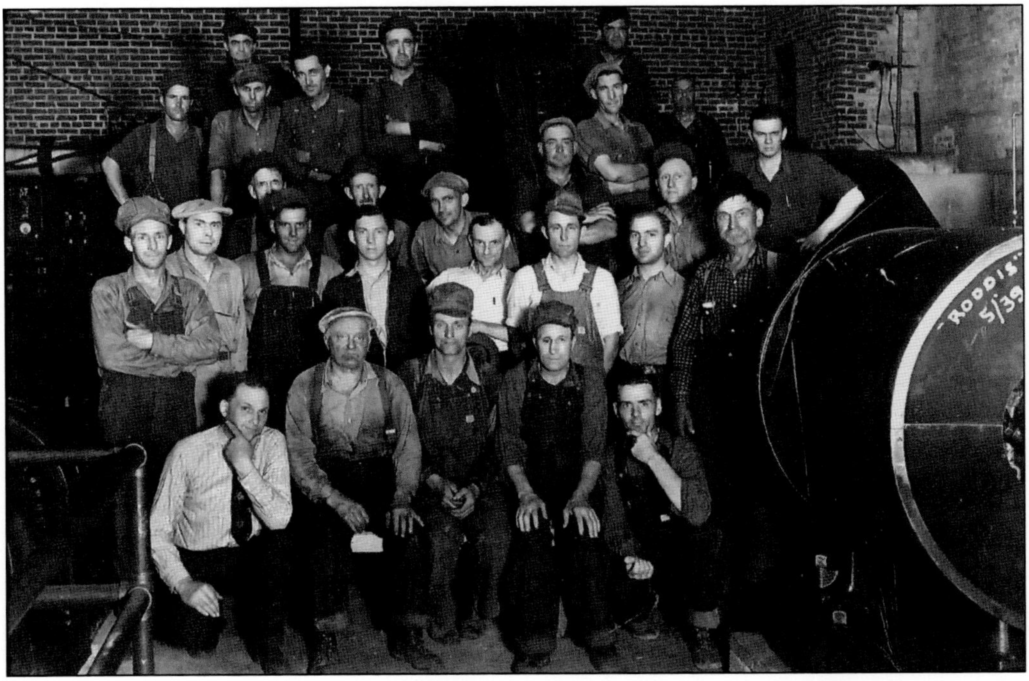

The Roddis Power Plant crew in 1939 included, from left to right, (first row) William Krashnewski, Adolph Backaus, William Salzwedl, Steve "Czackler" Zac, and Charles "Koodles" Manthe; (second row) John VanderMolen, John Drachenberg, John Noble, Kenny Zollar, Allie Rose, Frank Kotlow Sr., Philmore Pischer, and Phillip Schunk; (third row) Bill Meyers, Anton Peham, George Schrage, Bert Grossbier, Al Bercklin, and Ed Wendt; (fourth row) unidentified, Tony Miller, unidentified, Sam Muir, Adolph Paasch, Tom Verkilen, Reuben Weister, and Joe Leitner.

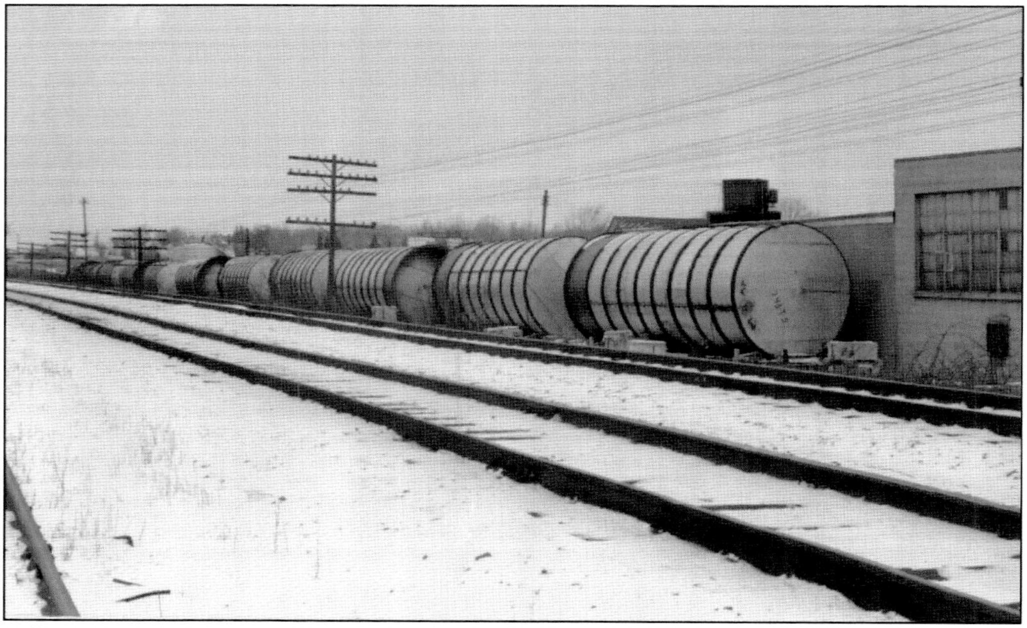

Felker Brothers moved to Marshfield from Sparta, Wisconsin, in 1903. They were manufacturers of galvanized steel products, such as stock tanks and well casings, for use on the farm and in the city. During World War II, they made parts for submarine chasers and ship deck parts for the US Navy. The company continues its operations today in the same location, producing stainless steel pipe for companies across the United States.

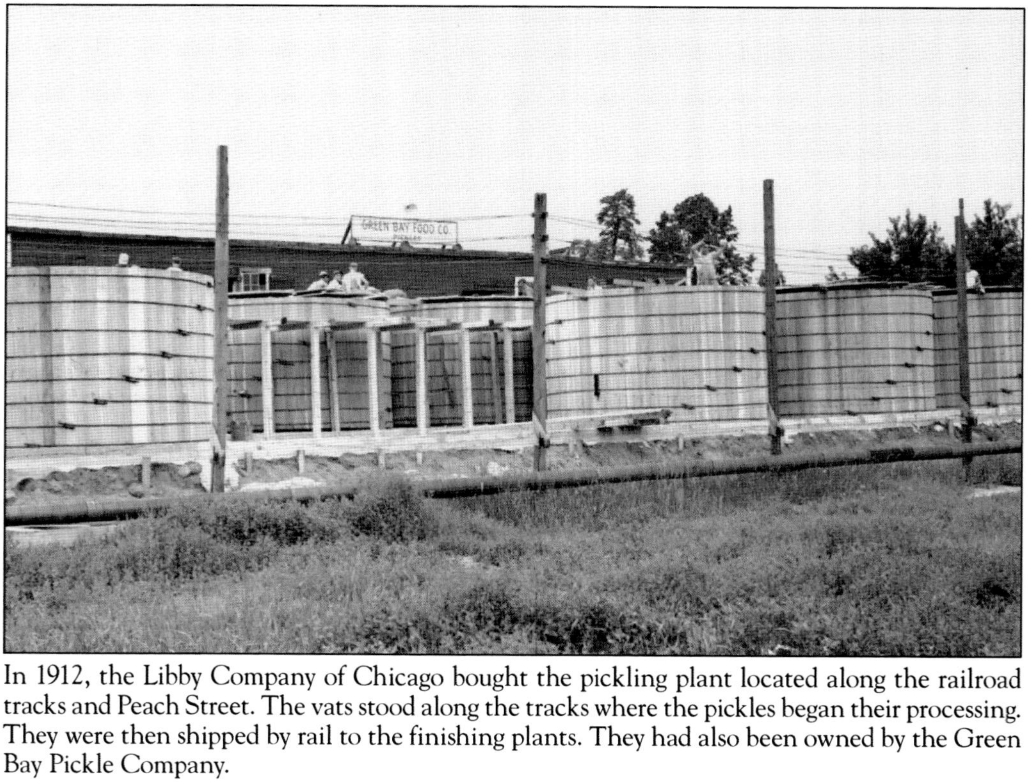

In 1912, the Libby Company of Chicago bought the pickling plant located along the railroad tracks and Peach Street. The vats stood along the tracks where the pickles began their processing. They were then shipped by rail to the finishing plants. They had also been owned by the Green Bay Pickle Company.

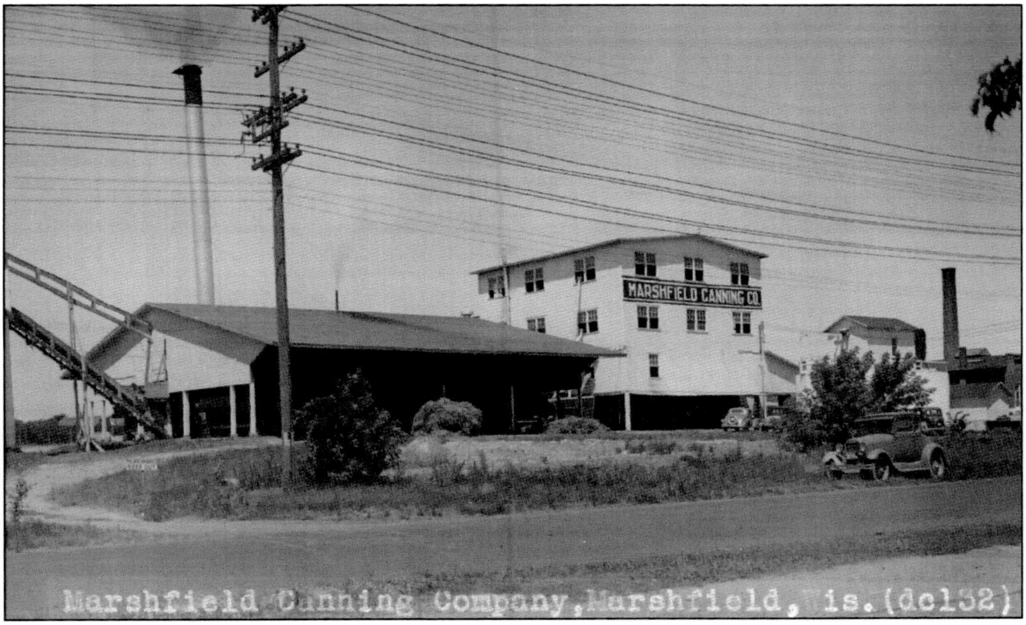

The Marshfield Canning Company was located on the southern edge of the city in the mid-1920s, employing 130 seasonal workers. During the World War II labor shortage, schools opened late in the fall so students could work in the fields. Pay was between 37¢ and 42¢ for women and 40¢ to 50¢ for men. In 1944, the company imported works from Barbados. In 1945, it was decided to use German POWs from camps nearby.

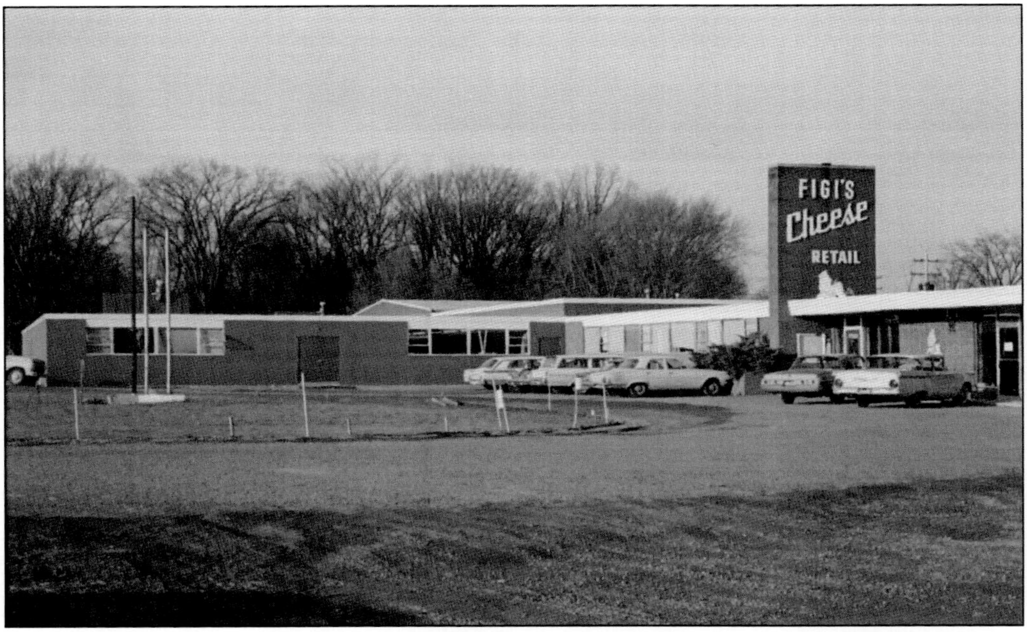

One of the largest businesses in Marshfield today is the Figi Company. Begun by John and Ann Figi in their apartment in 1945 with 43 cheese mail orders the first year, the company is now a nationwide catalog sales company as a subsidiary of The Charming Shoppers Inc. It sells a large variety of food gifts across the nation, all filled at shipping centers in Stevens Point, Neillsville, and Marshfield.

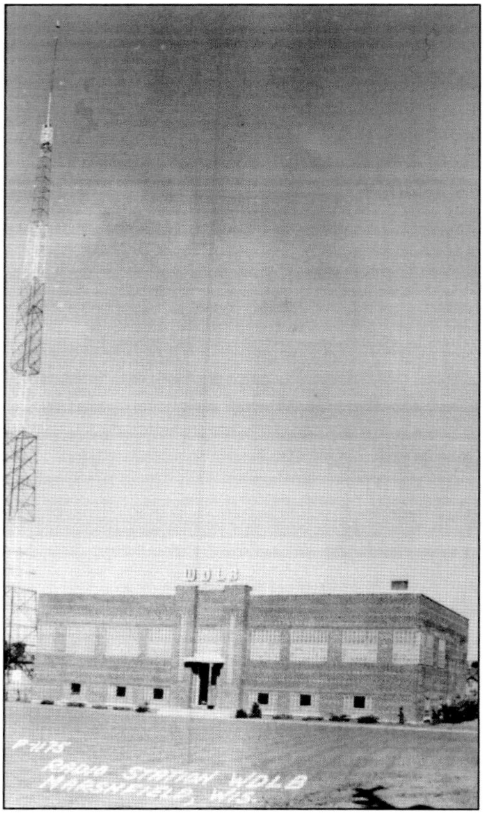

In 1945, the FCC granted a broadcast license to a group composed, in part, of Dr. Karl Doege, Lloyd Felker, Dr. L.A. Copps, George Meyer, and Corinne Kraus. They were assigned 1,450 kilocycles and the call letters WDLB. In 1966, they added 106.5 on the FM dial as WLJY, locally. In 1993, the group purchased the Spencer radio station and began a country format with the call letters WOSQ.

In the 1920s, W.L. Parkin purchased the McCrillis Ice Cream Company on West Ninth Street and began production. The specialties were molded ice cream designs. After a fire in 1941, a new brick building was erected. Today, ice cream is no longer produced here. It is now a brewpub known as West Fourteenth Street. A more formal dining area upstairs is known as Parkin Place.

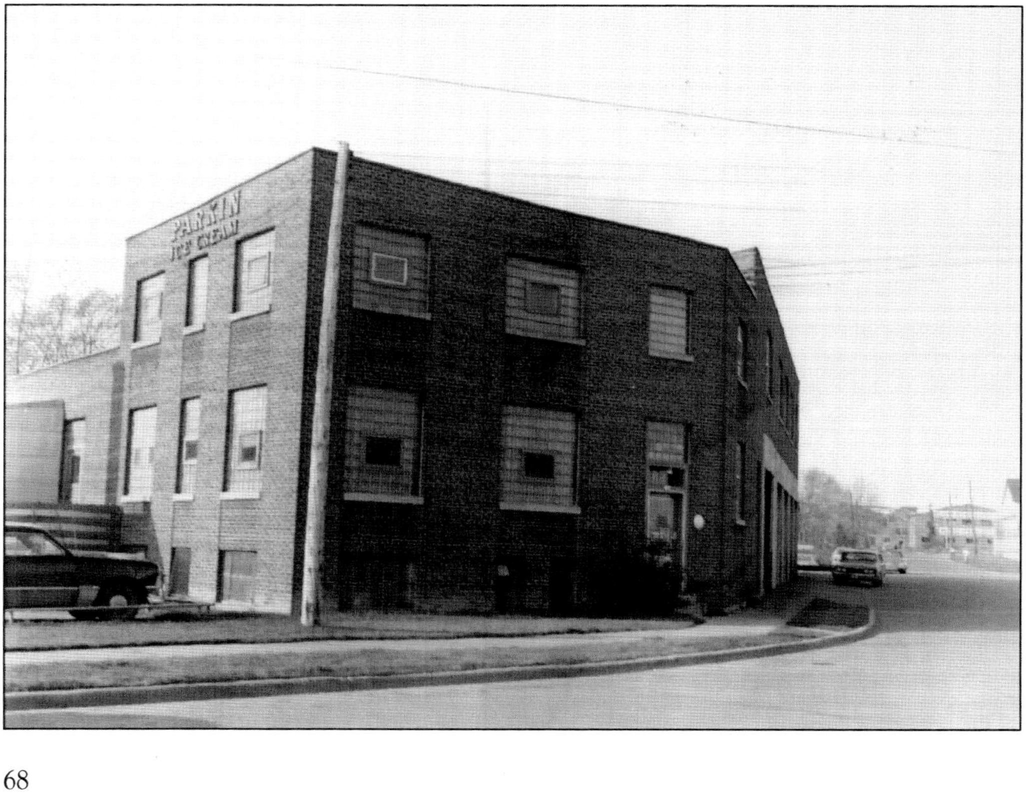

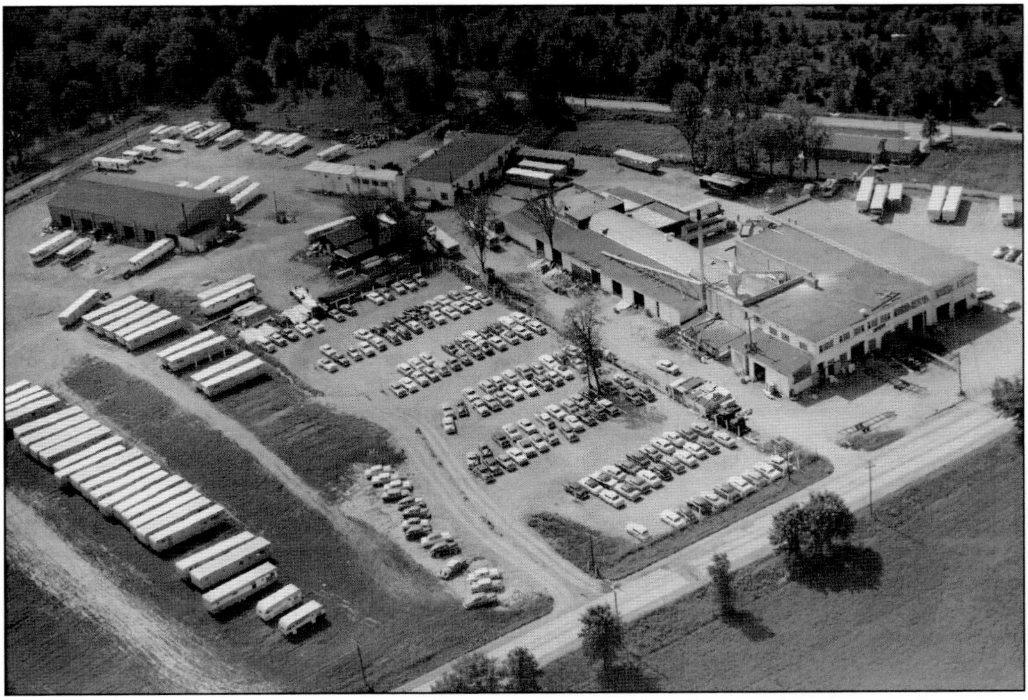

Elmer Frey built a trailer in his barn and sold it for a profit. Then, to his surprise, he got an order for another. In 1950, Rollohome Trailer Coach Company was born. The company sold 60,000 units in two years and pushed the sizes beyond 40 feet. Many were sold to house defense workers and military personnel. One was donated to the state to add to their fleet of seven traveling museums.

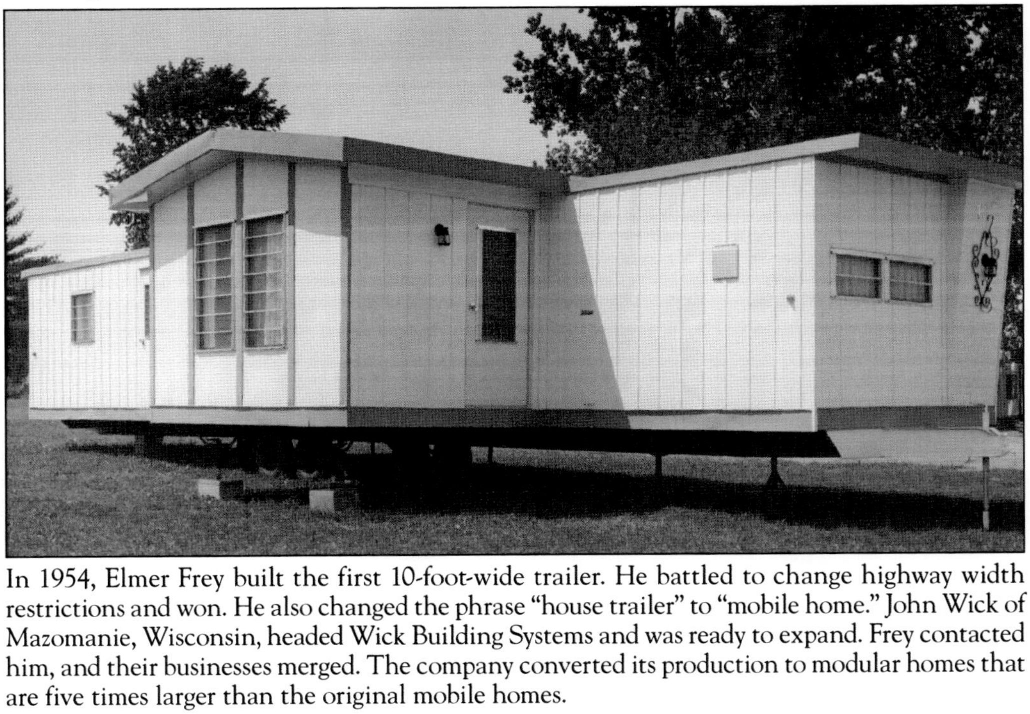

In 1954, Elmer Frey built the first 10-foot-wide trailer. He battled to change highway width restrictions and won. He also changed the phrase "house trailer" to "mobile home." John Wick of Mazomanie, Wisconsin, headed Wick Building Systems and was ready to expand. Frey contacted him, and their businesses merged. The company converted its production to modular homes that are five times larger than the original mobile homes.

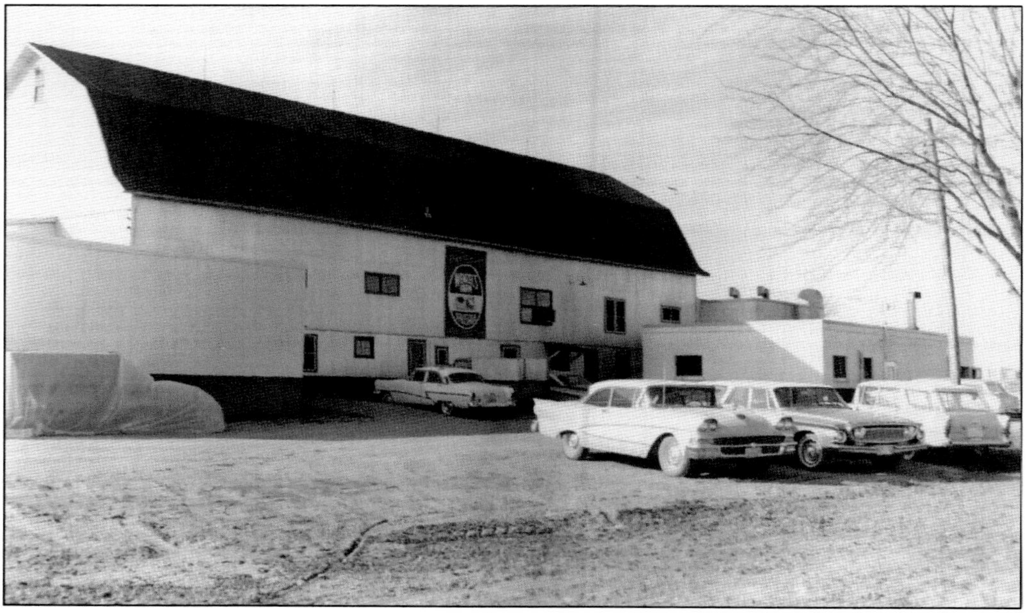

William Karl Wenzel was born near Berlin, Germany, in 1971 and was trained as a butcher. He came to Marshfield directly from Germany with his family in 1903. He operated several meat markets in Marshfield and Colby. His son William operated a veal business from the family farm. After William's death, his son Harry added a sausage company to the operation in 1949. The first sausage of Wenzel Farms was sold in 1949.

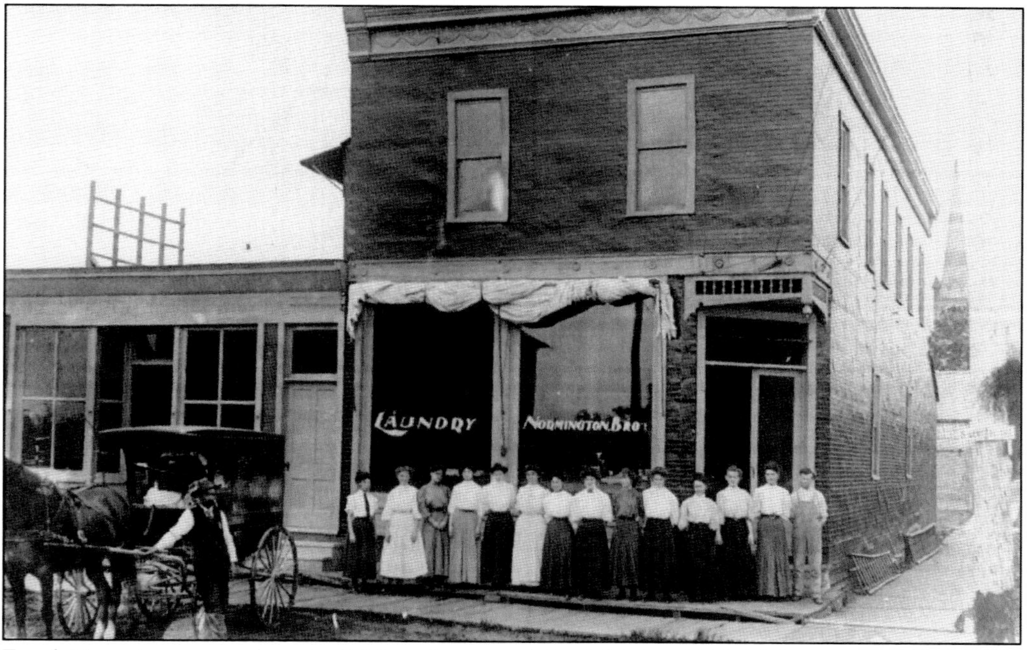

Frank Normington was born in 1872 and came to Marshfield in 1902. He had operated laundries in Milwaukee and Tomahawk. He bought a laundry operation from A. Rumenopp and opened his business on the corner of Sixth Street and Central Avenue. In 1959, they opened the first coin-operated laundry in the area. The building was sold to the Clinic for its expansion in 1968, and operations moved to the north side.

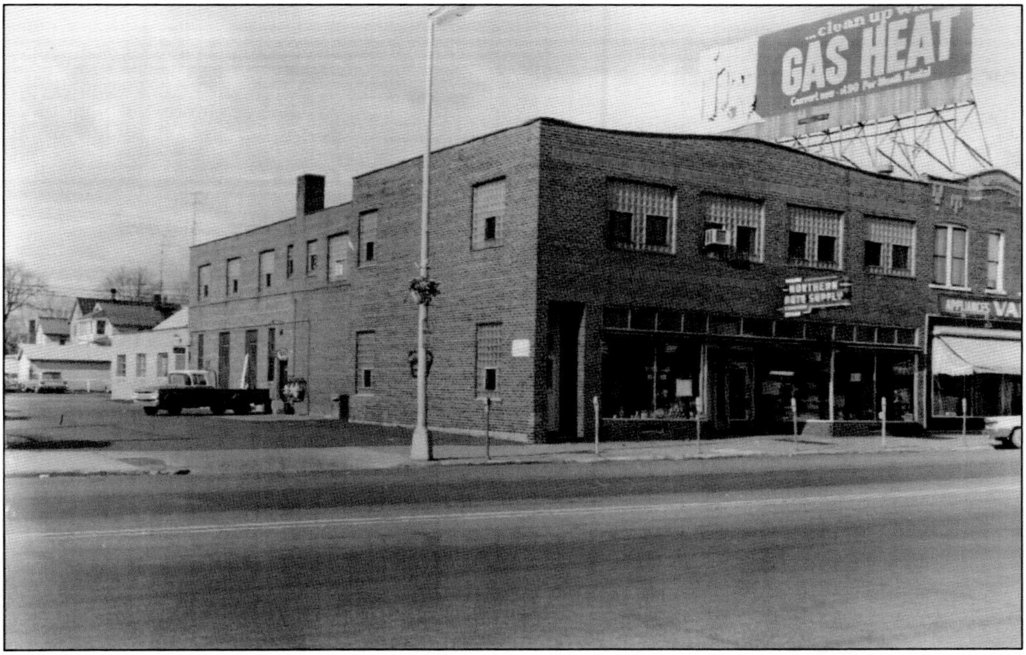

Northern Auto Supply Company was organized as a corporation in Marshfield in 1918. Under the leadership of E.M. Lee, the company grew. It opened its first branch in Stevens Point in 1931, then in Rhinelander in 1933, and Wausau in 1934. Over the next 20 years, stores were opened in 30 other cities across central and northern Wisconsin within 150 miles of Marshfield.

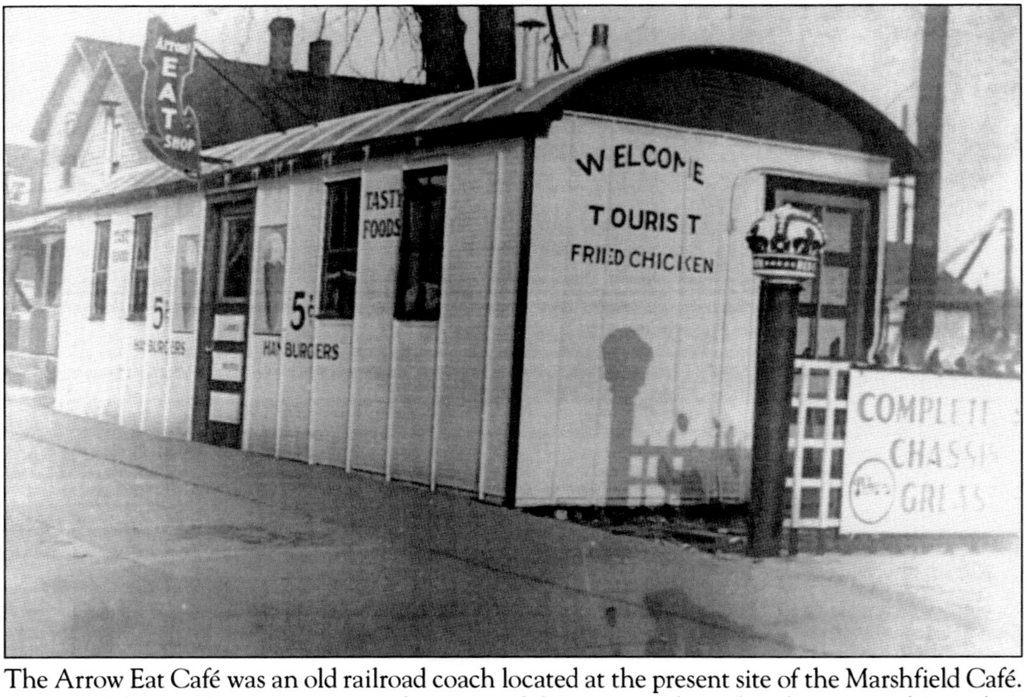

The Arrow Eat Café was an old railroad coach located at the present site of the Marshfield Café. It opened during the Depression and was noted for its 5¢ and 10¢ hamburgers and 30¢ plate lunches. Open from 6:00 a.m. to 10:00 p.m., it was located near the movie theater and caught the crowds after the first show. Today, it is the site of the Marshfield Café.

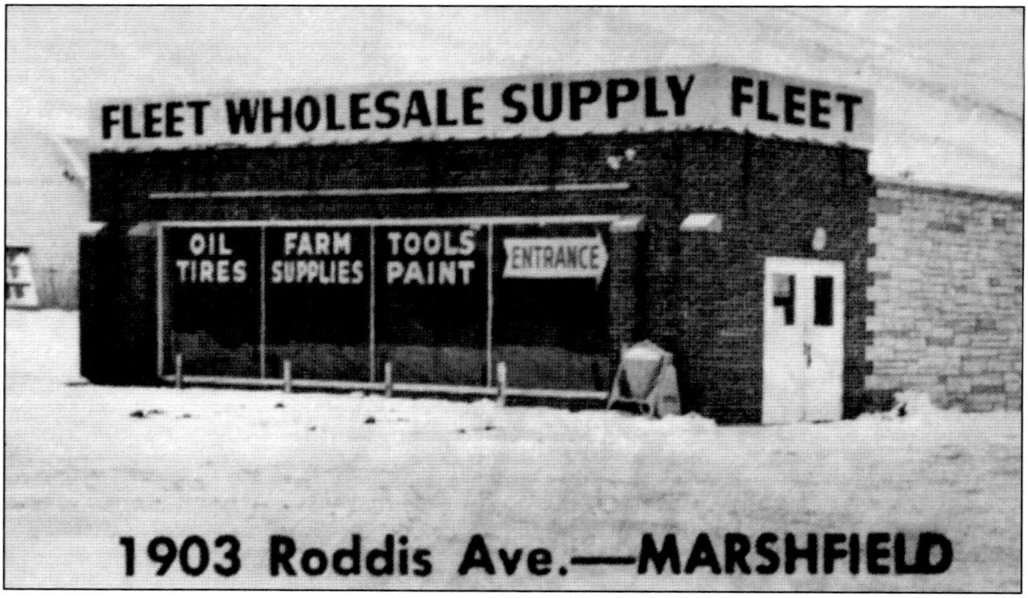

Marshfield was the location of the first Mills Fleet Farm Store, located on South Roddis Avenue. It was then known as Fleet Wholesale and Supply. From this beginning, the company has branched out into 31 stores in Wisconsin, Minnesota, Iowa, and North Dakota. The stores sell a wide variety of farm supplies, clothing, toys, yard and garden supplies, and housewares.

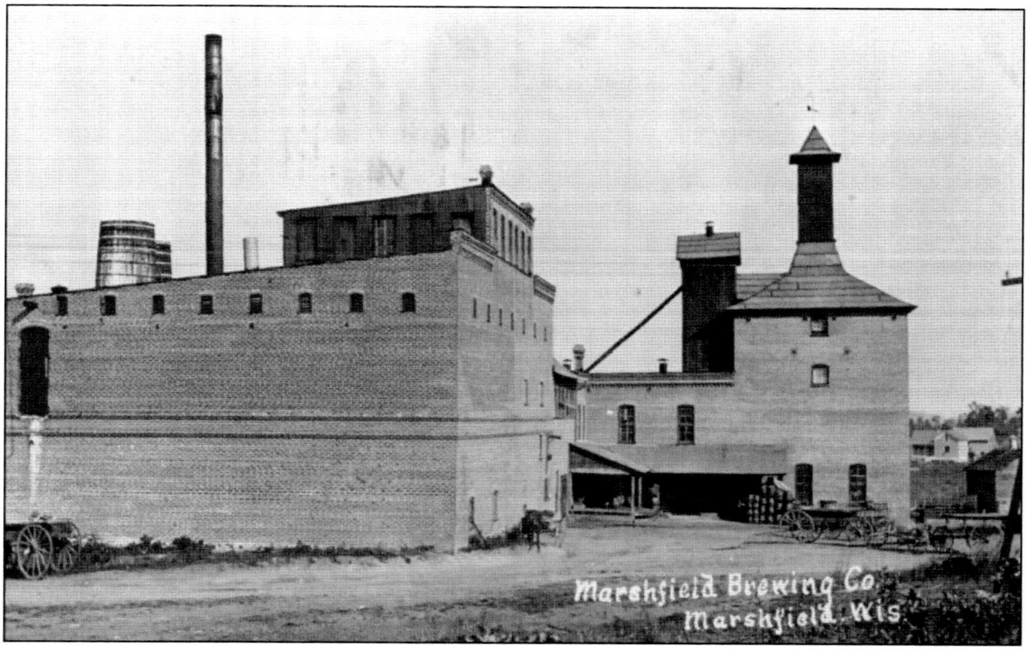

With many Germans populating the area, beer was always a popular drink. In 1890, the first barrel was sold from the Marshfield Brewery. The operation changed hands several times over its 77-year history but continued production, except during Prohibition, until it finally closed in 1967.

Five

HEALTH CARE INDUSTRY

Marshfield became the center of medical care when the first Marshfield Clinic was created in 1916. The city had always attracted doctors, and when many of them united into one organization no one knew nor expected it would grow into the nationally known and recognized health care and medical research facility it is today.

The Marshfield Clinic is the center for farm medicine research, which has identified conditions, such as farmer's lung disease, related to the inhalation of dust and fumes from working in and around silos. They are now involved in research in the field of genetics relating to the occurrences of diseases. In 1890, the Sisters of the Sorrowful Mother established a six-bed hospital, which has grown into the large hospital of today and continues the mission of the Sisters to minister to the sick and their families. The medical facilities in Marshfield continue to grow and expand into new areas of patient care and medical research. In 1909, the Wood County Board passed a resolution to build a "county insane asylum" at a location along County Highway A east of Marshfield. The facility opened in 1910.

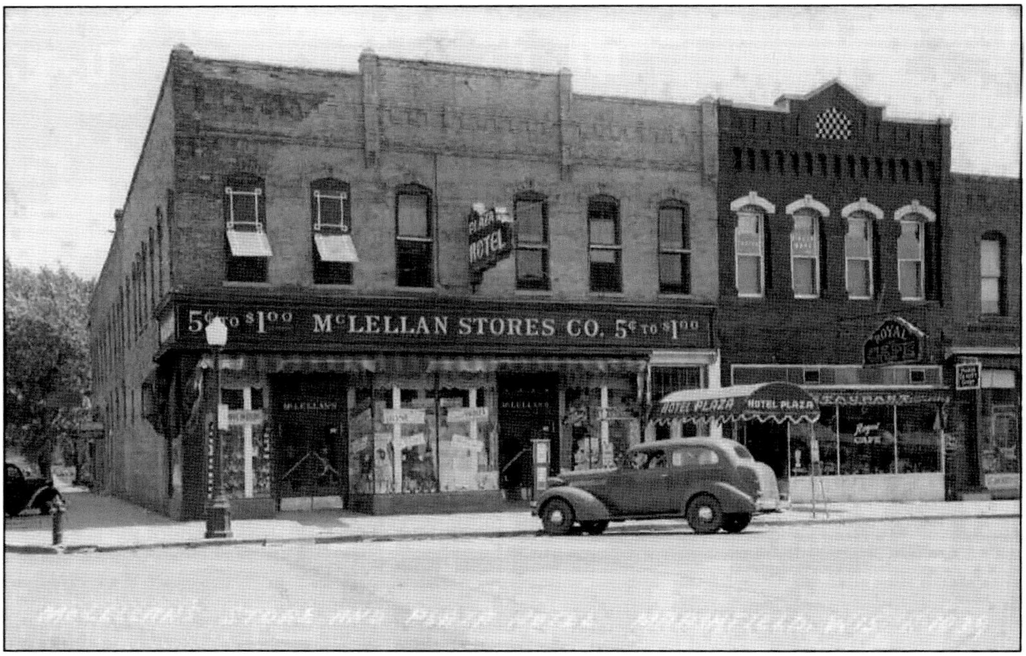

The Marshfield Clinic was first established in the Thiel Building on the southeast corner of Third Street and Central Avenue. It was created in 1915 when Dr. Karl W. Doege introduced the idea to his fellow doctors, Victor Mason and Hansford Milbee. The other seven doctors in the city of 7,100 were asked to join, and Drs. Walter G. Sexton, William A. Hipke, and Roy P. Potter accepted.

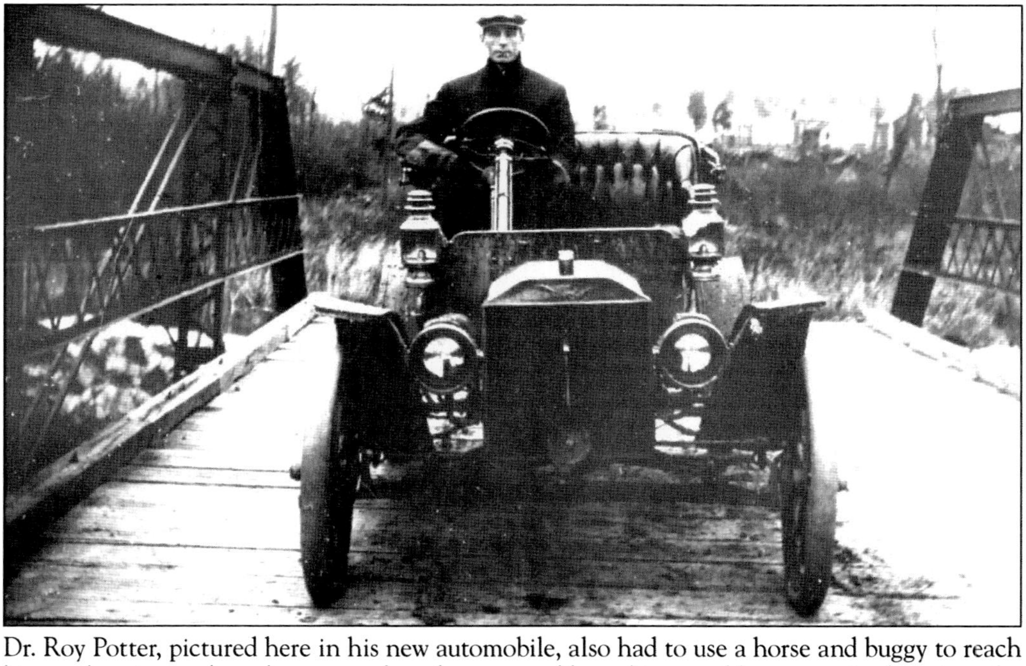

Dr. Roy Potter, pictured here in his new automobile, also had to use a horse and buggy to reach his rural patients when the unpaved roads were muddy and impassable to cars. In the winter he also used a horse-drawn sleigh. Doctors were on call all hours of the day and night and often delivered babies and performed minor surgeries in patients' homes.

Dr. Karl W. Doege was born in Stettin, Germany, in 1867, coming with his family to a farm near Thorp, Wisconsin, in 1881. He graduated from Western Reserve Medical School in Cleveland, Ohio, at the age of 23 and stopped at Marshfield on his way home. In 1890, when he set up his practice, Marshfield had recovered from its disastrous fire and boasted a population of 3,400 people, 10 hotels, 26 saloons, and a hospital.

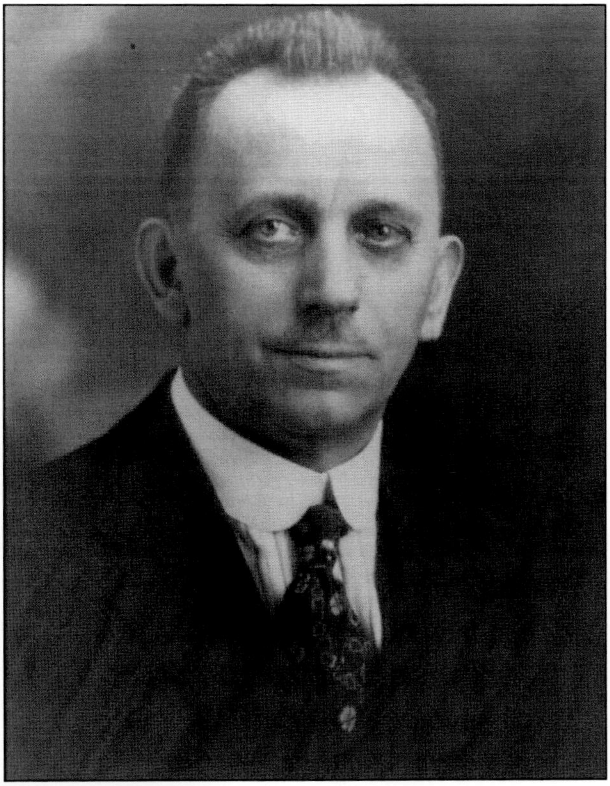

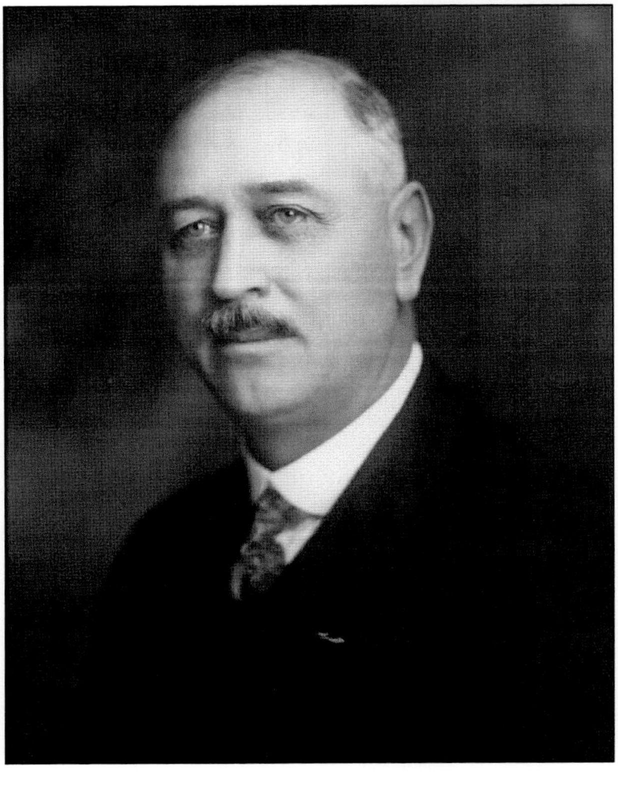

The son of poor Irish immigrants, Dr. Hansford H. Milbee was born in Canada in 1870. He received his medical degree from Trinity Medical College, part of the University of Toronto, in 1896. He first practiced near Hudson, Wisconsin, moving to Marshfield in 1901. He preferred non-surgical treatment to surgery. He was one of the first to use an X-ray machine in Marshfield.

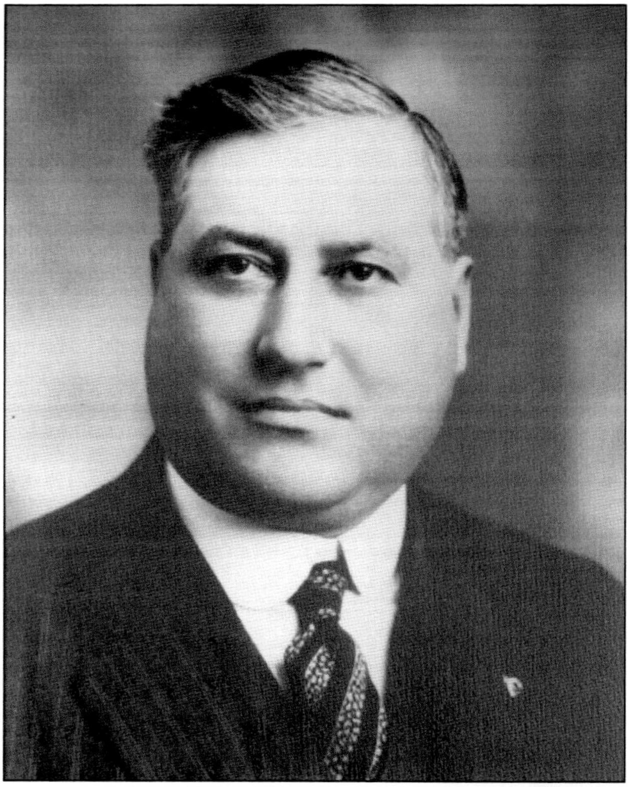

Dr. Victor Mason was born in Portsmouth, England, in 1860. He immigrated in 1874 to Canada and later to Michigan. In 1889, the family moved to Marshfield and lived next door to Doctor Milbee. He graduated from the University of Toronto with a medical degree in 1906. After two years of education in Europe, he returned to Marshfield to set up practice in the "Doctor's Block." He specialized in surgery.

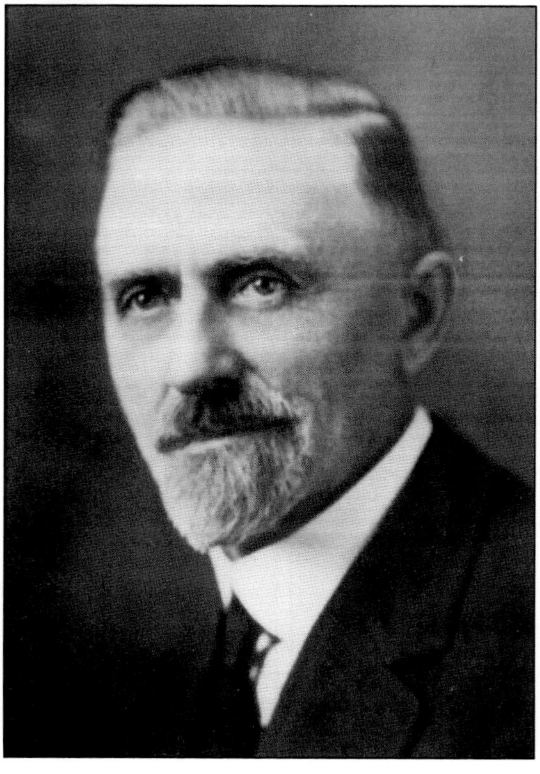

Dr. William Hipke was born in 1865 in New Holstein, Wisconsin. He graduated from the University of Illinois in 1891. He studied ophthalmology and otolaryngology in Vienna in the early 1900s and set up his practice in Marshfield on East Second Street. He was the first eye, ear, nose, and throat specialist at Marshfield Clinic. He retired at the age of 70.

Dr. Walter Gresham Sexton was born in 1886. When his parents died, eight-year-old Walter was sent to live with his cousin William Sexton, a pioneer pharmacist in Marshfield. After graduating from the University of Wisconsin, he attended Johns Hopkins University and graduated in 1911. Dr. K.W. Doege invited him to join his practice as a urologist.

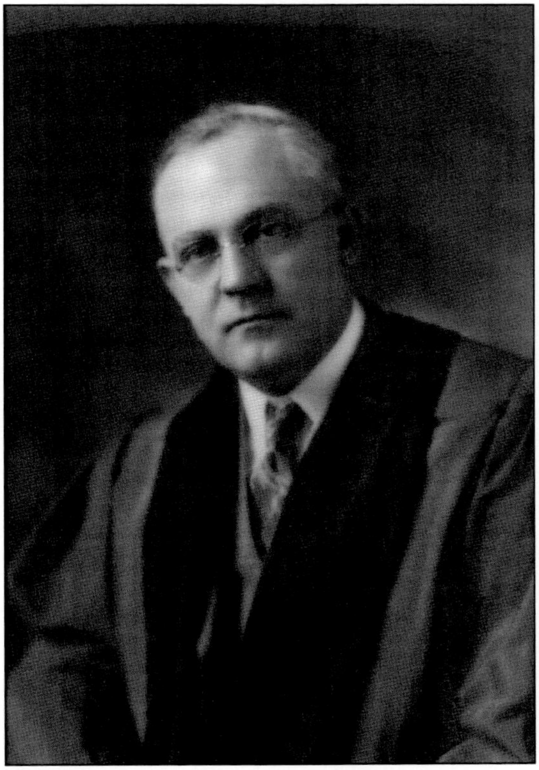

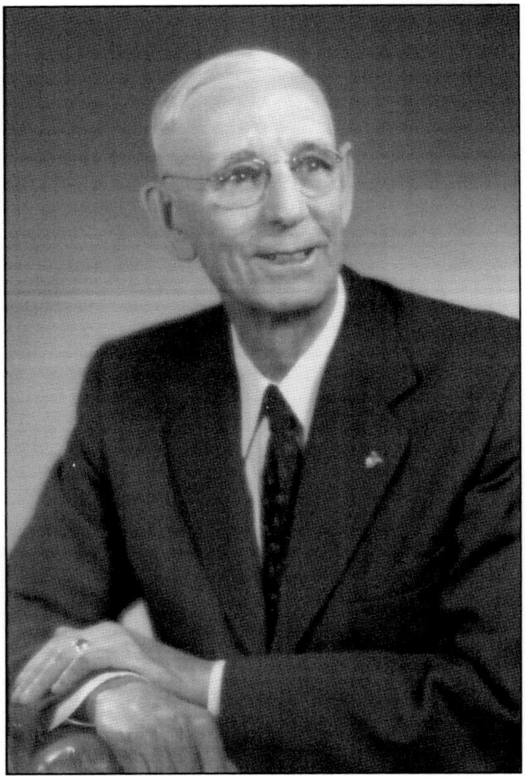

Dr. Roy Potter was born in Mauston, Wisconsin, in 1879. He dropped out of high school and worked for a doctor, learning to compound prescriptions. He decided to become a pharmacist but transferred to Milwaukee Medical College, where a shorter program would give him his medical degree. He lost one year to tuberculosis but still graduated at age 23. He came to Marshfield in 1910 and became a radiologist.

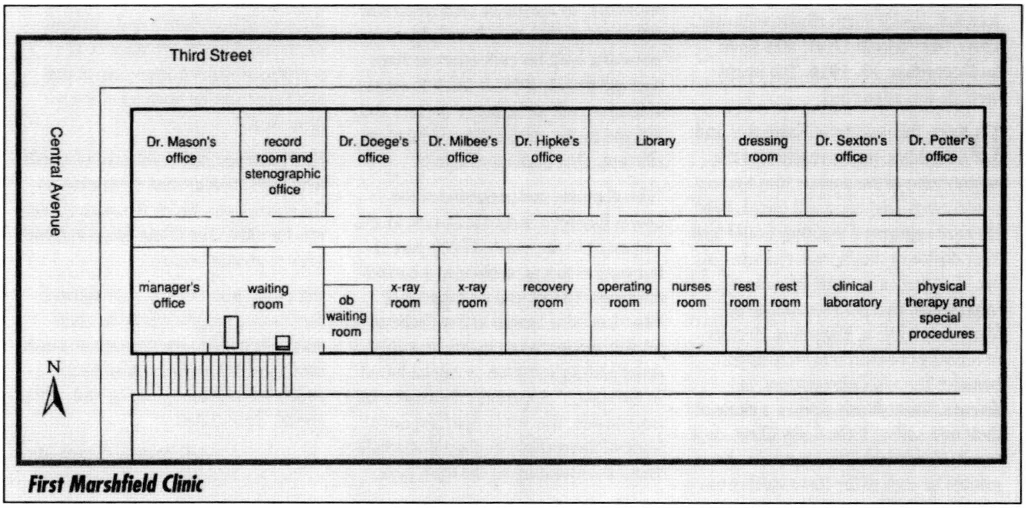

The floor plan of the 1917 Marshfield Clinic shows the efficient organization of space. The complex was laid out to accommodate modern equipment, such as an X-ray machine, as well as the specialties of each doctor. The library indicates a commitment to keep abreast of the latest medical advances and research.

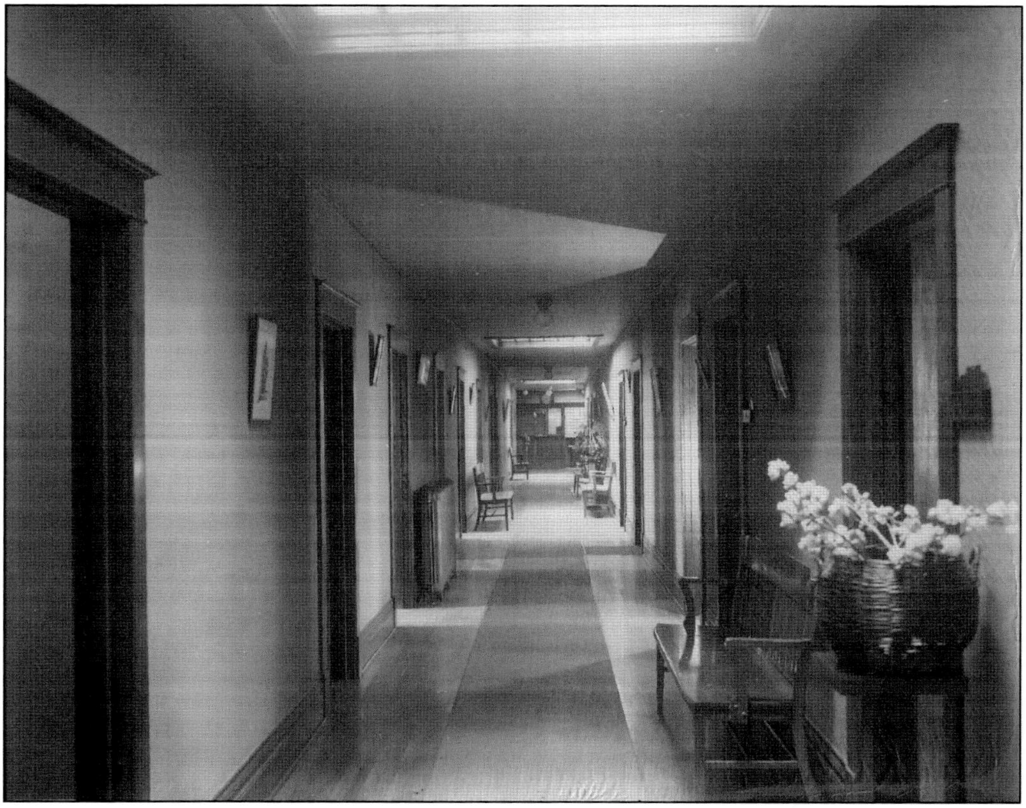

The use of skylights to illuminate the long main hallway of the Marshfield Clinic added not only light but also a sense of style that remains as a hallmark in the present facilities. The use of art as decoration in both the hallways and offices, and the existence of an art gallery in the building, show this commitment to a pleasant surrounding for the patient.

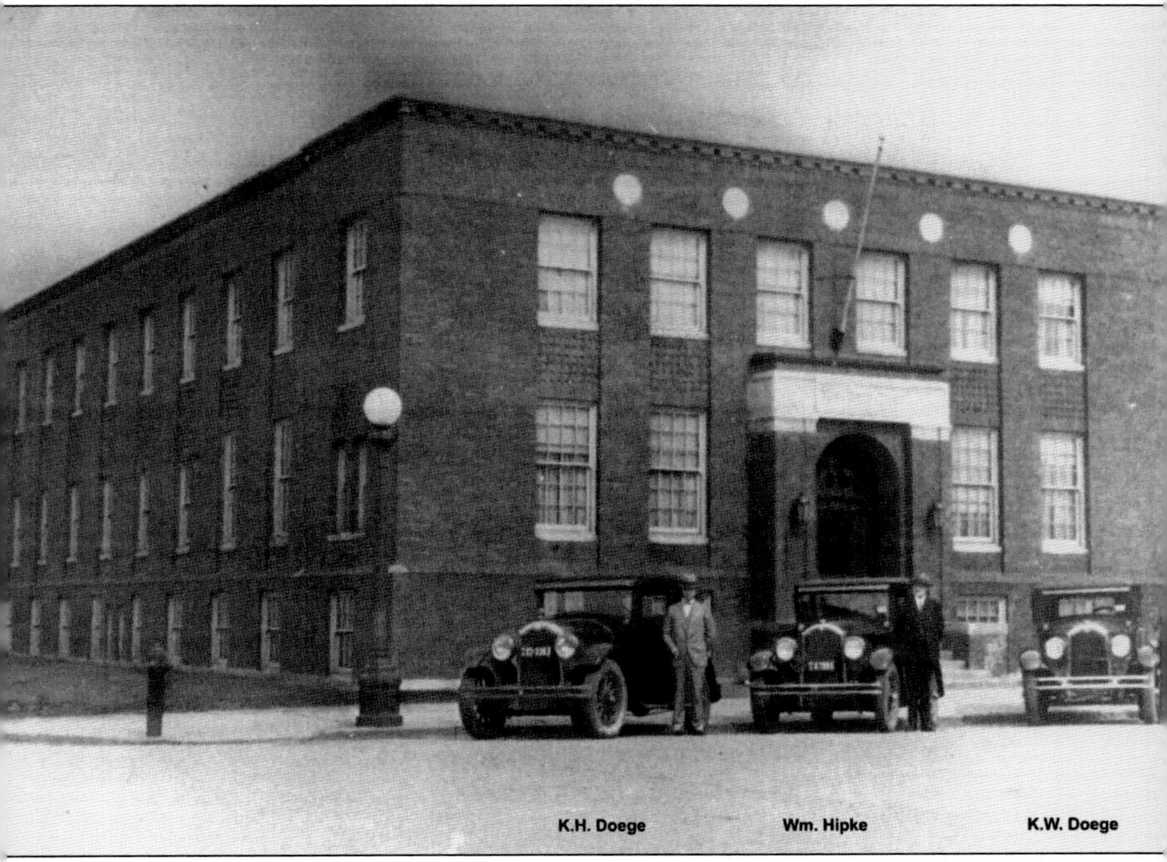

In 1926, due to its rapid patient growth, the Marshfield Clinic constructed a new building at the northwest corner of South Central Avenue and West Seventh Street, today part of city hall. This allowed the doctors to design a building that suited the medical profession from the ground up.

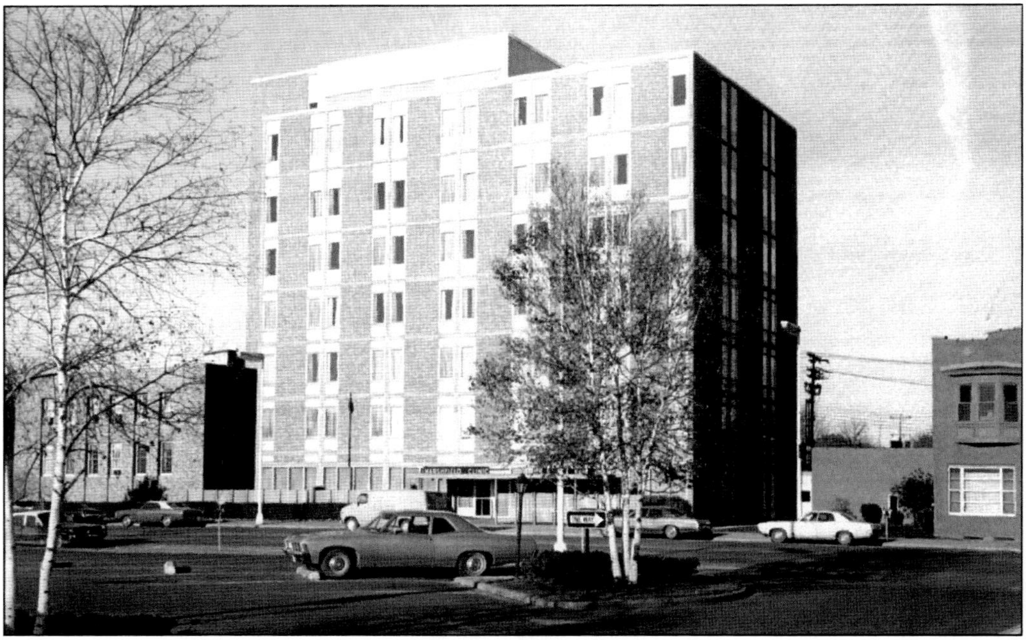

In 1958, a new building was constructed next to the 1927 structure. The new four-story building, plus the addition of three floors in 1964, indicated continual growth. By 1975, it again outgrew its location. A new location had to be found that would allow for future growth.

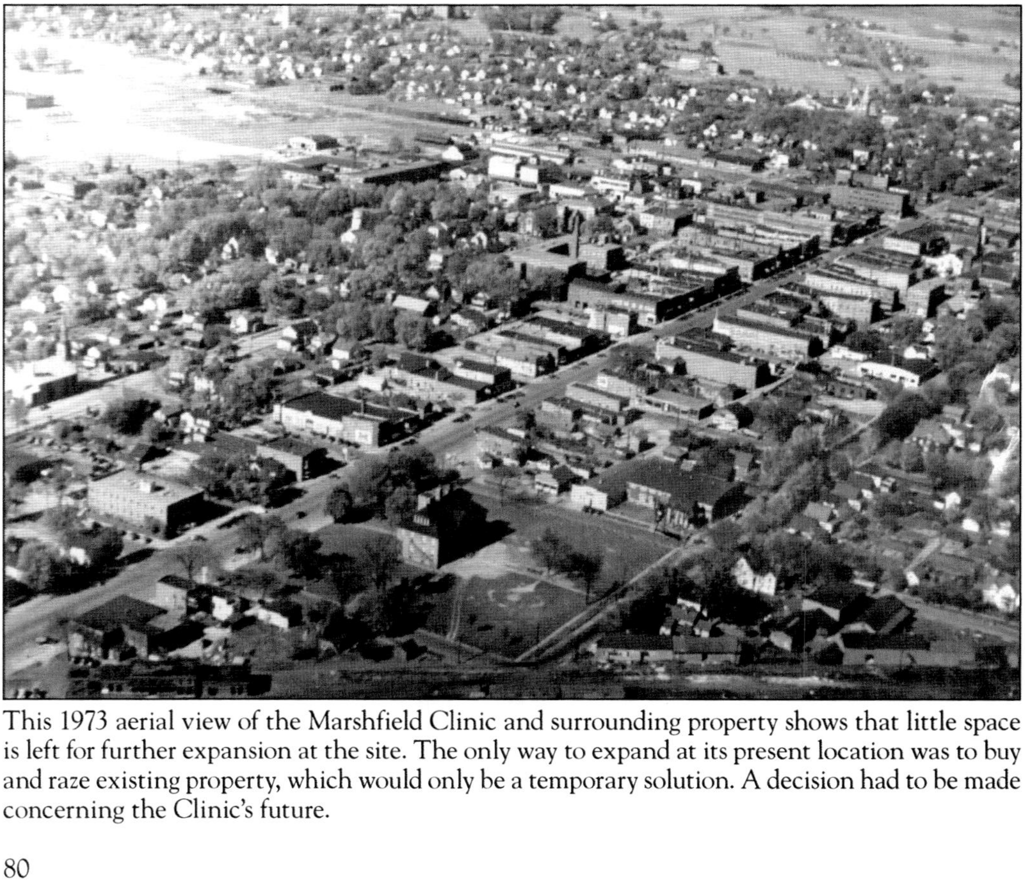

This 1973 aerial view of the Marshfield Clinic and surrounding property shows that little space is left for further expansion at the site. The only way to expand at its present location was to buy and raze existing property, which would only be a temporary solution. A decision had to be made concerning the Clinic's future.

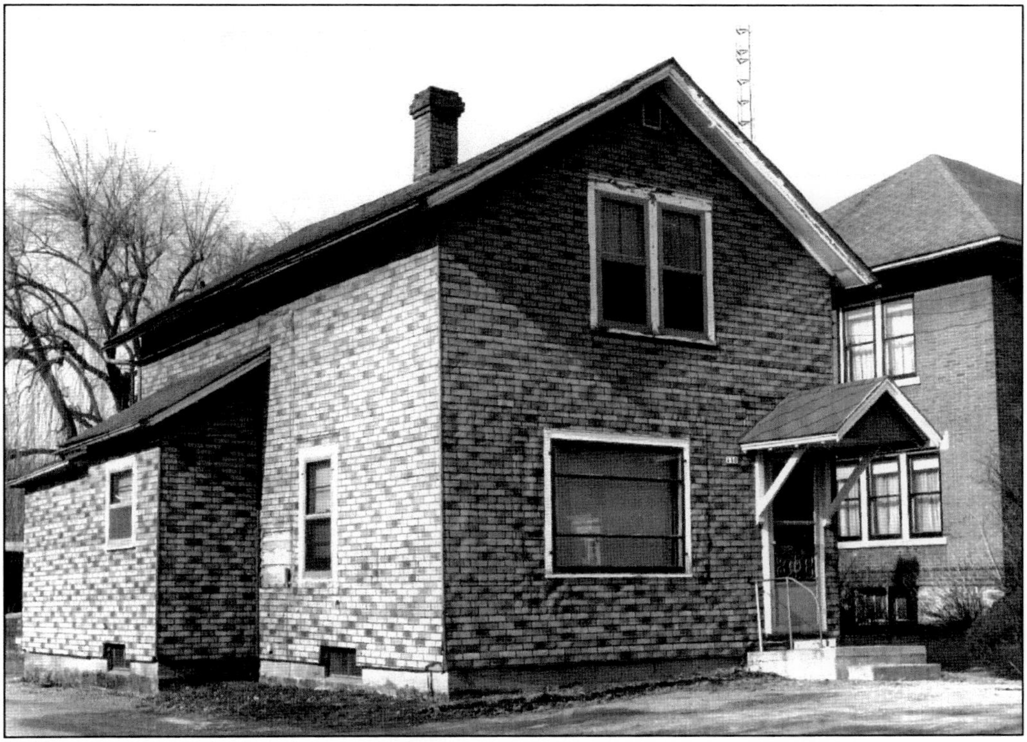

This structure was known as the Brown House and housed the animals for the medical research facility and the graphic arts department. It was located at 110 West Sixth Street and was condemned in the late 1960s as being unsafe for the animals. The graphic arts department was moved next door to a building called the Parsonage, and this building was razed.

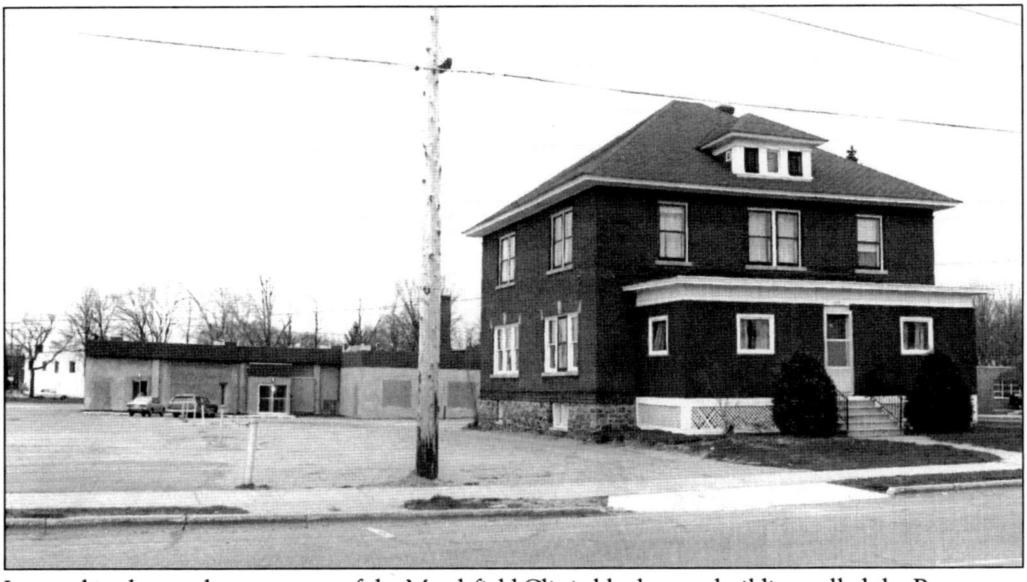

Located in the northwest corner of the Marshfield Clinic block was a building called the Parsonage. It was formerly part of the Immanuel Lutheran Church property when the church had been located in this area before moving across the street. In the late 1960s, it housed the Marshfield Clinic's stenographic and graphic arts departments.

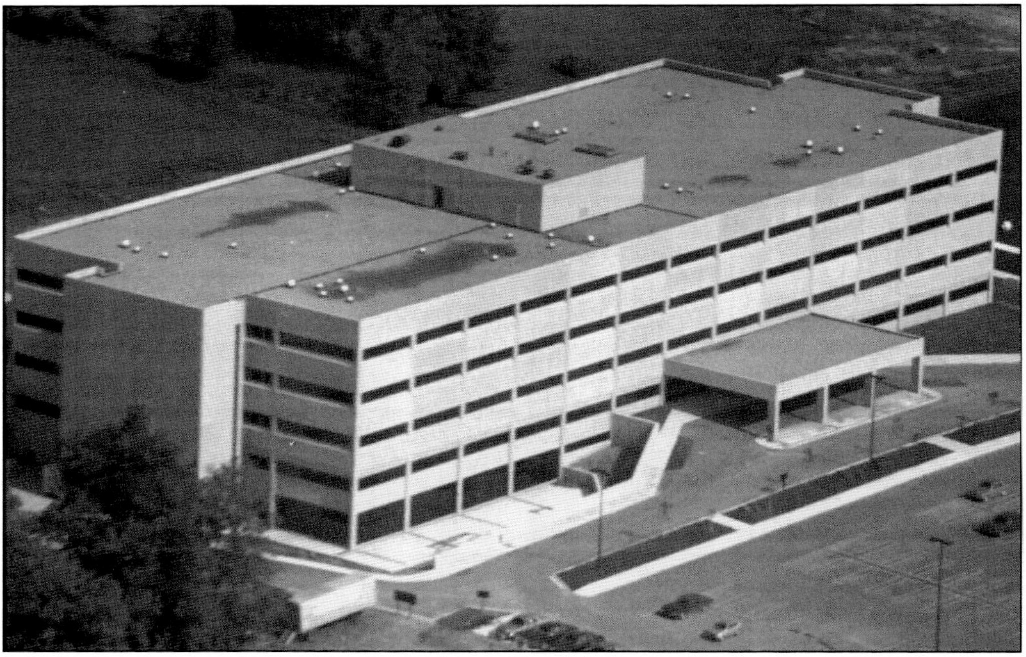

In 1975, the decision was made to move the Marshfield Clinic to a location with ample space for future development east of St. Joseph's Hospital on Marshfield's northwest side. The new facility contained 560,000 square feet. This was a far cry from its beginnings on the second floor of a downtown retail store. Phenomenal growth had been experienced in a period of only 60 years.

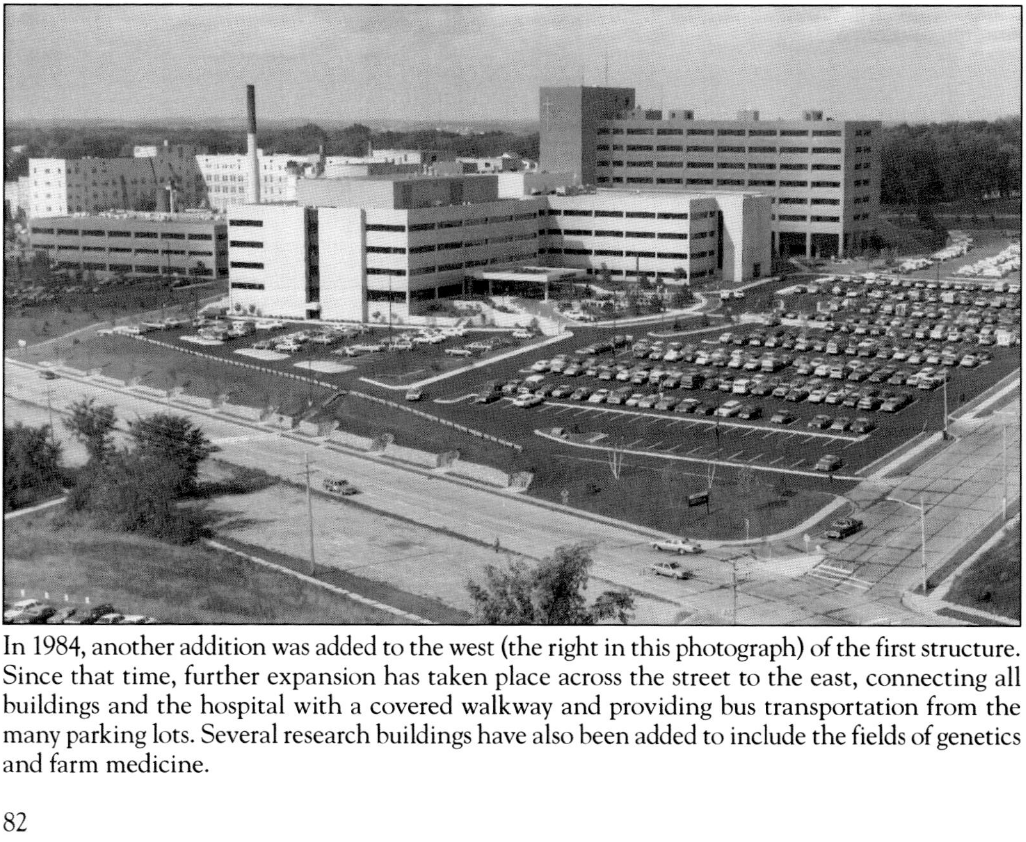

In 1984, another addition was added to the west (the right in this photograph) of the first structure. Since that time, further expansion has taken place across the street to the east, connecting all buildings and the hospital with a covered walkway and providing bus transportation from the many parking lots. Several research buildings have also been added to include the fields of genetics and farm medicine.

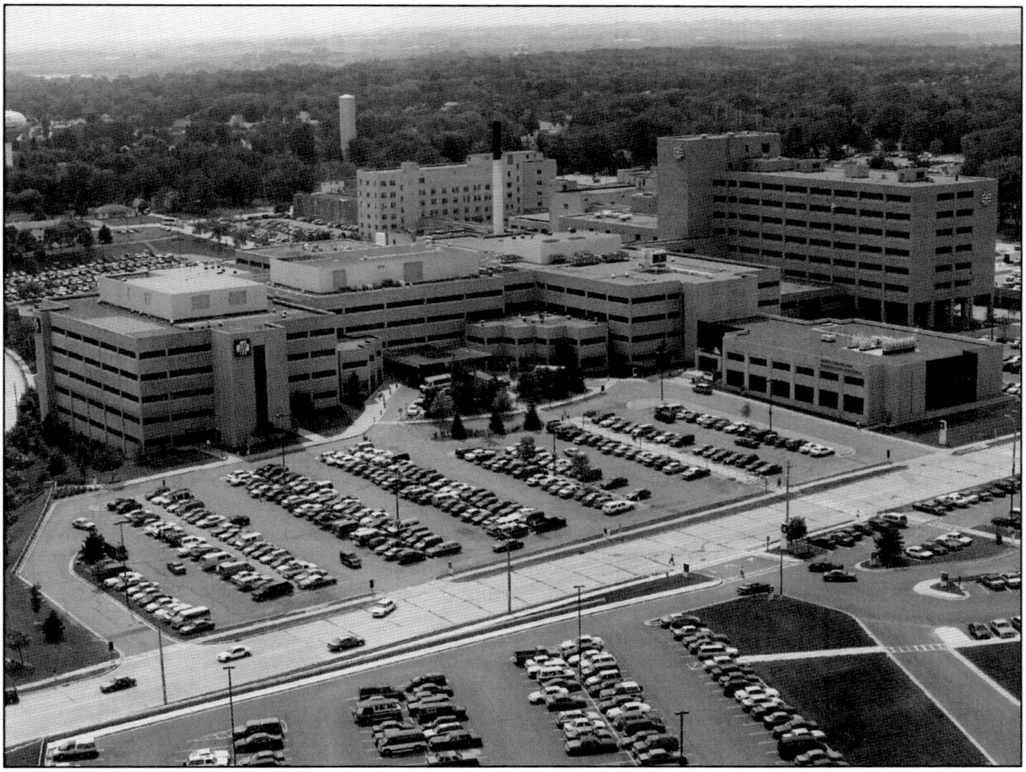

Situated to the east of the main complex of the Marshfield Clinic are the Clinic Foundation and the National Farm Medicine Center, where farm-related diseases and accident prevention are studied. A disease known as farmer's lung was first identified here after it had often been mistaken for tuberculosis.

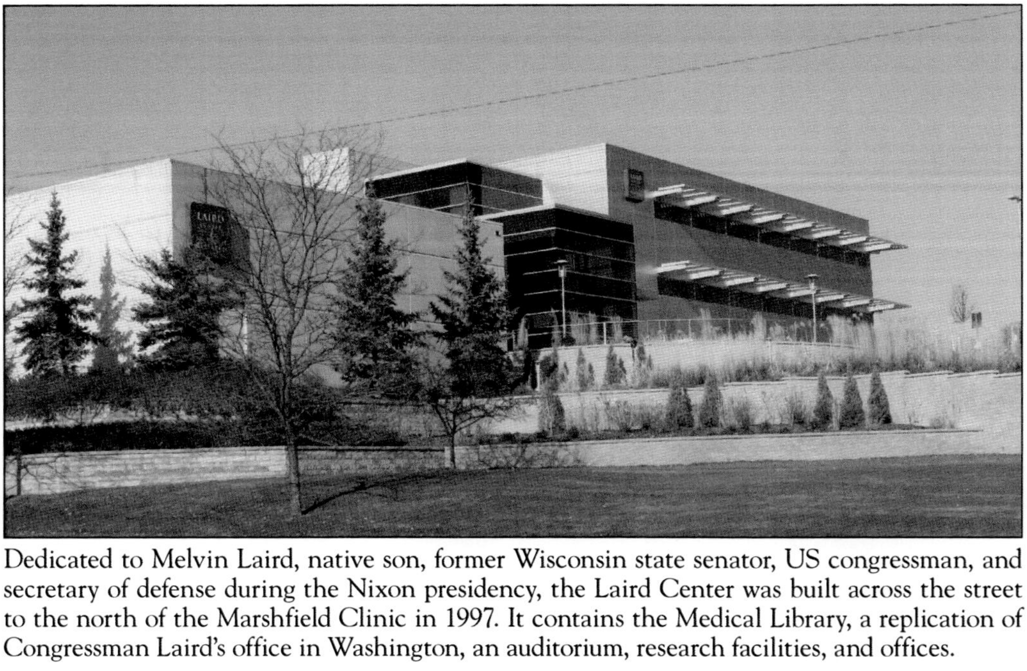

Dedicated to Melvin Laird, native son, former Wisconsin state senator, US congressman, and secretary of defense during the Nixon presidency, the Laird Center was built across the street to the north of the Marshfield Clinic in 1997. It contains the Medical Library, a replication of Congressman Laird's office in Washington, an auditorium, research facilities, and offices.

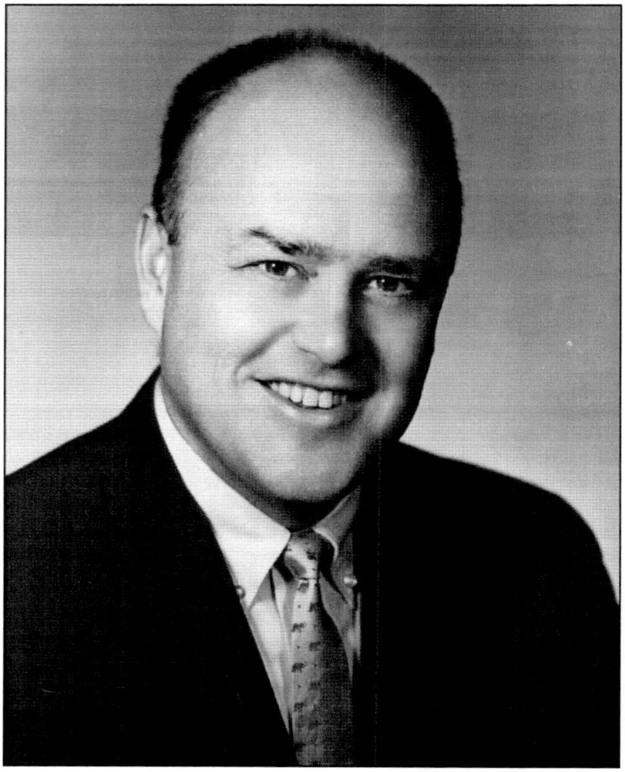

Melvin Laird Jr., as the ranking member of the House Appropriations Committee, worked for adoption of a special report by that committee to make the Marshfield Clinic a regional medical center so that it could receive priority in establishing facilities to treat heart disease, cancer, and stroke cases ahead of all other medical clinics in the state.

The Wood County Asylum was located east of Marshfield on County Highway A. It was built in 1910 and had a capacity of 250 mental patients. The care was considered protective in nature, and work therapy was utilized. The facility closed in 1974, and 100 patients moved to a facility on North Chestnut Avenue. It became licensed as a psychiatric hospital and nursing home in 1974.

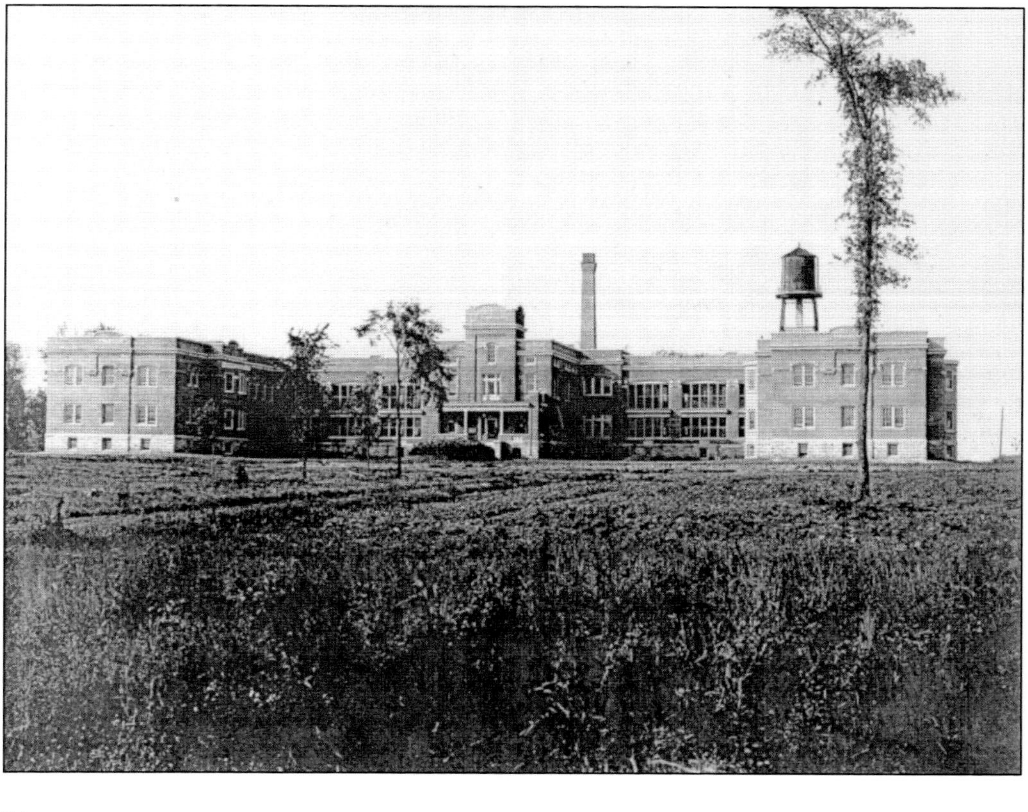

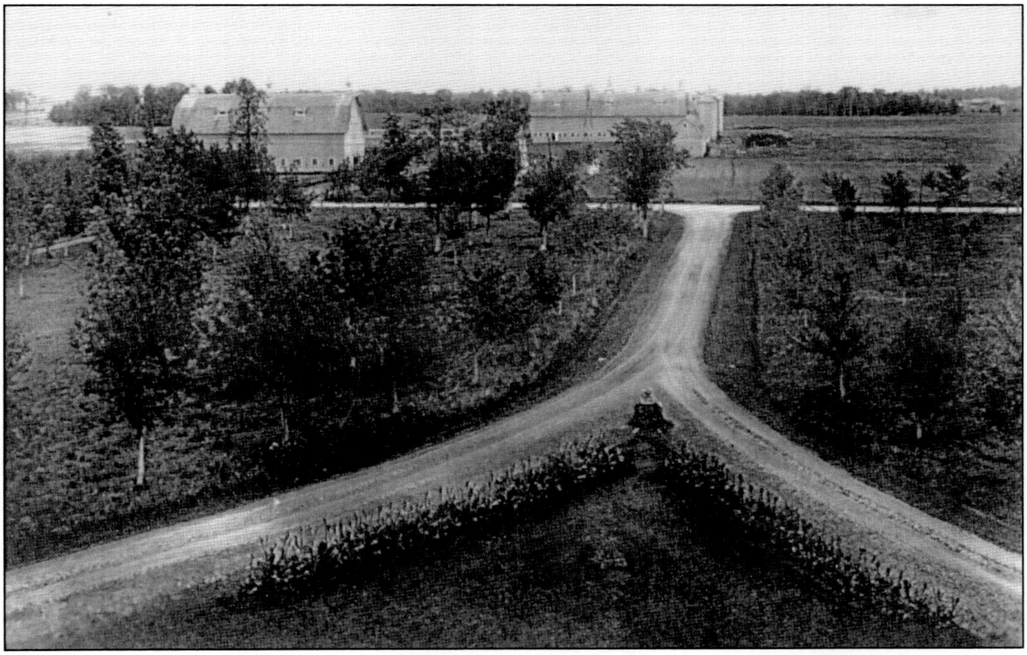

The grounds included 640 acres of prime farmland with barns, one of which still stands today east of County Highway A. The facility raised cattle, hogs, and horses and grew much of the food for the patients. It became one of the most respected operations in the county. A tunnel connected the hospital grounds with the farm to prevent injury to patients as they crossed the highway.

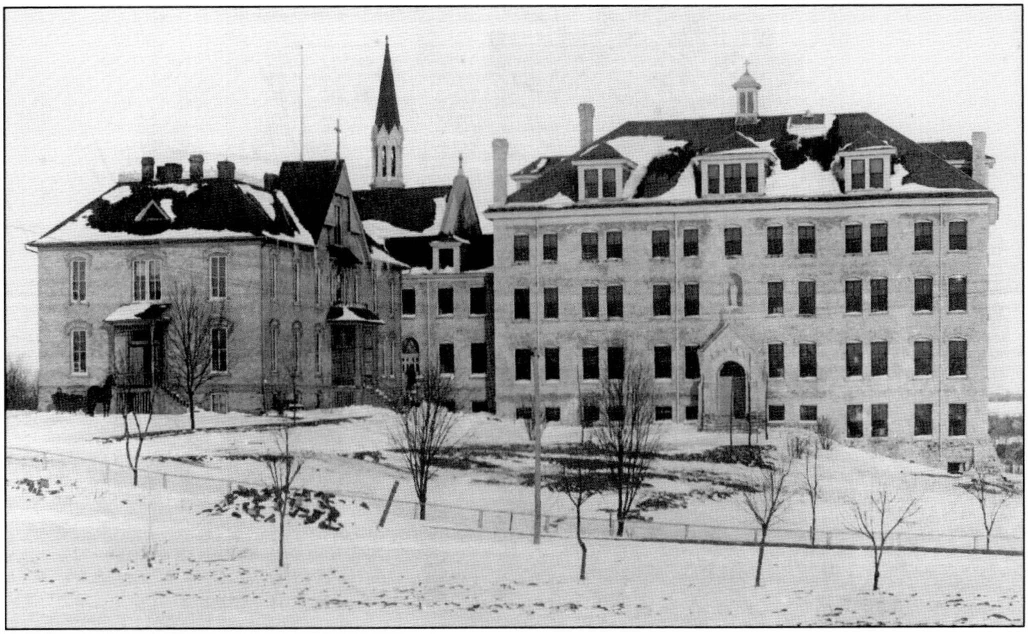

In 1890, the Sisters of the Sorrowful Mother were invited to Marshfield by Fr. Geyer of St. John's Catholic Church to begin a hospital in the city. He called upon his parishioners to supply horses and scoops to excavate the basement and haul stones for the foundation. The building was to be completed in late fall of 1890. It was apparent that this would not happen, so a house was purchased to serve as the hospital.

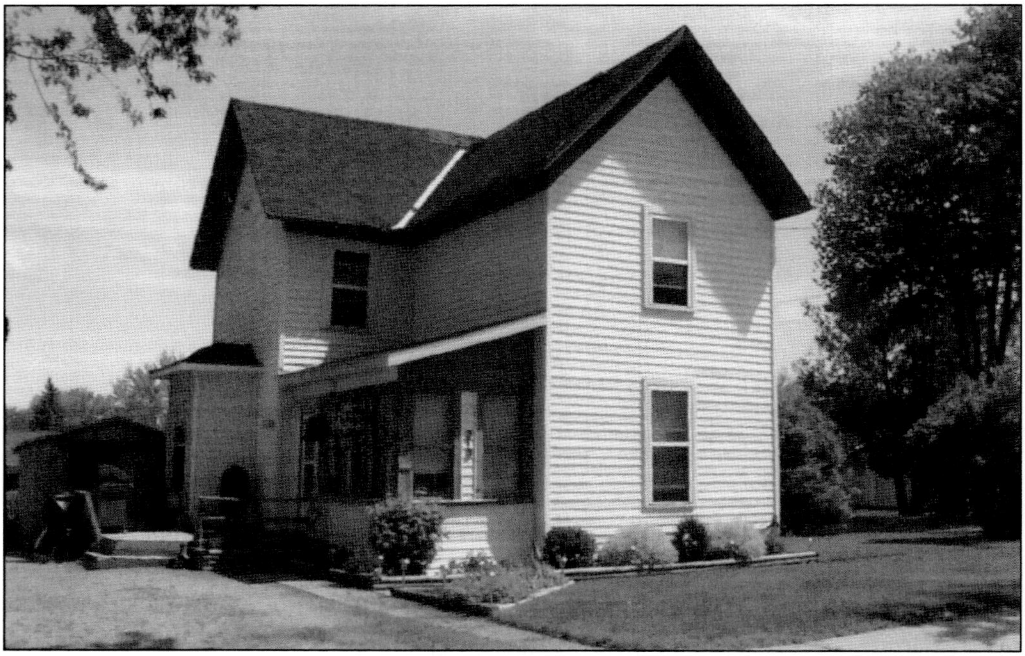

The home was located near St. John's Catholic Church. The bottom floor was converted into six patient rooms and the upper floor into living quarters for the five nuns. The home still stands at 313 East Blodgett, where it is now a private residence. The hospital was ready for occupancy on February 5, 1891, and the nuns moved in, ready to treat patients.

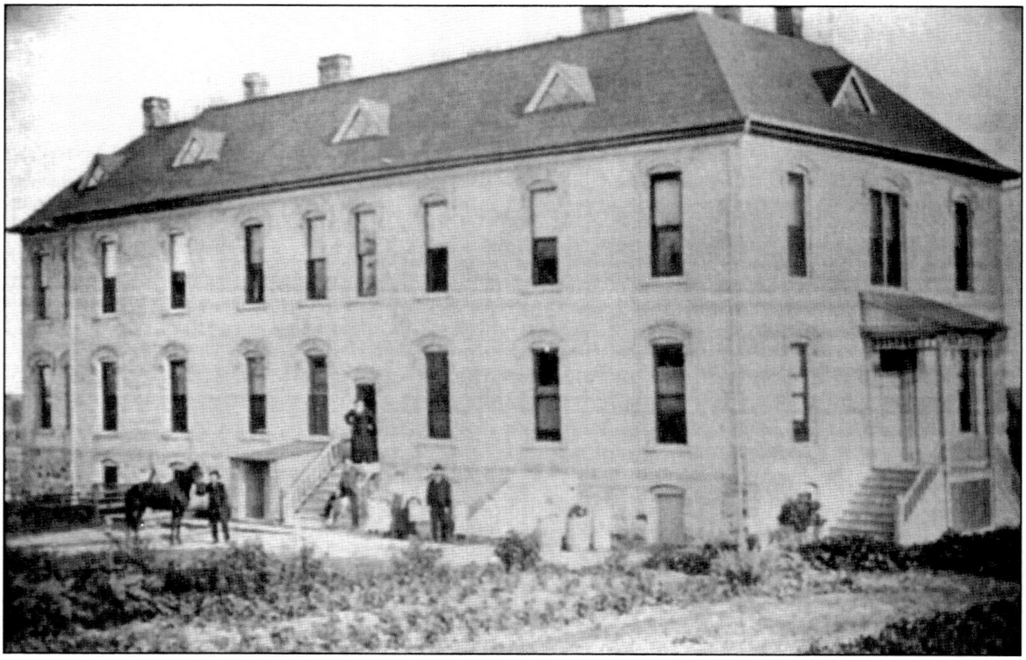

Attracting patients was challenging at first. Most people looked upon the hospital as a place to die. During the first year, they had one patient. The number rose to four the next year. The nuns mainly treated lumberjacks and mill workers. They also instituted a plan in which a patient would be treated as often as necessary for a single yearly fee.

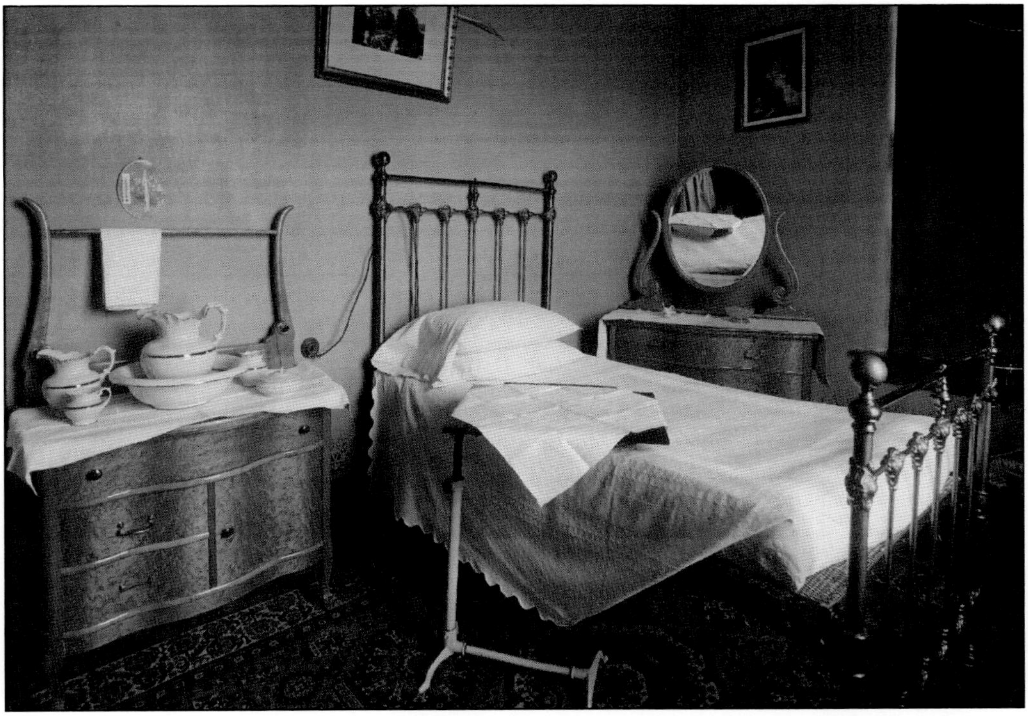

This is a typical room in the hospital. Palm fronds are tucked behind the picture, an indication that this is a Catholic hospital keeping with the custom of the blessed palms on Palm Sunday. The room is equipped with all the necessities for patient comfort, including a call button attached to the bedstead.

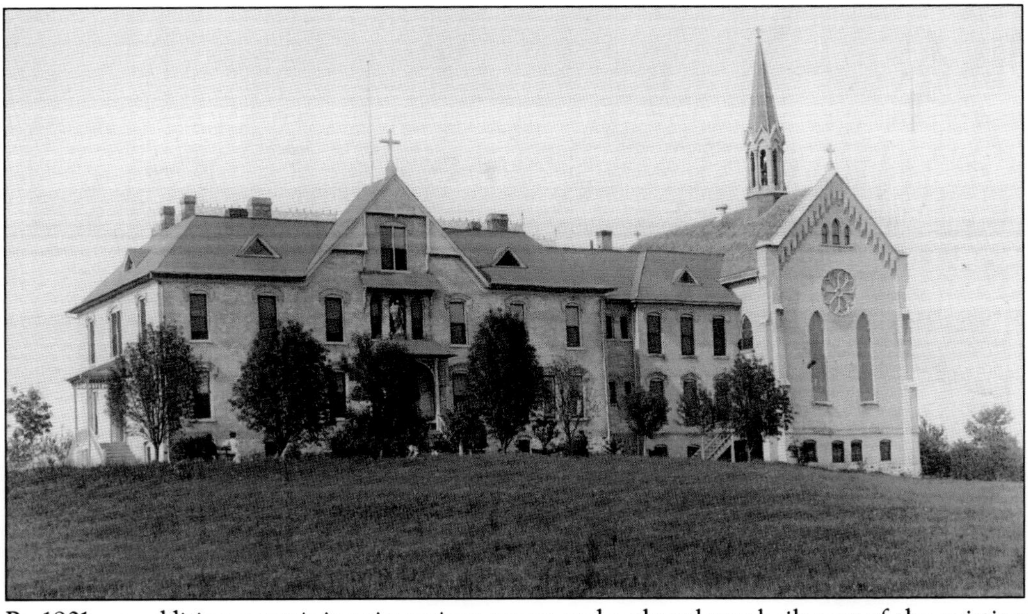

By 1901, an addition containing six patient rooms and a chapel was built east of the existing structure. By this time, more people were being referred to the hospital by doctors in town who had been upset at first when the nuns brought in a Catholic doctor from Wichita, Kansas, to run the hospital. There were no Catholic doctors in town at the time.

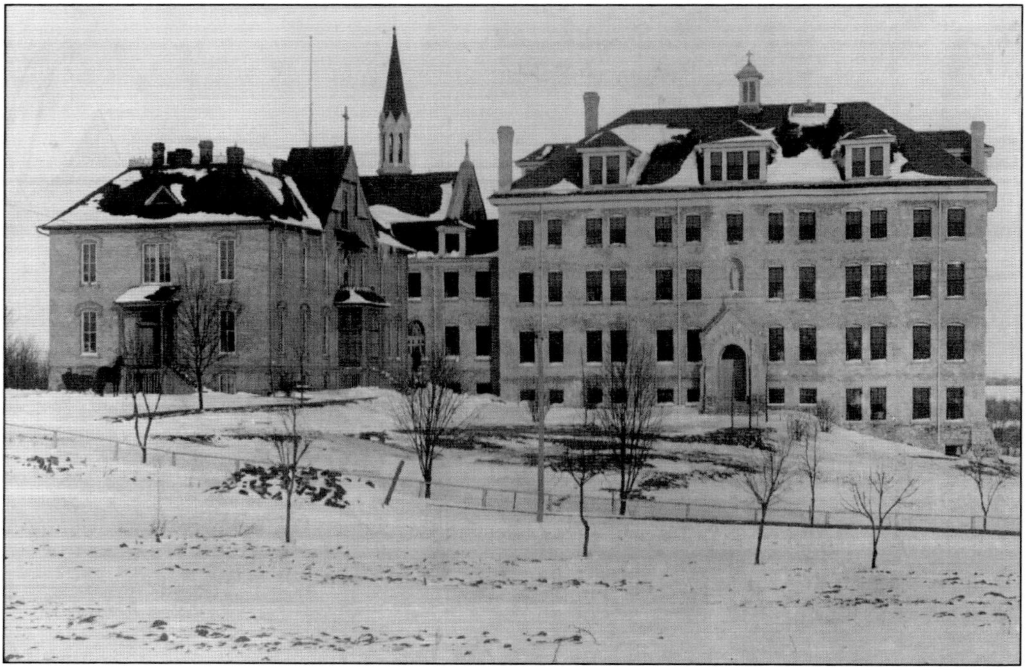

By 1918, the hospital had expanded once again. The addition of more patient rooms plus the beginning of the School of Nursing added greatly to the structure. The first class to graduate from the school consisted of three nuns. It was also the first year that a layperson, Coba Kelly, was admitted to the school. She graduated in 1921.

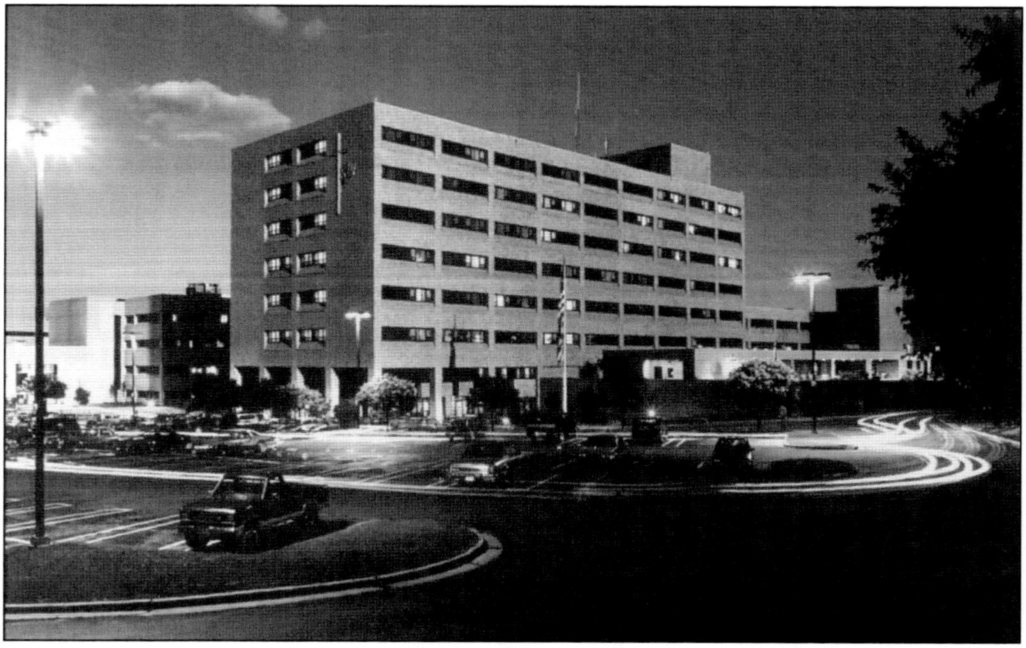

This is a view of the hospital in the 1980s. There have been several additions to the structure, and related buildings have been added to the grounds. A Ronald McDonald House sits across the street to the west, a hospice unit was built to the south, and a House of the Dove was located on campus until a new facility opened on the south side of the city in 2011.

Six

Churches

From the beginning, due to the dominance of the German, Norwegian, French Canadian, and Irish nationalities, the Lutheran and Roman Catholic Churches dominated the scene. As the population grew and included other ethnic groups, all major religions, including the Jewish faith, became represented.

The early Lutheran services were usually conducted in German. This practice continued until the World War I era and the rise of anti-German sentiment. During this time some churches added the term English Lutheran to their name to emphasize the language change.

Beautiful church buildings were erected throughout the city, reflecting the architectural styles of their eras. They have served their congregations well and some have been replaced by newer buildings that reflect the changes in church architecture in the late 20th century. Some of the early churches still remain, but today serve many different purposes. A drive around the city will show the churches built in 1880 and those built in the 1990s.

In the early days of the city, the churches provided not only a place to worship, but also a place for social interaction through their sponsorship of youth groups and adult activities throughout the year. This role continues today and is an important part of the life of the community.

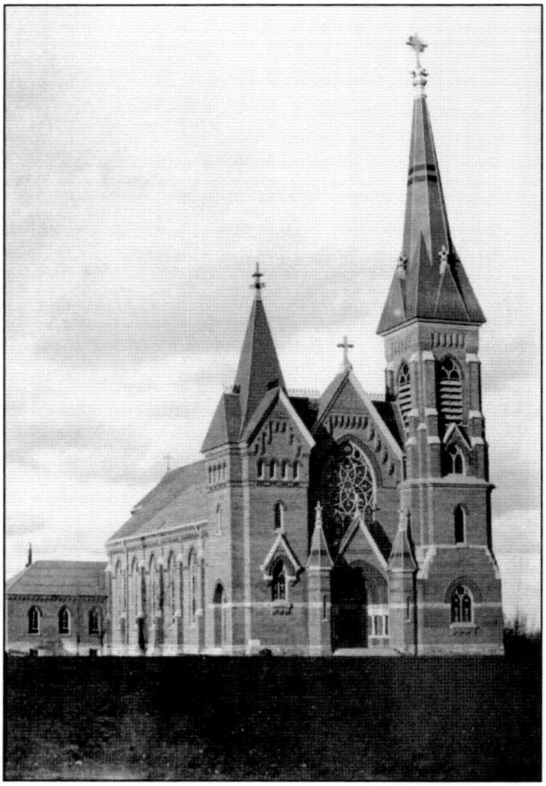

Marshfield was united in the 1880s by two factors: the German language and Catholicism. Many of the early settlers were German, French, and Irish Catholics. Services were held as early as 1874. The first priest arrived in 1878, and by 1881 St. John the Baptist Church was built. The original structure is now the rectory. The current church was constructed in 1892 when Father Eisen was pastor.

When Father Eisen died in 1907, a very large part of the population of Marshfield turned out to escort his remains to the Catholic cemetery located across from what was to become St. Joseph's Hospital. He had been a very popular priest and was well respected throughout the city. His efforts to educate the children set an example to all who followed.

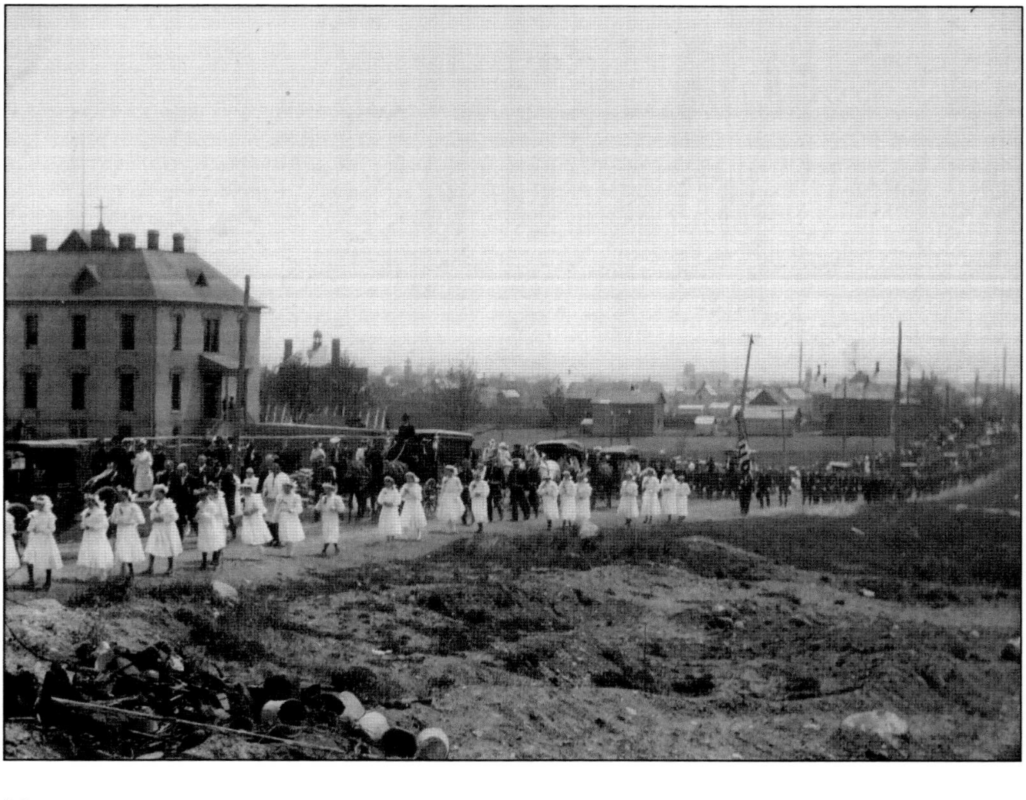

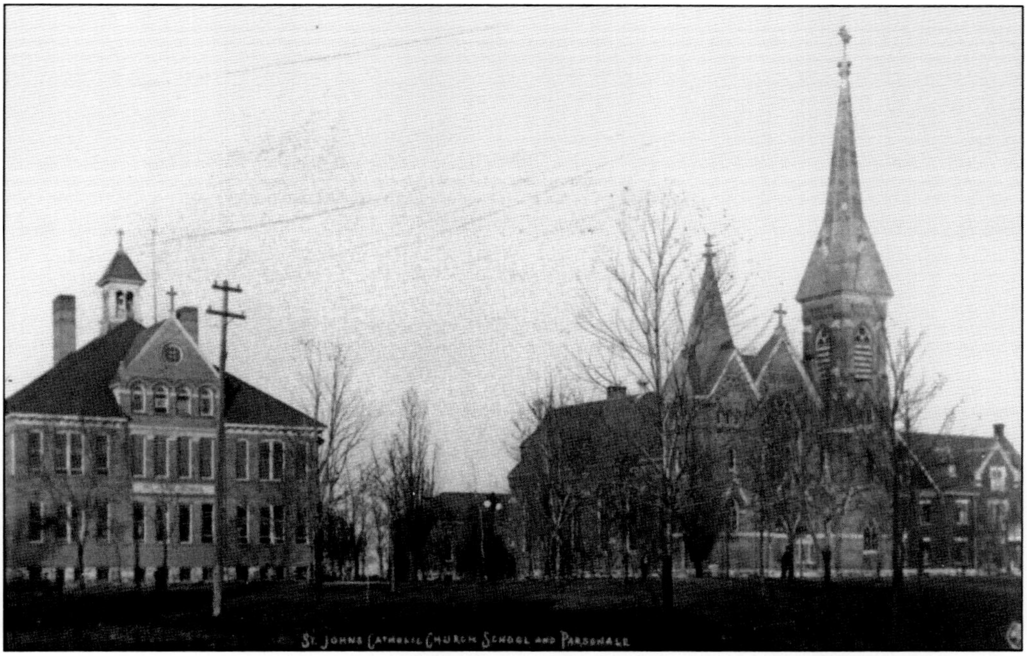

St. John's Catholic Church is located on the block bounded by West Blodgett, North Walnut, West Cleveland, and North Chestnut, north of Columbia Park. The school is located on the western portion of the block, the church in the center, and the rectory to the east. Across the street to the south is Columbia Park, once known as City Park, with a band shell for summer concerts.

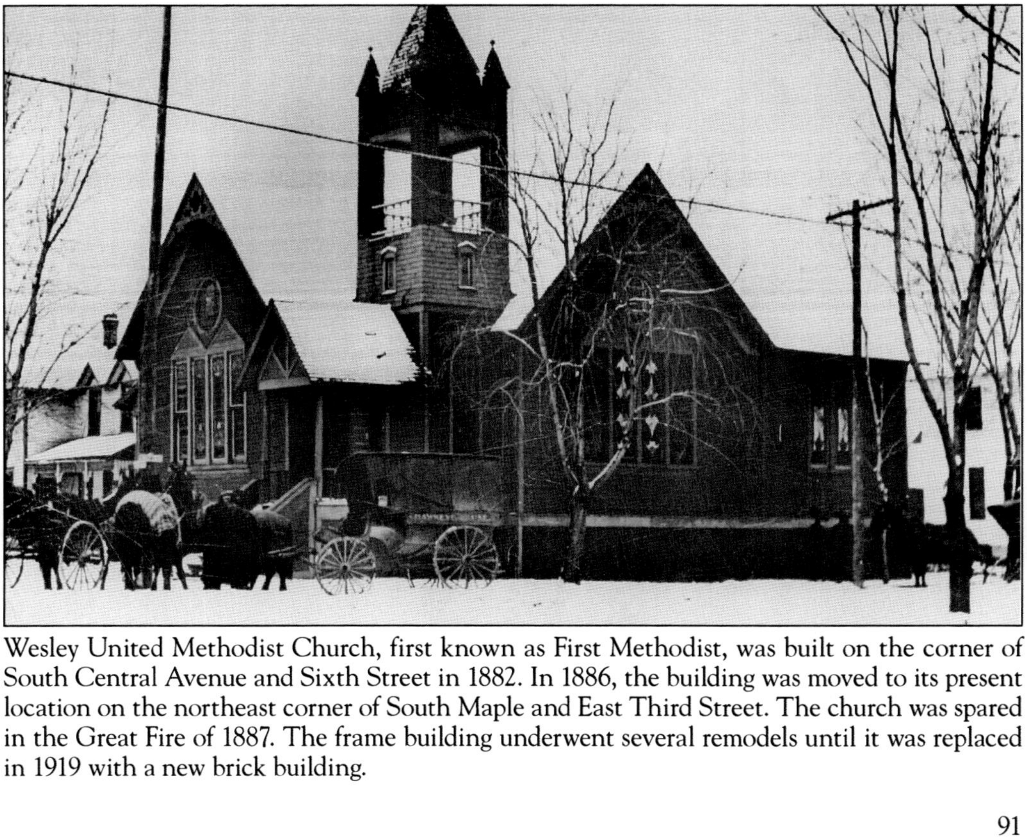

Wesley United Methodist Church, first known as First Methodist, was built on the corner of South Central Avenue and Sixth Street in 1882. In 1886, the building was moved to its present location on the northeast corner of South Maple and East Third Street. The church was spared in the Great Fire of 1887. The frame building underwent several remodels until it was replaced in 1919 with a new brick building.

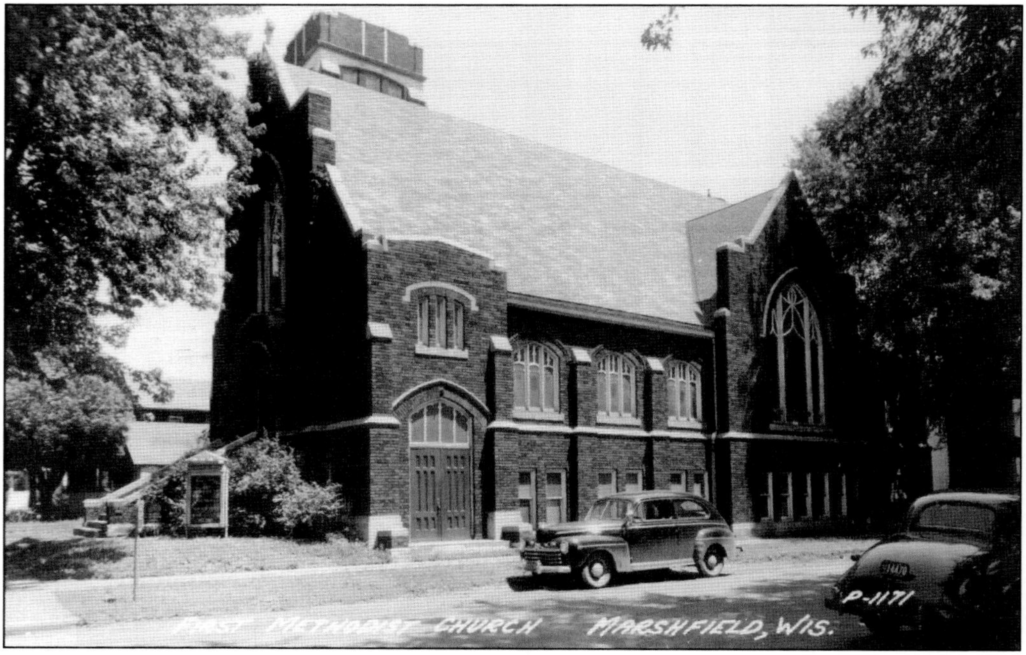

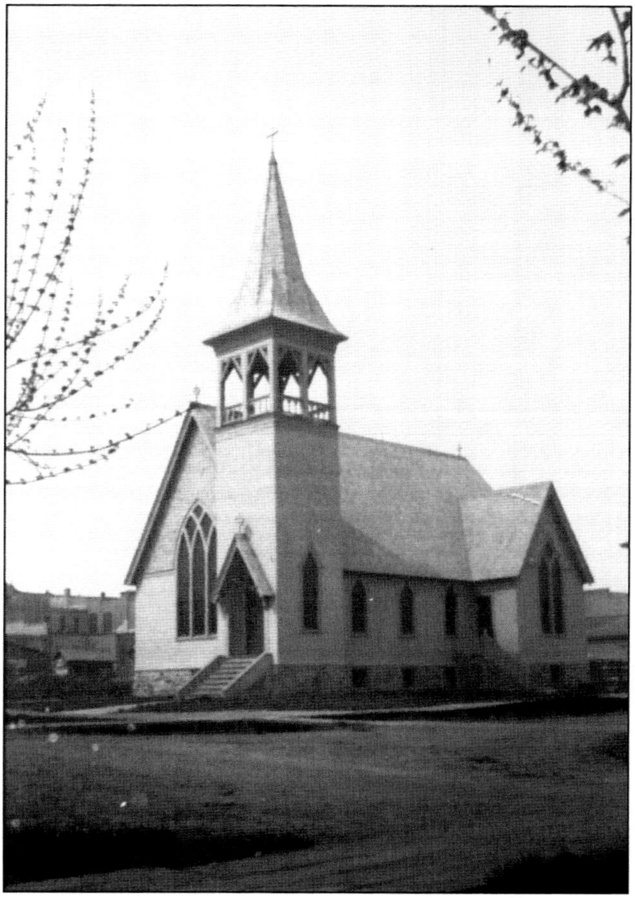

Services were held in the new, red-brick Methodist Church in 1922. The building continues to serve its congregation today. From 1947 to 1990, its Sunday services were broadcast on the local radio station, WDLB, as a program called *Radio Church*. In 1968, with the merger of the Methodist and Evangelical United Brethren Churches, the name became Wesley United Methodist Church.

St. Alban's Episcopal Church was located on the northwest corner of East Third Street and South Maple Avenue, across from the First Methodist Church. The pretty wooden building was erected in 1898. W.H. Roddis was the driving force behind the building project. The Guild Hall was built on the corner of East Second Street and South Maple in 1914 and later sold to the Elks Club as their meeting hall.

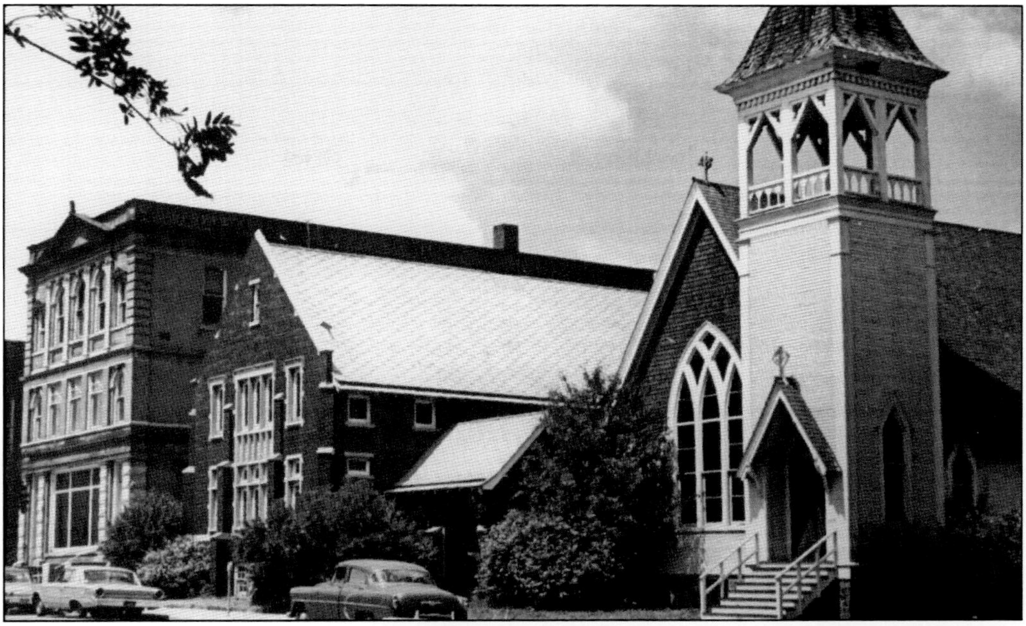

This photograph, taken around 1960, shows the Guild Hall that was built in 1921 to replace the one sold to the Elks. It contained meeting rooms and the church office. The building to the left was the Marshfield Telephone Exchange. Today, a public parking lot is located here. St. Albans built a new church on the east side, at the corner of South Felker Avenue at Fifteenth Street in 1962.

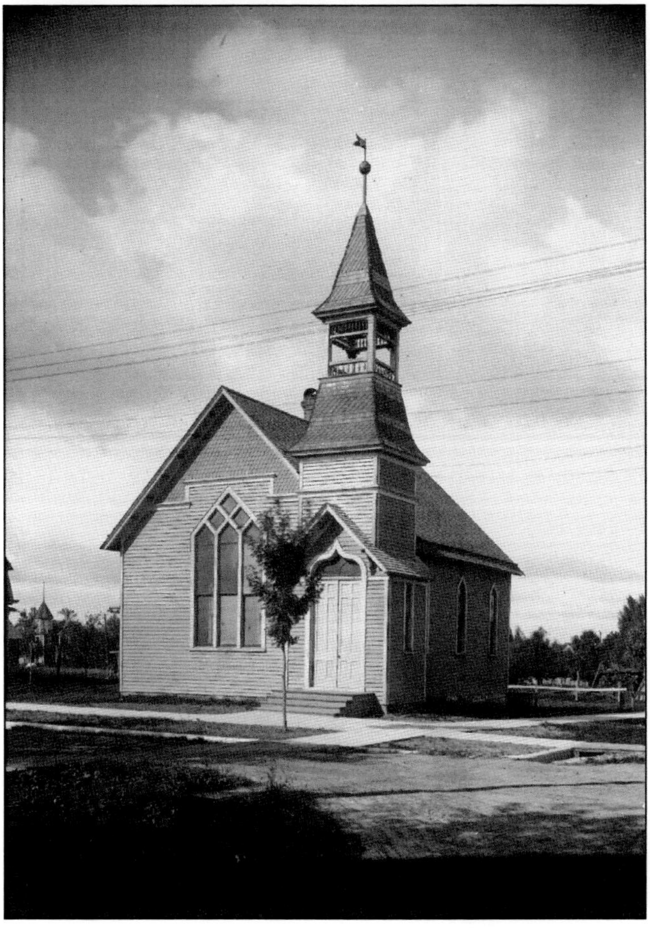

This church is the original Zion Methodist Church, located on the southwest corner of South Cherry and East Ninth Street. Earlier it was known as the German Evangelical Church. Built in 1892, it is quite similar in design to the original St. Albans Episcopal Church. The major differences visible are the size of the upper steeple and the shape of the windows.

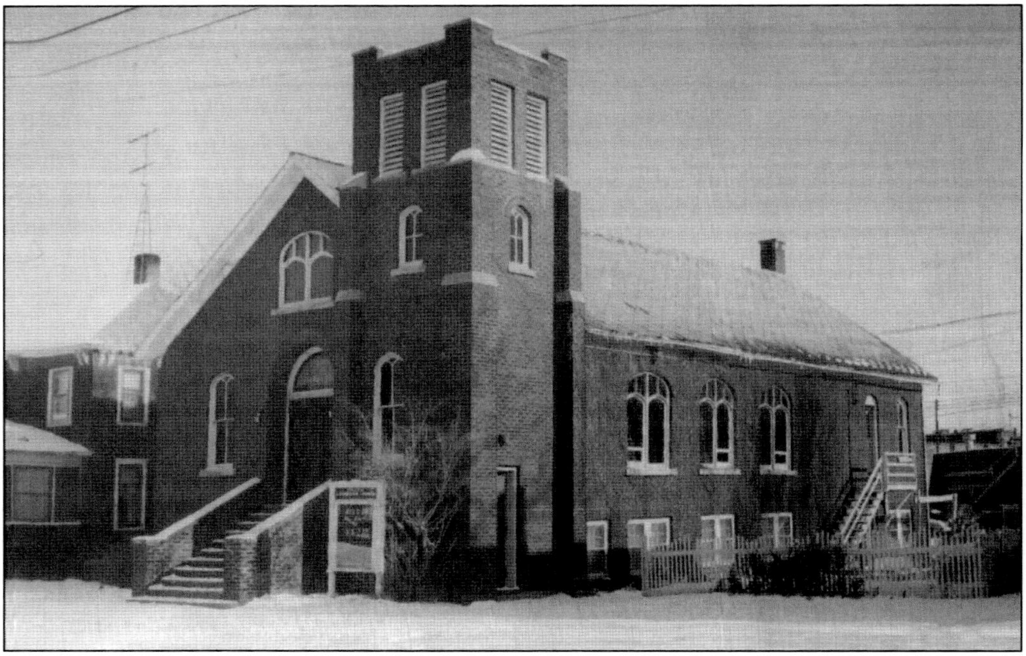

St. Matthew's Lutheran Church started in 1921 and held services in the Seventh-day Adventist Church at 500 West Fifth Street. In 1923, the congregation moved into this building on South Chestnut Street, now occupied by the Baltus Oil Company offices. It had been called First English to set it apart from the German-language churches. In 1954, it combined with Trinity Lutheran to create Faith Lutheran Church.

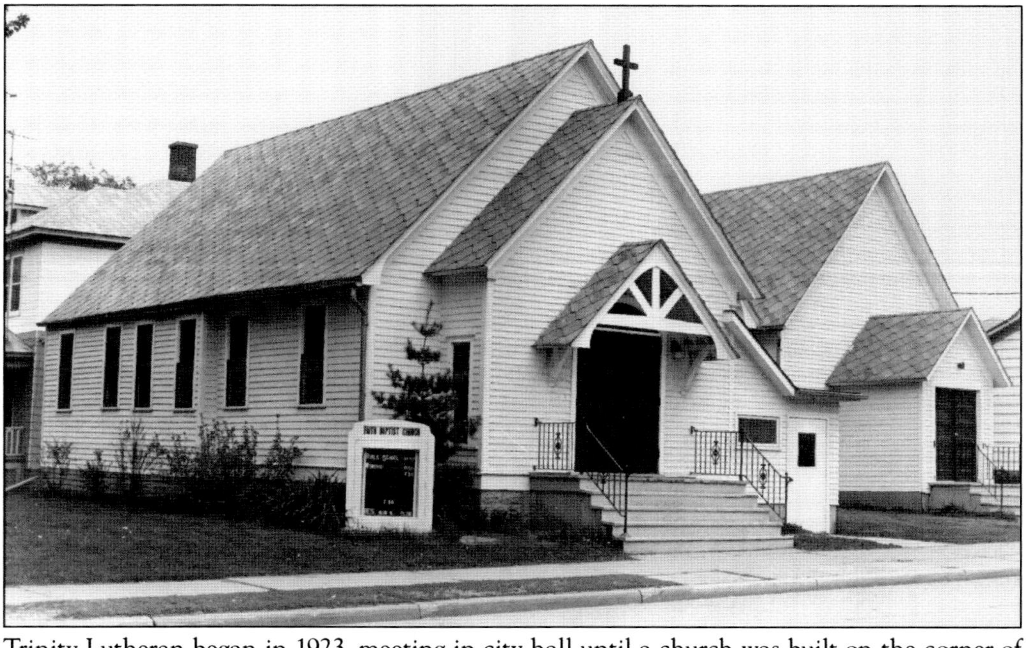

Trinity Lutheran began in 1923, meeting in city hall until a church was built on the corner of East Fourth Street and South Cedar Avenue. It called itself Trinity English Lutheran. In 1952, it moved into the vacant Slidre Lutheran Church in town to serve as a parish hall. It vacated the building in 1954 when it joined with St. Matthew. Today, it is a television production studio.

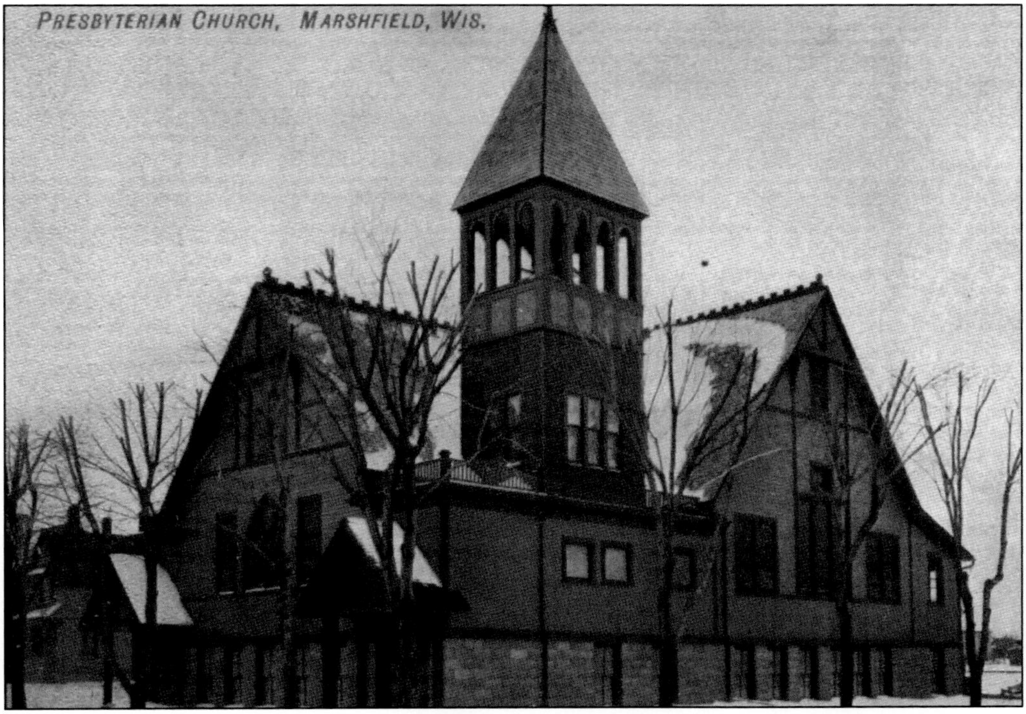

The First Presbyterian Church of Marshfield was a wooden building constructed in 1882 on the northwest corner of South Chestnut and West Third Street. Among its pastors was Reverend Melvin R. Laird, who came in 1911. He married Helen Connor at the church, and their son Melvin Jr. became secretary of defense under President Nixon. This building burned several times and was replaced by a brick structure in 1924.

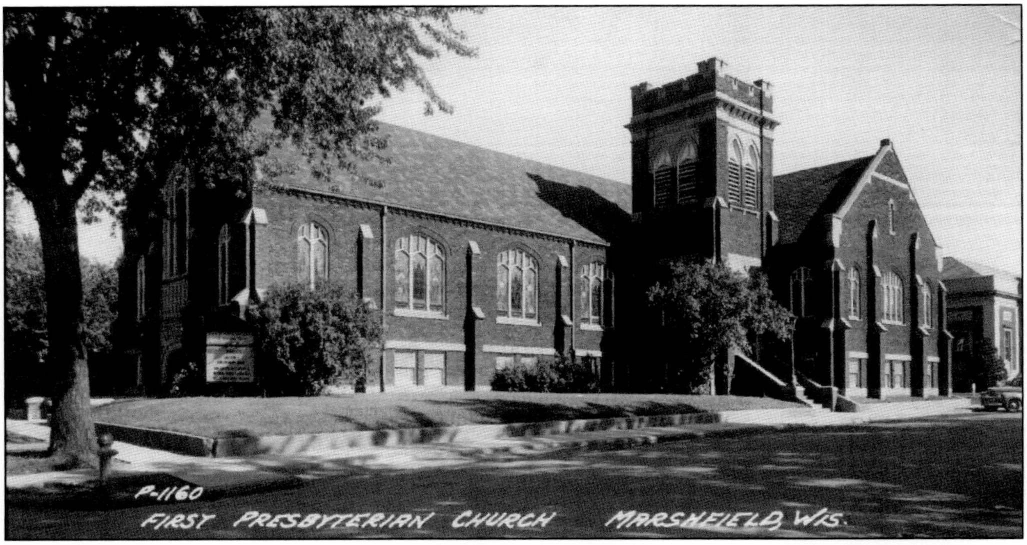

The first brick First Presbyterian Church opened in 1924 and continued to serve its congregation until 2003, when a new church was built at the western edge of the city, on the southwest corner of Adler and Lincoln Roads. The old church building on South Chestnut became the Chestnut Center for the Arts and contains classrooms for art instruction as well an area for various types of performing groups.

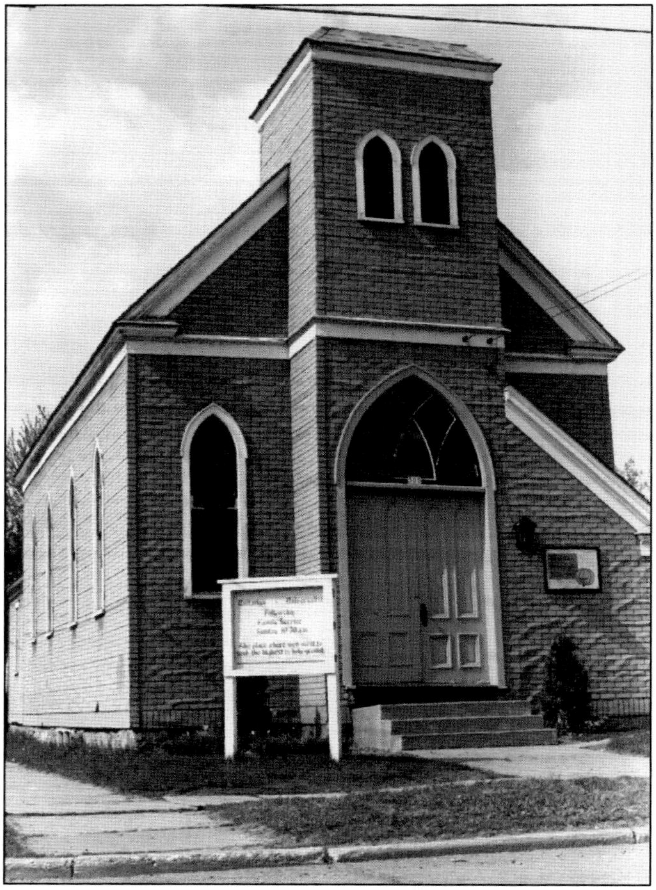

This structure is located on the southwest corner of South Pine Avenue and West Fifth Street. It was originally built in 1890 as the Independent Scandinavian Evangelical Congregation in the town of Cameron, south of Marshfield. The structure was moved into town and purchased by the Seventh-day Adventists in 1903. In 1969, it became the meeting place of the Unitarian Universalist Fellowship and today is a private residence.

This building on West Depot Street has had many uses. Originally built as a home in 1888, it was purchased by the Alliance Missionary Church in 1936. In 1952, the congregation moved to a new location on Park Street. The building was sold to the city for use as a youth center for a single year before it was sold to the VFW. It still operates today as their meeting hall.

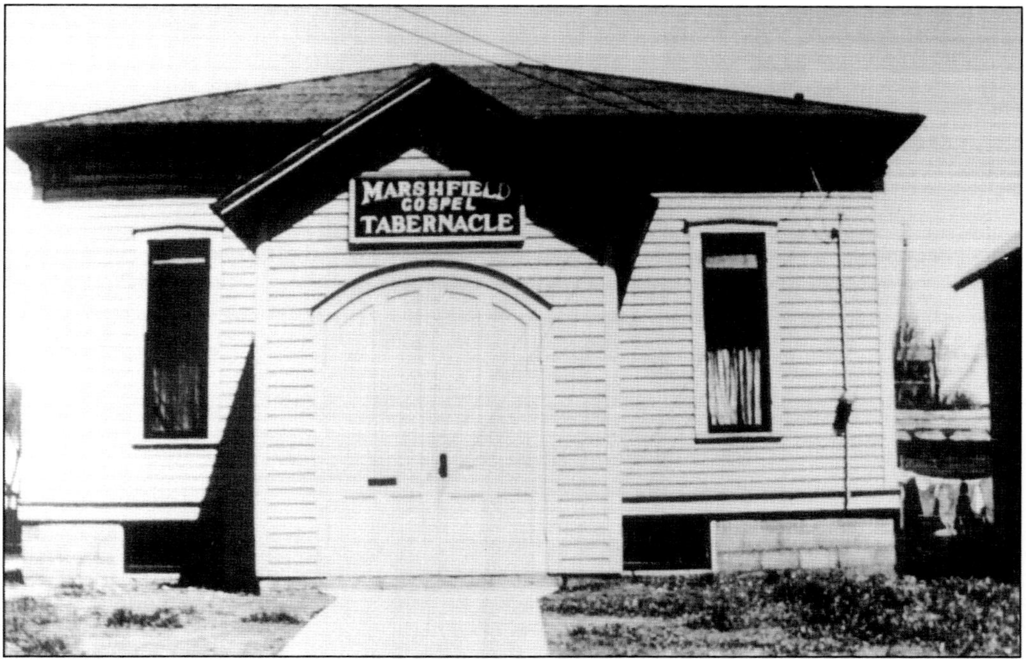

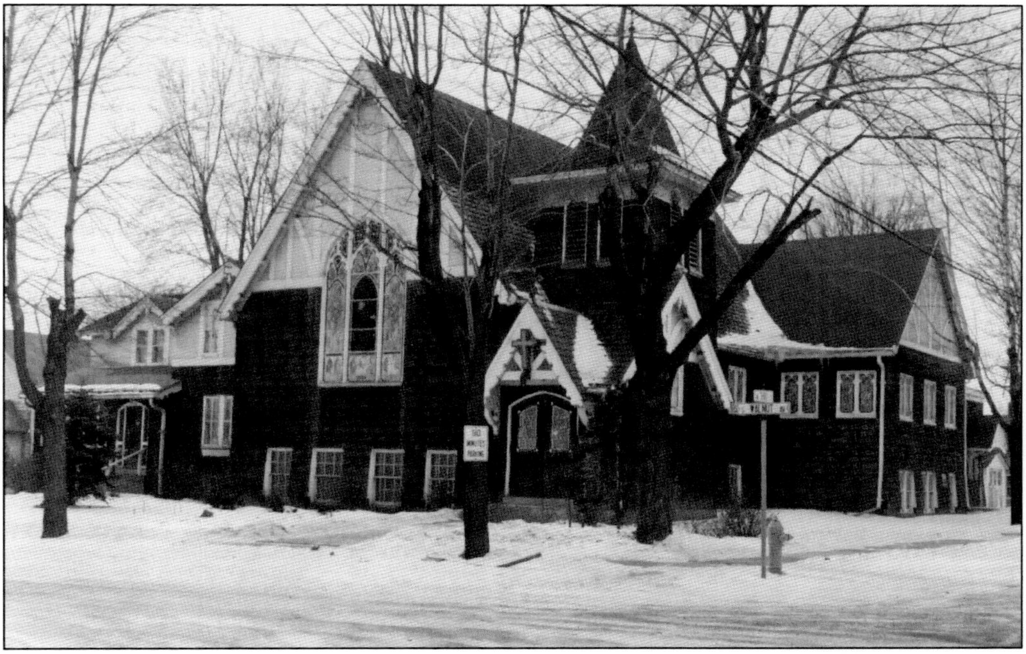

The Calvary Bible Church is located across Walnut Street from the Upham Mansion, home of the North Wood County Historical Society. The church was built in 1928 as Christ Lutheran Church. The Bible Institute—which had conducted meetings in a former bank building on the corner of West Third Street and Central Avenue since 1944—purchased the church in 1968.

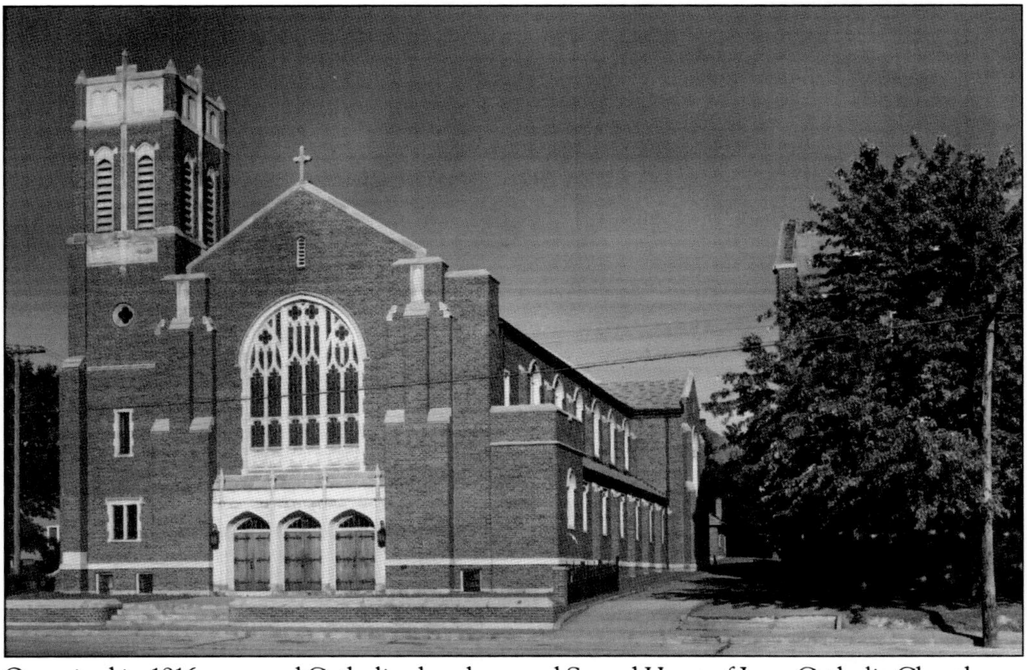

Organized in 1916, a second Catholic church named Sacred Heart of Jesus Catholic Church was located on the south side of the city. A convent and school were constructed by 1917. Masses were celebrated in the school auditorium until 1932, when the auditorium became too small to serve the congregation.

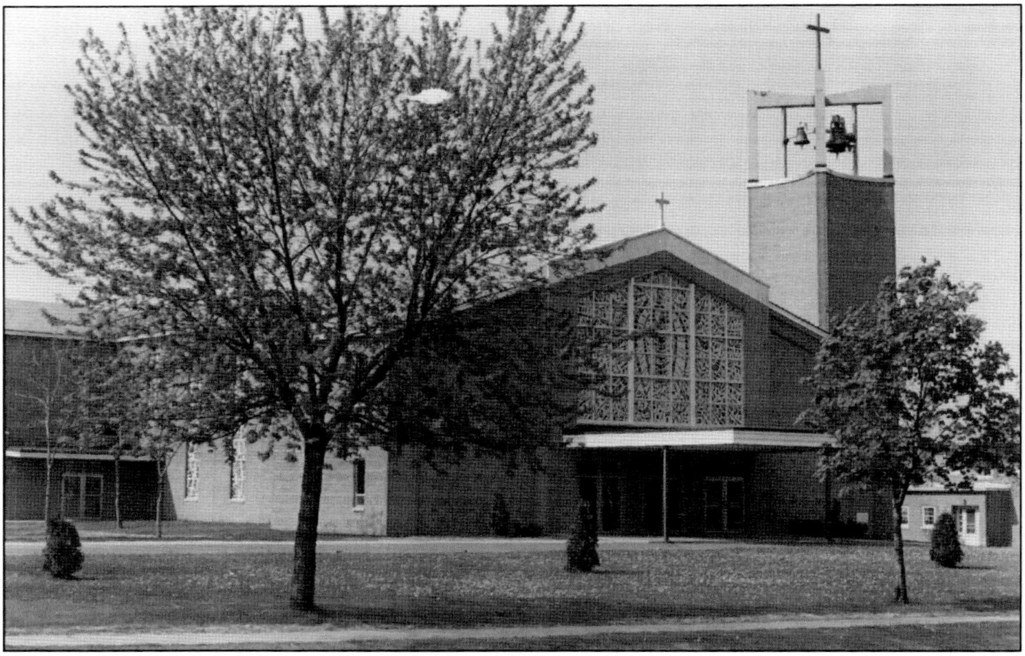

The youngest of the Catholic parishes is Our Lady of Peace, located on the southwest side of the city. The church was dedicated in 1949, and the celebration included an address by Bishop Fulton J. Sheen of television fame. The school opened that fall. In 1951, Columbus High School, located next to the grade school, opened as a joint project of the three Catholic parishes.

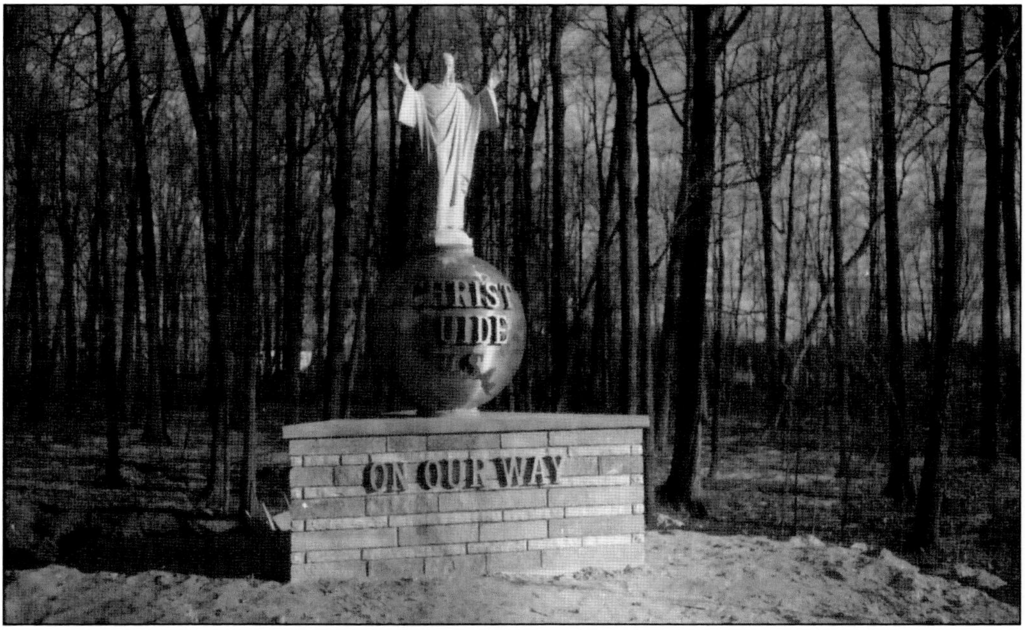

Praschak Wayside was donated to the city in 1964 by Henry Praschak. Located at the southern entrance to the city, it was dedicated as a public park and contained a statue of Jesus. In 1986, the Freedom From Religion Foundation demanded the removal of the statue. To comply with the legal decision, the Knights of Columbus purchased the area containing the statue, which sits inside a fence surrounded by public land.

Seven

Schools

Marshfield had its first settlers in 1872. By 1873 a school, taught by Clara Davis, had been organized in the front room of a residence. From its earliest days, Marshfield valued education. The city continued to grow with mainly a German immigrant population that considered education important. The first public school building, a one-room frame structure located in the present *News Herald* parking lot on the corner of Third Street and South Chestnut Avenue, opened in 1877. It was difficult to reach, as the only access was via an elevated plank walkway from Depot Street. It was so narrow that students had to walk single file.

In 1881, the first multiroom public school was built on South Central Avenue in what became known as Washington Square. Other schools followed: St. John's Catholic School in 1882 and the Evangelical Lutheran Day School in 1884.

In 1888, a second public school was opened. Prior to 1900, less than one-third of all American children over 14 attended school and even fewer graduated from high school nationally. Marshfield had already opened a permanent high school in 1890, and within one year it was overcrowded. A student who missed three consecutive days would lose his or her spot to someone on the waiting list.

In 1897, with state accreditation, McKinley High School was opened on Third Street and South Oak Avenue. In 1917, a second Catholic grade school was opened on South Central, followed by a third in 1949 and a Catholic high school in 1951.

Marshfield's high esteem of education was well known. It was almost home to a state teacher's college or normal school. However, that honor went to Stevens Point instead. Marshfield valued education for all of its students, even those facing challenges. In the 1920s, evening adult education classes were taught at the new Purdy Junior High. A school for the "deaf and dumb" opened in 1912. The beginnings of what would later be called "special education" classes began in 1921. A new high school opened on the east side after McKinley burned in 1936. In 1968, it was replaced by the present high school and the building was converted to a junior high school. A two-year campus of the University of Wisconsin opened in 1964.

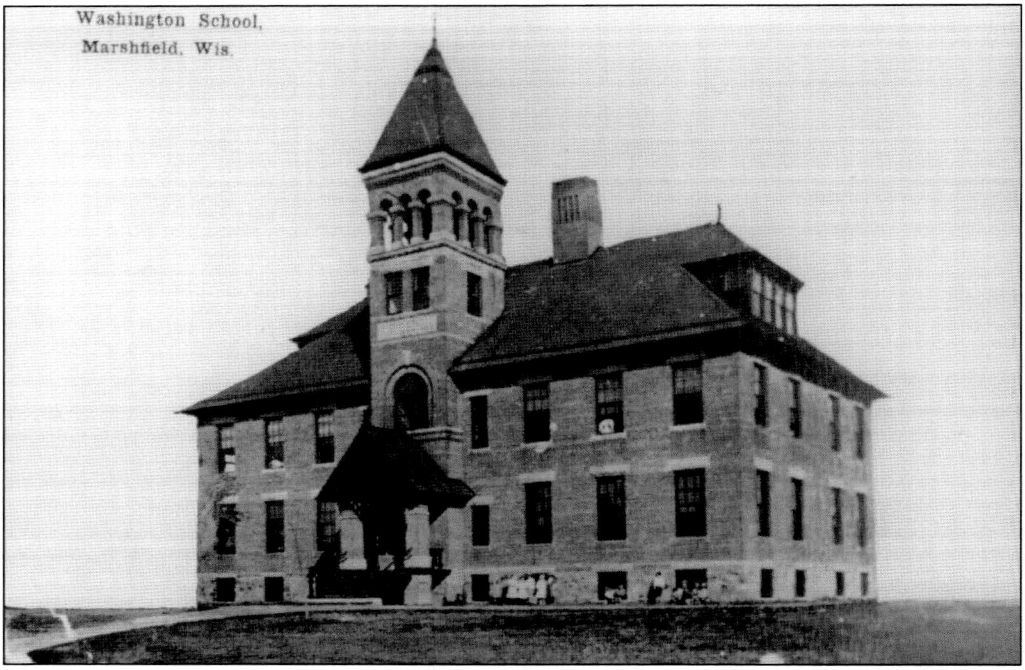

By 1881, the city's population had reached 800 and a new school was needed. A site was selected between Sixth and Seventh Streets on South Central Avenue. It was first known as the Central Avenue School. The original school became too small by 1886, and a new school opened on the site in 1890. The original building was slowly moved to Second Street and South Maple Avenue to serve as the city hall.

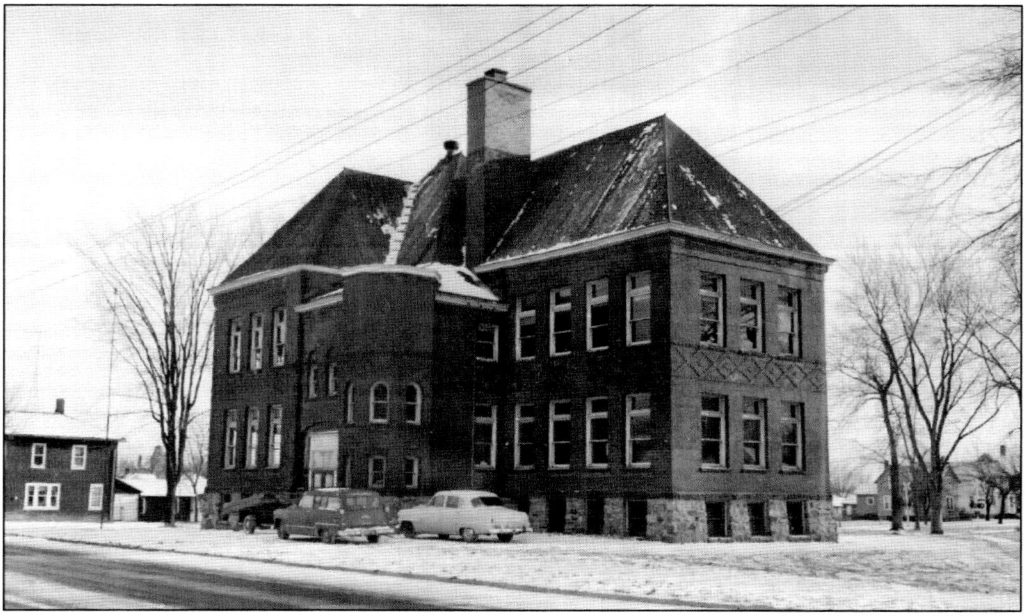

In 1894, Lincoln Elementary School was built on the corner of East Fourth Street and South Vine Avenue, the area occupied today by the former fire station. The school opened on February 3, 1896. In this view, the circular tower that extended beyond the roof line has been removed. Only the base remains visible behind the cars.

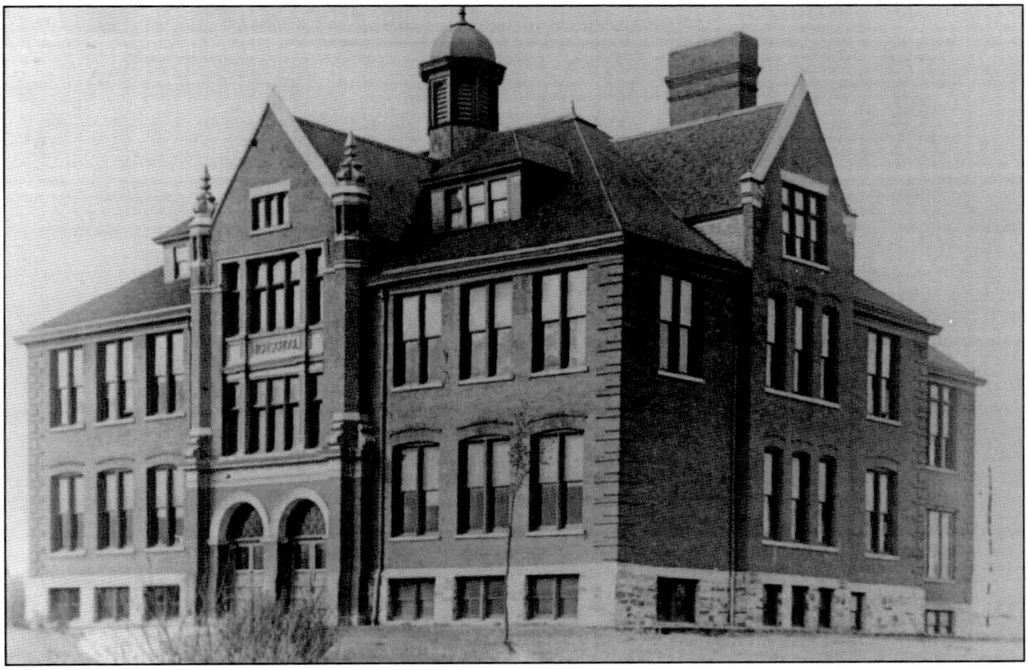

By 1898, crowding was again a problem. A site was purchased on Oak Street between West Fifth and West Sixth Streets from the Fox River Land Company, and construction began. When the school opened on January 29, 1900, it had an enrollment of 120 students and four teachers. The principal was J.B. Borden. One of the teachers was Margaret Ashmun, who became a well-known children's author.

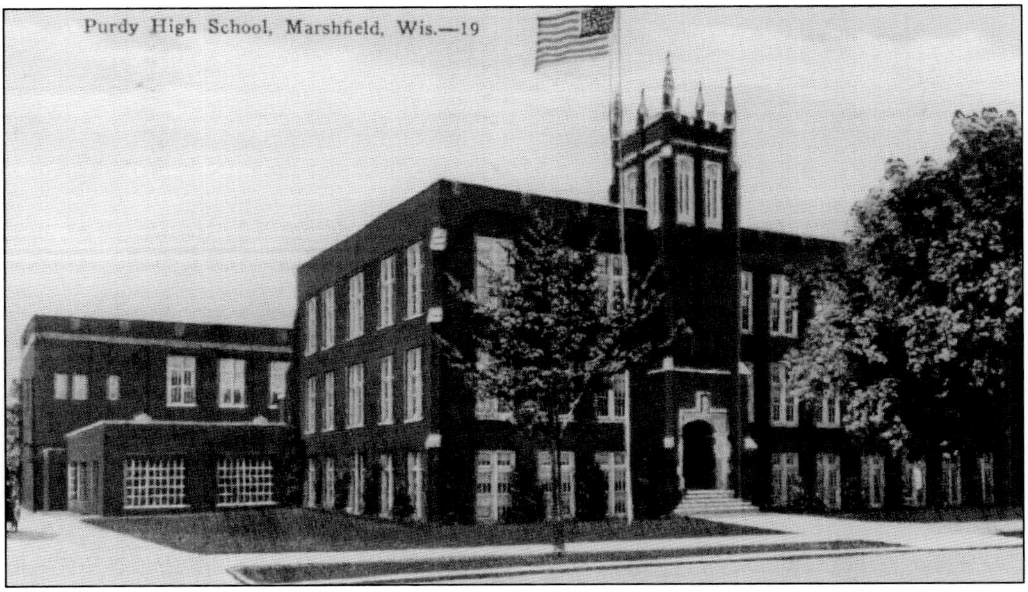

The school board decided to build a new junior high school on the southeast corner of East Third Street and South Chestnut Street in 1918. Because of World War I, construction was postponed. After the war, the Krasin Brothers built the school, which was named in honor of war hero Willard Purdy. The facility opened in 1920 with an enrollment of 200, plus 100 in the vocational school.

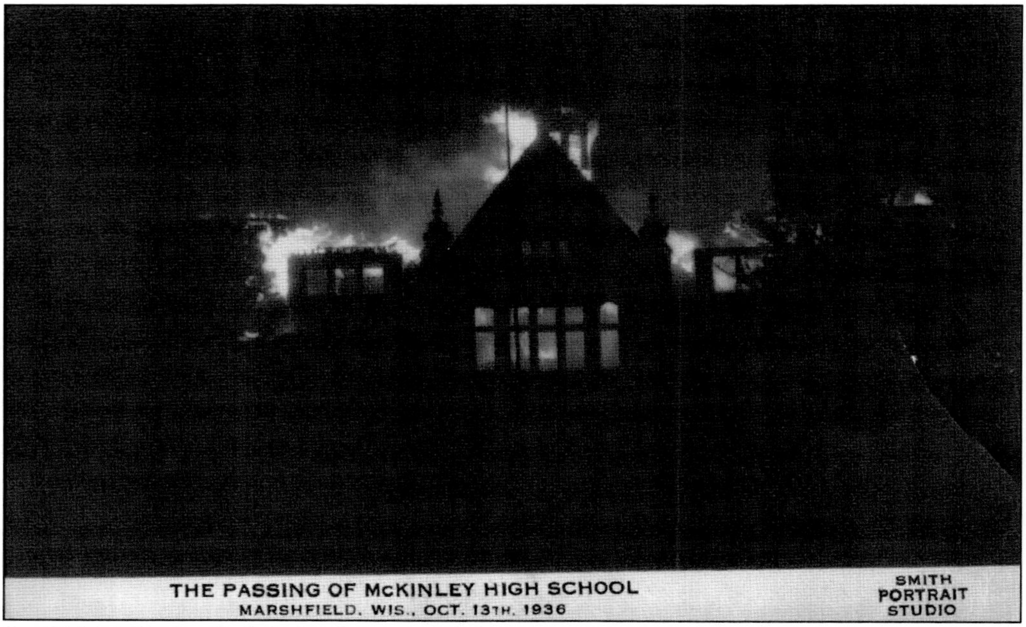

By 1935, McKinley High School was crowded once again. It was deemed too old to remodel, so a new school was considered. On the evening of October 13, 1936, McKinley High School burned. Only a shell remained of the brick building. The students, however, only missed one day of class. They were moved to Purdy Junior High School, thus putting over 1,000 students in a building designed for 400.

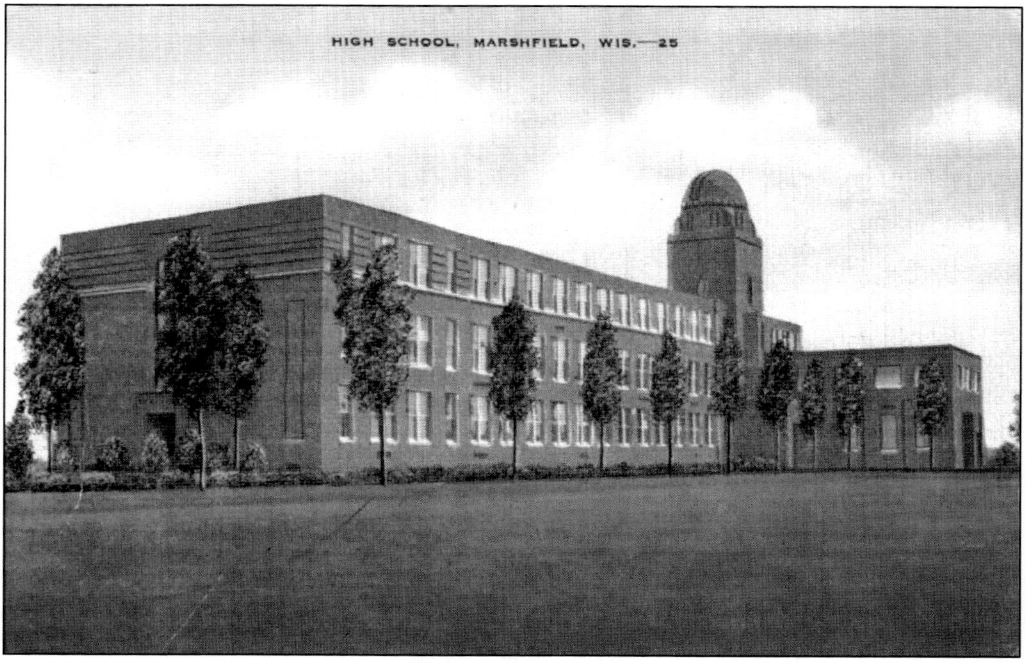

It took the school board months to select a new site from a list of 21 possibilities. Finally, they decided on the 17-acre Vannedom-Roddis site on East Fourth Street and South Palmetto Street. They purchased the property for $7,700 in 1937. In 1938, $200,000 in PWA money was granted to cover 45 percent of the projected cost. Construction was completed in the spring of 1940.

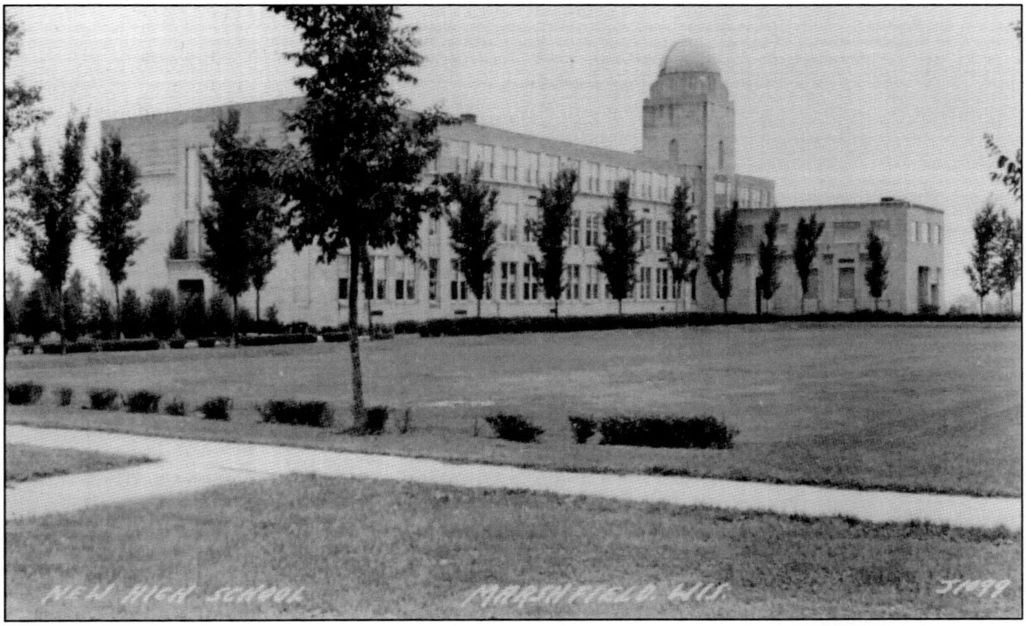

The City of Marshfield received a WPA grant of $127,637 for landscaping. It included an underground water supply system to flood the two hockey rinks and in-ground sprinklers to water the grass. Facilities also included tennis courts and a concrete stadium seating 4,000 people. The stadium was dedicated to Fred A. Beell, professional wrestling champion and the only Marshfield police officer to die in the line of duty.

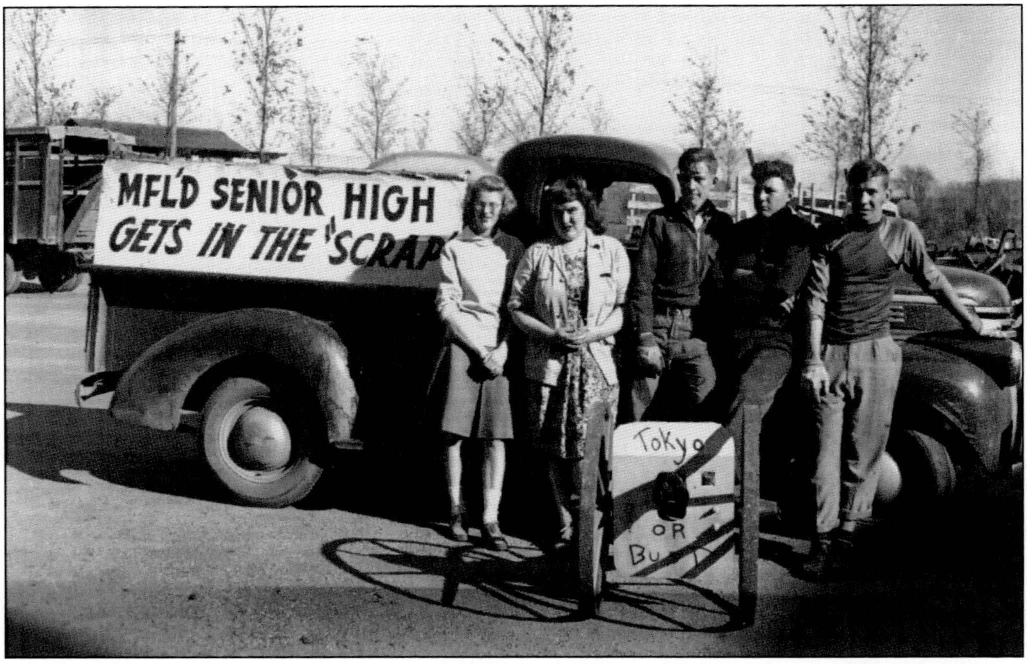

Not everything concerning students was about crowding and new schools. After World War II began, concerns shifted to the well-being of the troops from the Marshfield area serving in the Pacific. These students show their support in a scrap drive. According to the sign, it's "Tokyo or Bust."

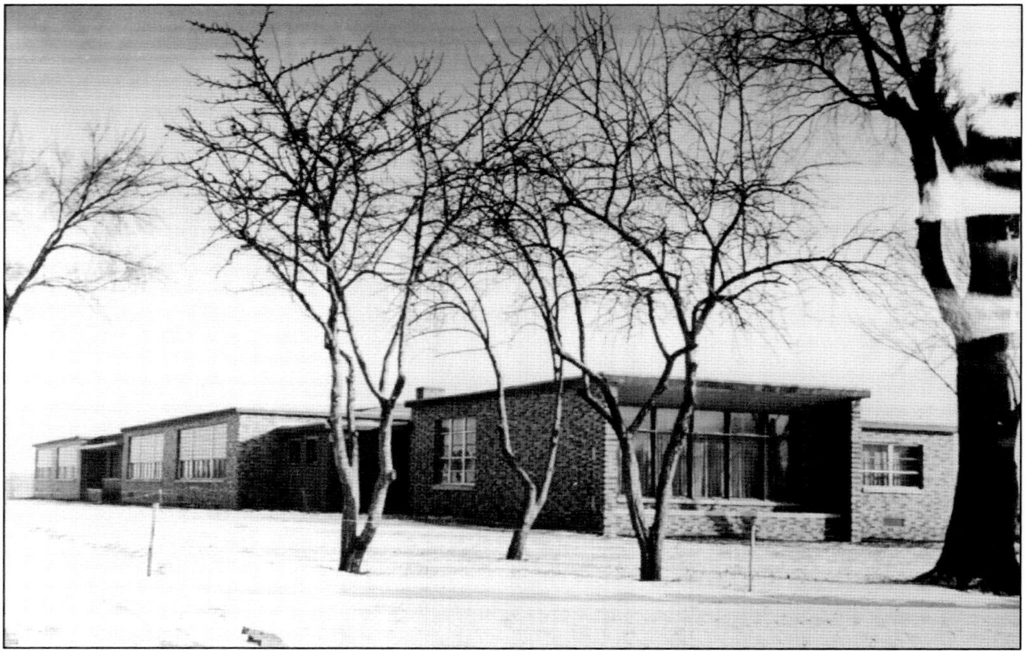

In 1948, the State Department of Public Instruction recommended a modernization of the district. In 1952, a new school called Madison Elementary opened on the north side of North Apple Street, south of East Doege Street. It would contain 10 classrooms, a pair of kindergarten rooms, a multipurpose room, and other educational facilities.

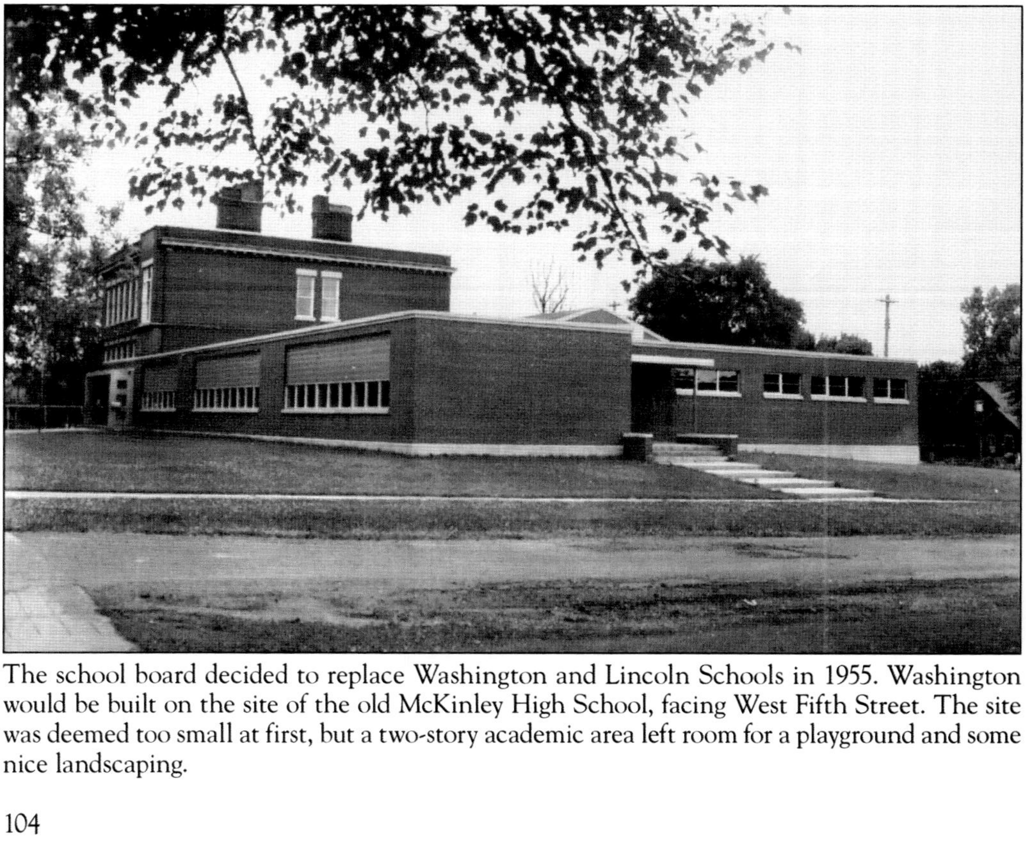

The school board decided to replace Washington and Lincoln Schools in 1955. Washington would be built on the site of the old McKinley High School, facing West Fifth Street. The site was deemed too small at first, but a two-story academic area left room for a playground and some nice landscaping.

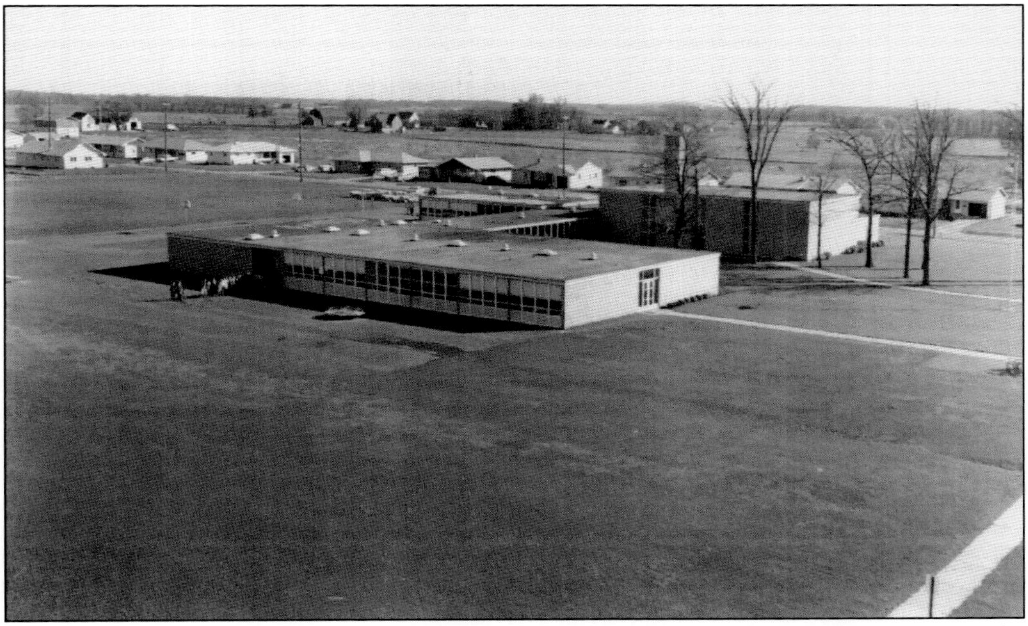

Lincoln School was to be built in one of the fastest growing areas of the city, the southeast side. The site selected was at the corner of East Seventeenth Street and South Felker Avenue. Lincoln's design was similar to Washington School but on a single level. Both schools opened in 1957.

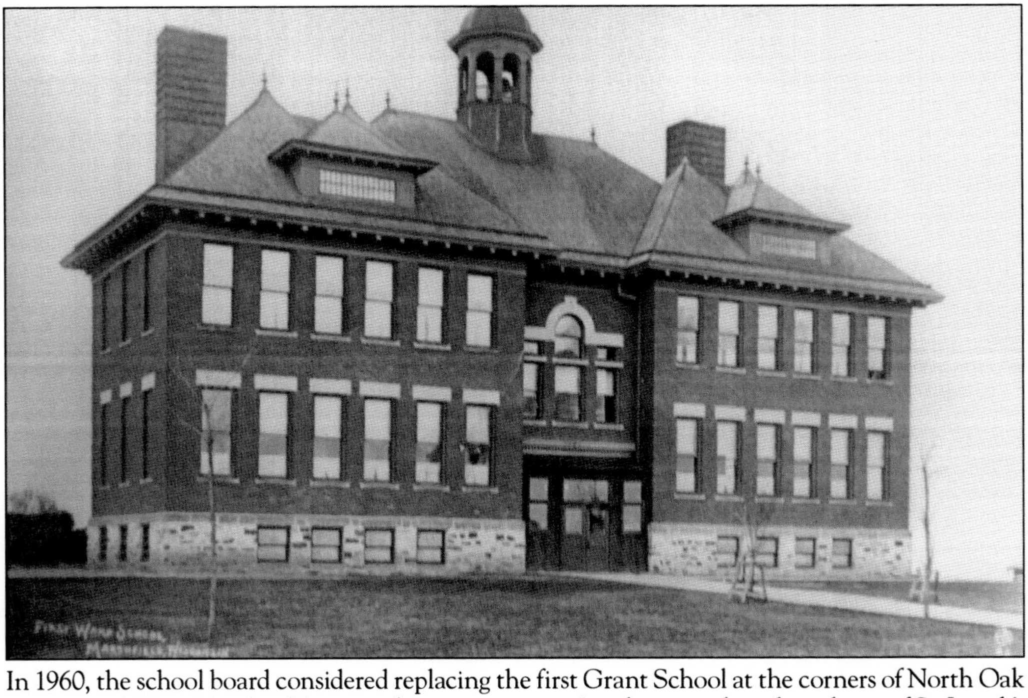

In 1960, the school board considered replacing the first Grant School at the corners of North Oak Avenue and West Cleveland Street with a new structure. Land was purchased northeast of St. Joseph's Hospital, east of North St. Joseph Avenue and West Upham Street. The second Grant School was completed in 1963. When the first school came down, the playground equipment remained. The area is now Grant Mini-Park. In 1990, the second school was sold to the Marshfield Clinic as part of a land swap of 14 acres of land for a third Grant School, which opened in 1992.

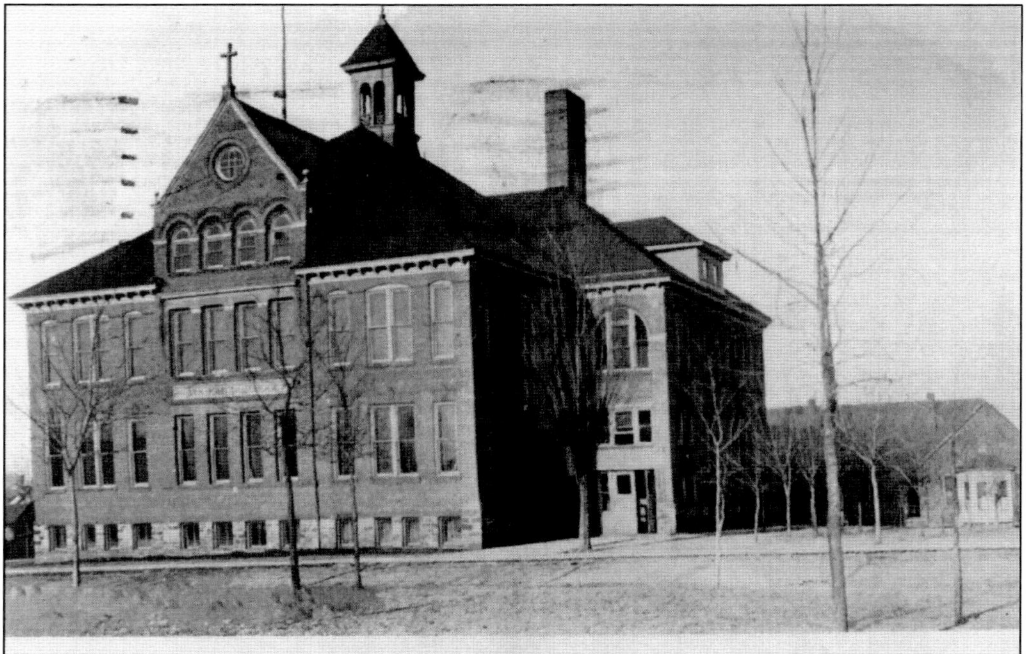

St. John's School, Marshfield, Wis.

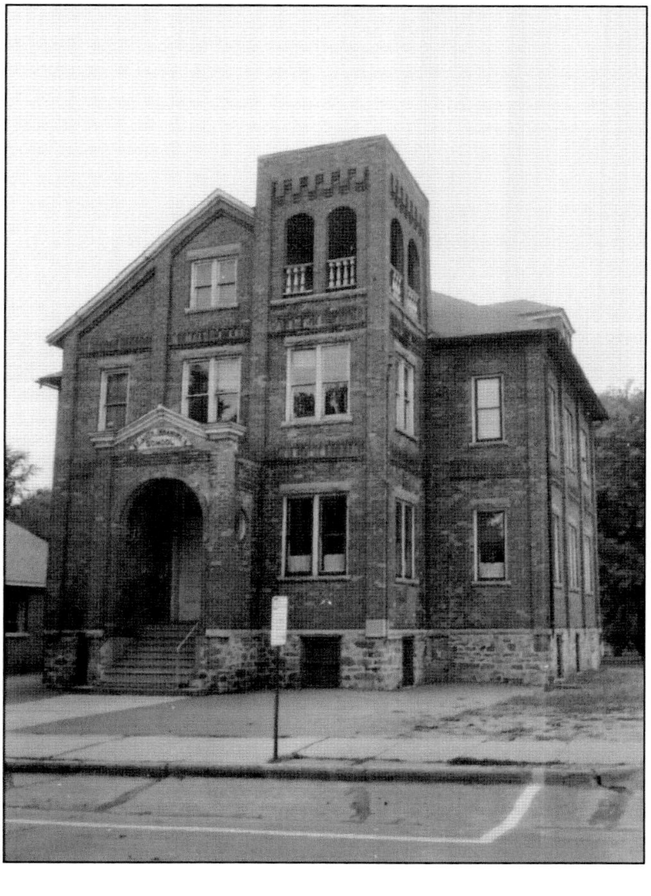

Parochial schools in Marshfield date back to 1882, when St. John the Baptist Catholic Church built a school, St. Johannes Schule, which reflected the German heritage of the area. The first school had classrooms on the first floor and living quarters for the nuns above. By 1896, a brick building was erected on the corner of North Walnut and West Blodgett Streets.

The second parochial school was Immanuel Lutheran School, begun in 1886 in the church. In 1892, the building was moved across the street to the corner of Sixth and Chestnut Streets and became the school building. Lots behind the church were purchased, and a new school was erected in 1906, but it burned. The school closed during the Depression and reopened in 1941. A new school was built in 1958.

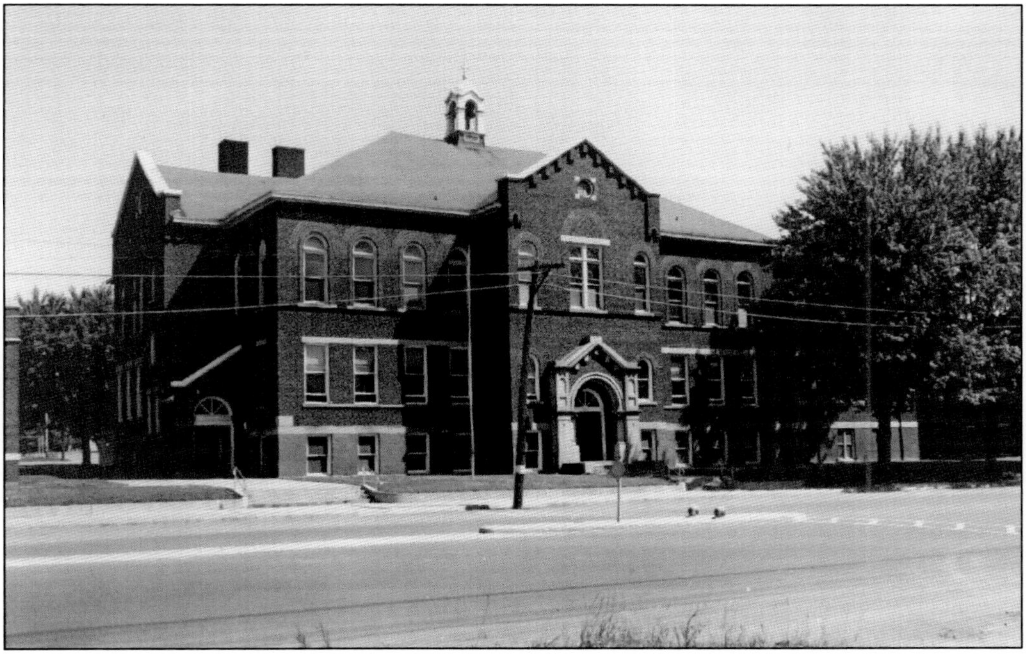

In 1917, a second Catholic school was opened with 152 students. It was located at the corner of South Central Avenue and East Eleventh Street. The school served as both the church and school until 1932. With enrollment in 1932 of 346, it served the needs of the Catholic families of the south side of Marshfield. The school was staffed by School Sisters of Notre Dame.

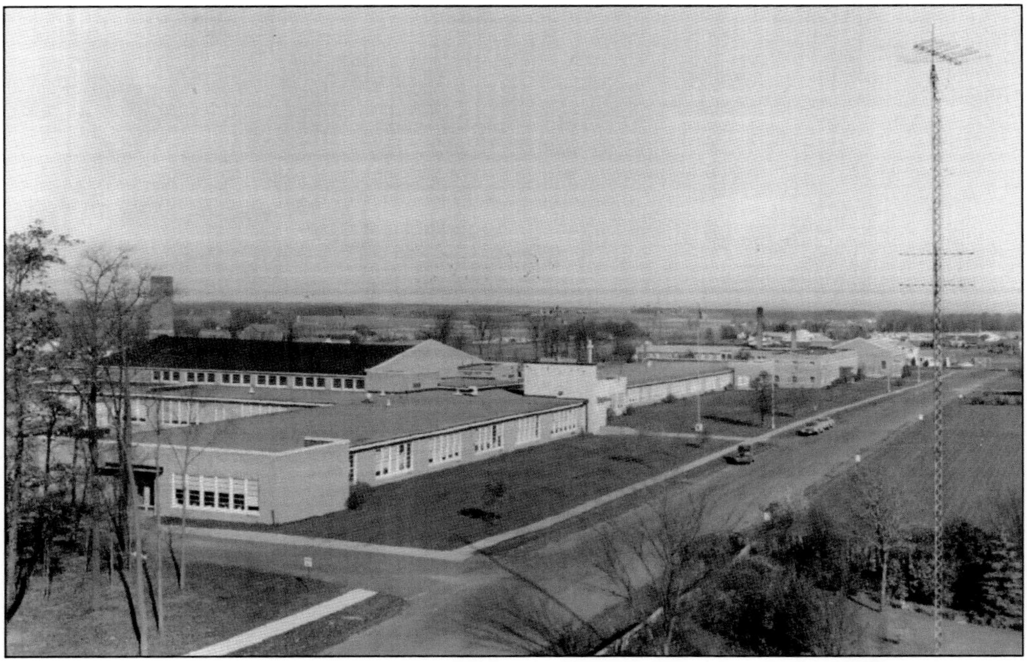

Ground was broken in 1951 on Van Ertle Street (now Columbus Avenue) for a Catholic four-year high school, fulfilling a dream held since 1928. The school was named Columbus and opened to students in the fall of 1953 when 365 students, grasping maps of the building so they could find their classrooms, entered the doors. Enrollment reached an all-time high in 1964 at 650 students.

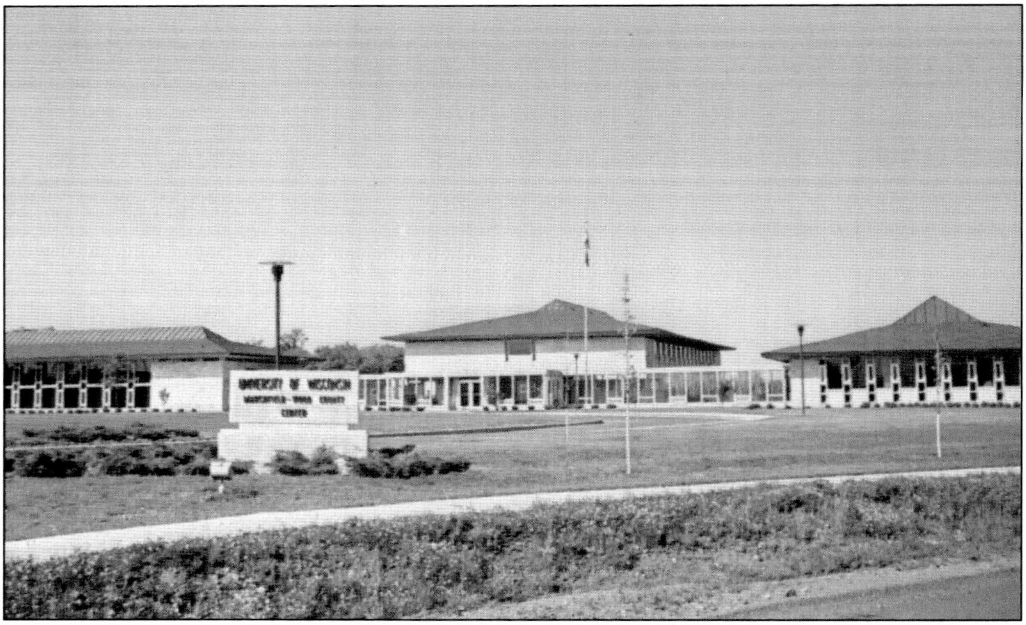

The University of Wisconsin Center–Marshfield/Wood County opened in 1964 with 141 students attending. It is a freshman-sophomore campus affiliated with the University of Wisconsin system. In 1971, the Helen Connor Laird Fine Arts Building was added. Students attend the school for two years and then transfer to a four-year campus to finish their degree. A continuing-education program offers non-credit classes to the community.

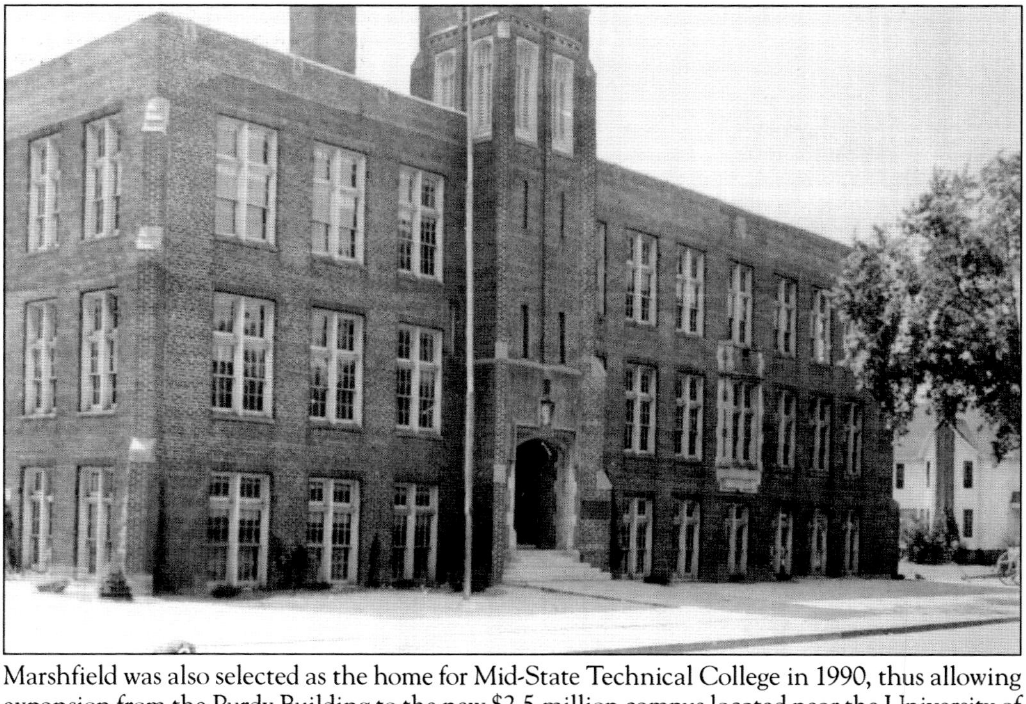

Marshfield was also selected as the home for Mid-State Technical College in 1990, thus allowing expansion from the Purdy Building to the new $2.5-million campus located near the University of Wisconsin Center on South Linden Street. The county board had earlier opposed the Marshfield location in favor of one in Wisconsin Rapids.

Eight

Growth of City Government and Services

Marshfield grew from a railroad stop of shacks, saloons, brothels, and a single mud street to a city of families, businesses, churches, and schools. As the city changed, its citizens expected the government to keep pace. Marshfield was incorporated in 1883 and elected its first mayor, L.A. Arnold. The first action taken by the new common council was the purchase of a fire cart, hose, and pump. Extensive water lines, however, were still a distant dream. In 1888, the Marshfield Electric Company was established by William Upham. By 1890, a total of 200 stores and homes had electric lights, as did Central Avenue, six years before the service was available in Milwaukee. The city bought the company in 1900. In 1883, a volunteer fire department was organized that was eventually based at city hall on East Second Street and South Maple Avenue. A library was started in the 1880s and was operated by various private organizations until 1901, when a library was added to the new city hall at East Third Street and South Maple Avenue. A new library was opened in 1960 and enlarged later. A new library–community service complex is presently in the planning stages. City streets began to be paved with bricks from A Street (now Arnold Street) to Ninth Street in 1914 and were finished by 1919.

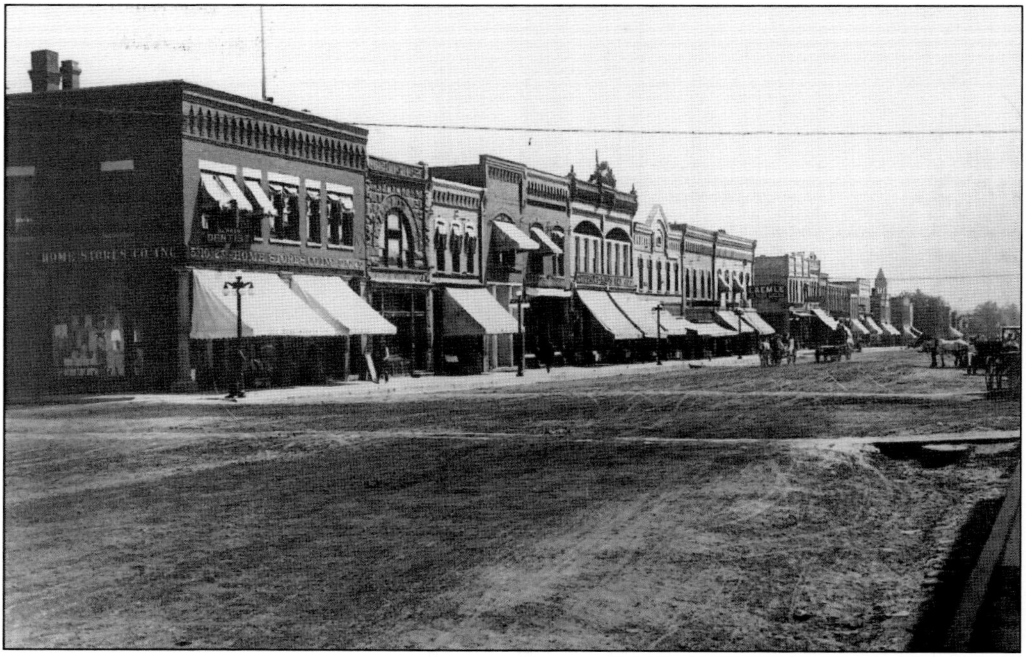

The city streets in Marshfield were unpaved until the 20th century. The soil in the city has a clay base, so after any rain or in the spring as the snow melted, they became quagmires, unsafe for man or horse. In dry weather, they were hard baked or dusty, a constant problem for the merchants and their merchandise.

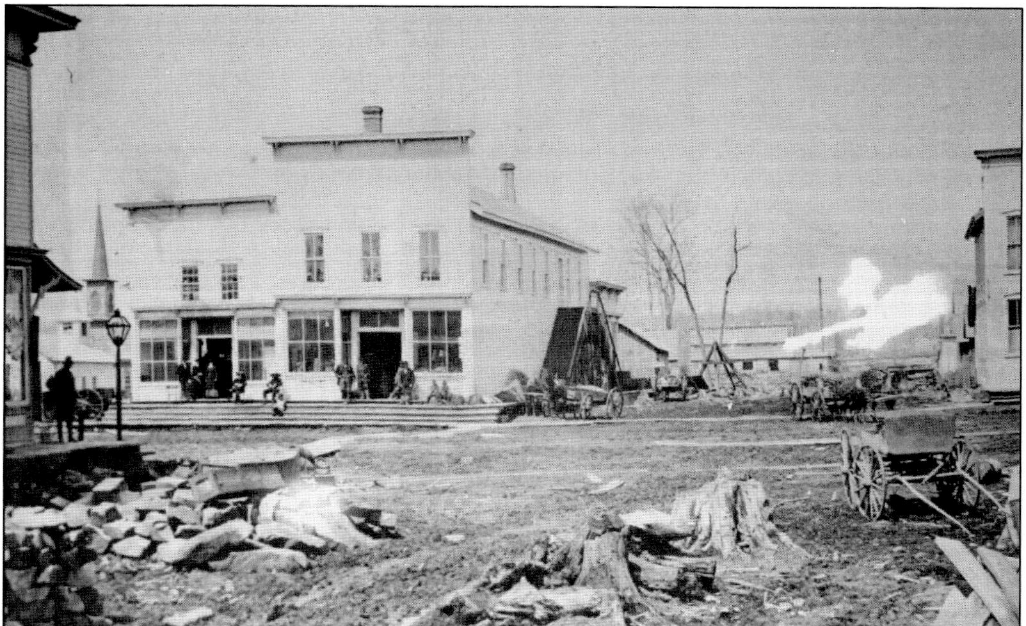

In a matter of 30 years, this corner would not be recognizable to the gentlemen sitting in front of the store on the southwest corner of West Second Street and South Central Avenue. The steeple of the First Presbyterian Church on South Chestnut Street is visible in the background. By 1919, the street would be paved with brick and the sidewalks would have replaced the boardwalks.

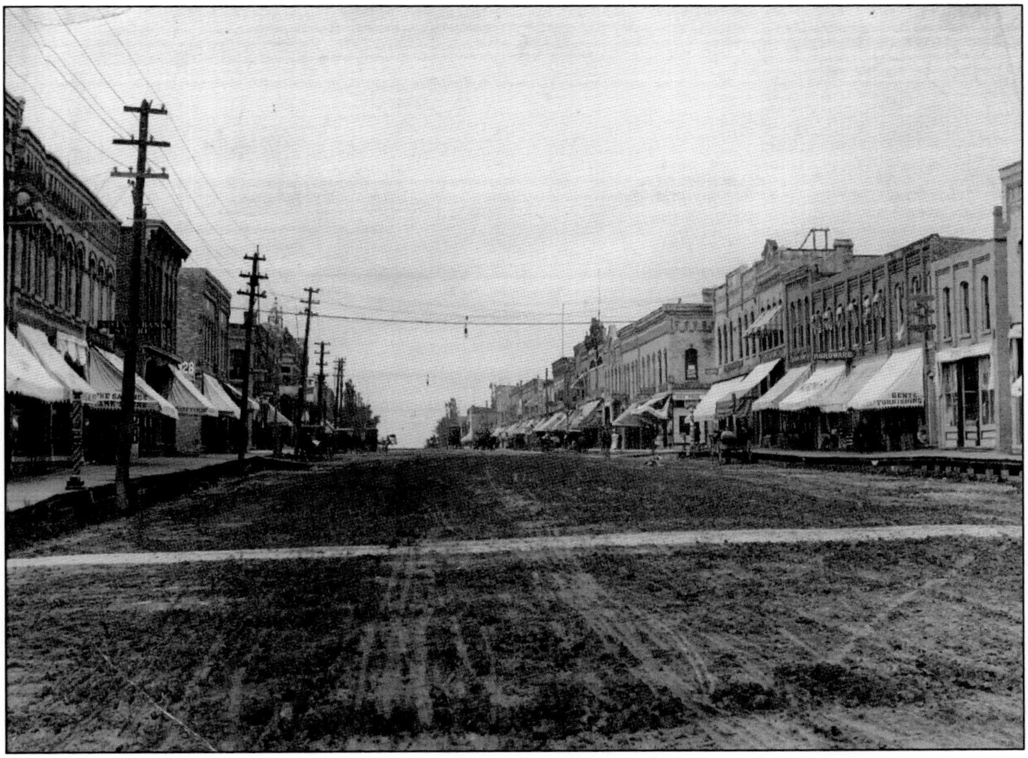

This view north on Central Avenue was taken after 1890, as lights can be seen hanging over the middle of the street. Boardwalks, rather than sidewalks, can be seen on either side of Central Avenue. The traffic is also light enough that a dog can take a rest in the street without concern. The view is looking north from near Third Street.

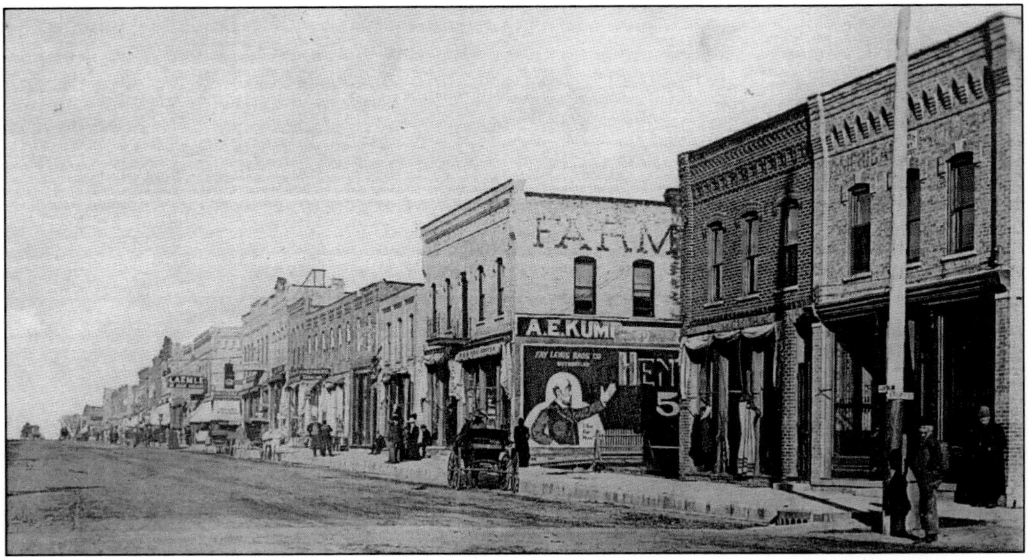

Viewed from a position only one block farther south, it is clear that many changes have been made on Central Avenue. The boardwalks have been replaced by cement sidewalks raised above the street. Storm sewers have been placed under the street, as is indicated by the sewer grate to the right of the photograph.

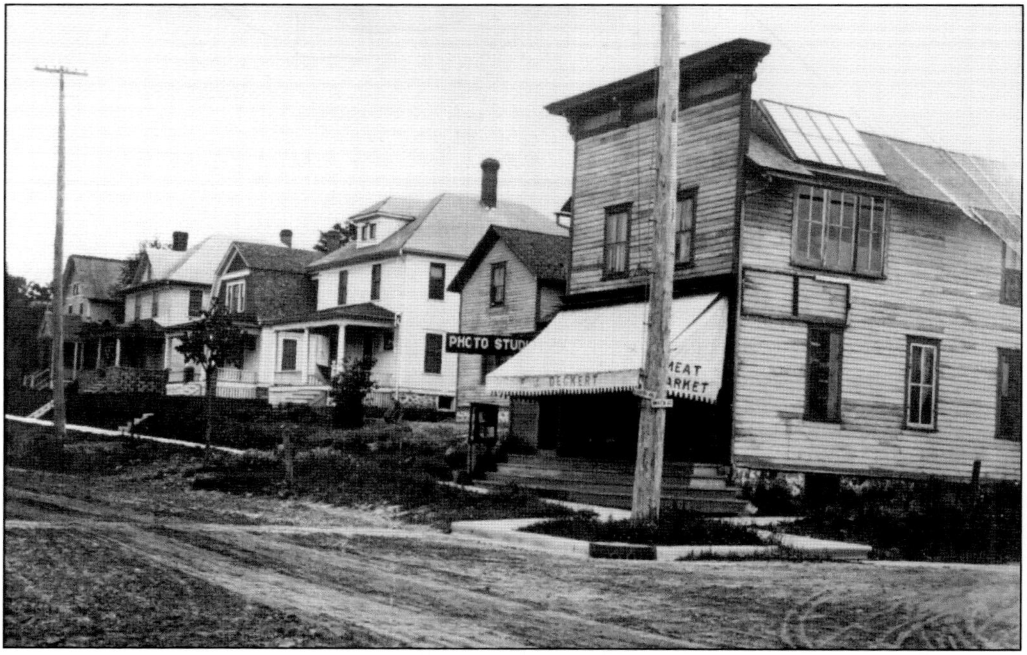

This view is of North Central Avenue at B Street, today's Blodgett Street. Improvements such as sewers and sidewalks were not confined to the business areas. This area of the city was a mix of small businesses and homes. The photographic studio above Deckert's Meat Market can be recognized by the large windows designed to let in the natural light needed for photography.

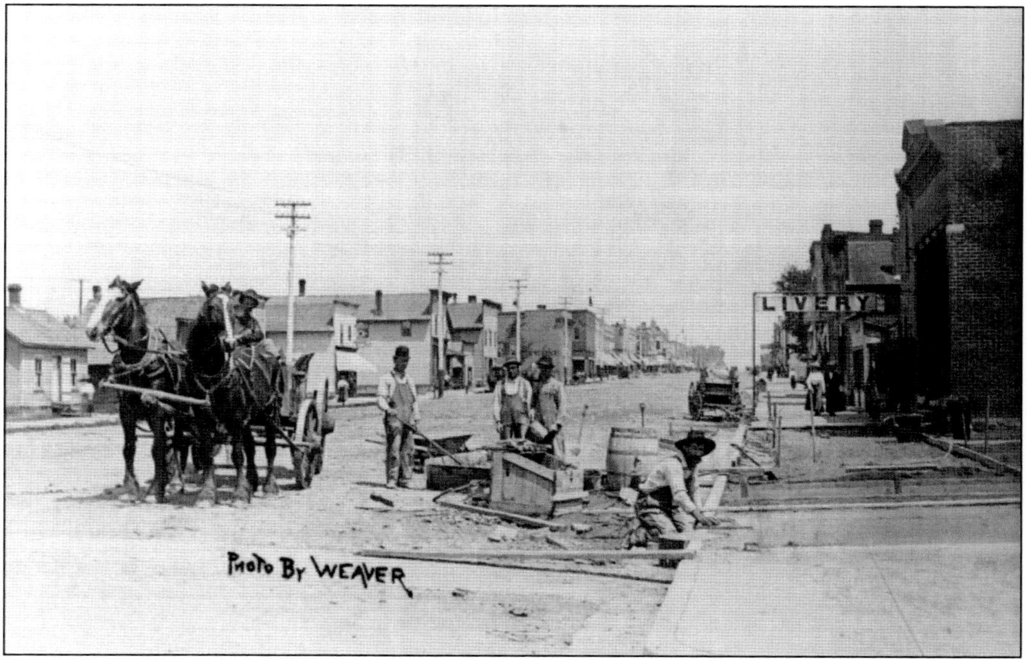

In the early 1900s, the city began to pave the sidewalks in the downtown area. Gradually, this work continued into the residential sections to the east and west of Central Avenue. These men are laying cement on the south end of Central Avenue. Notice that curb, gutter, and sewers have already been installed.

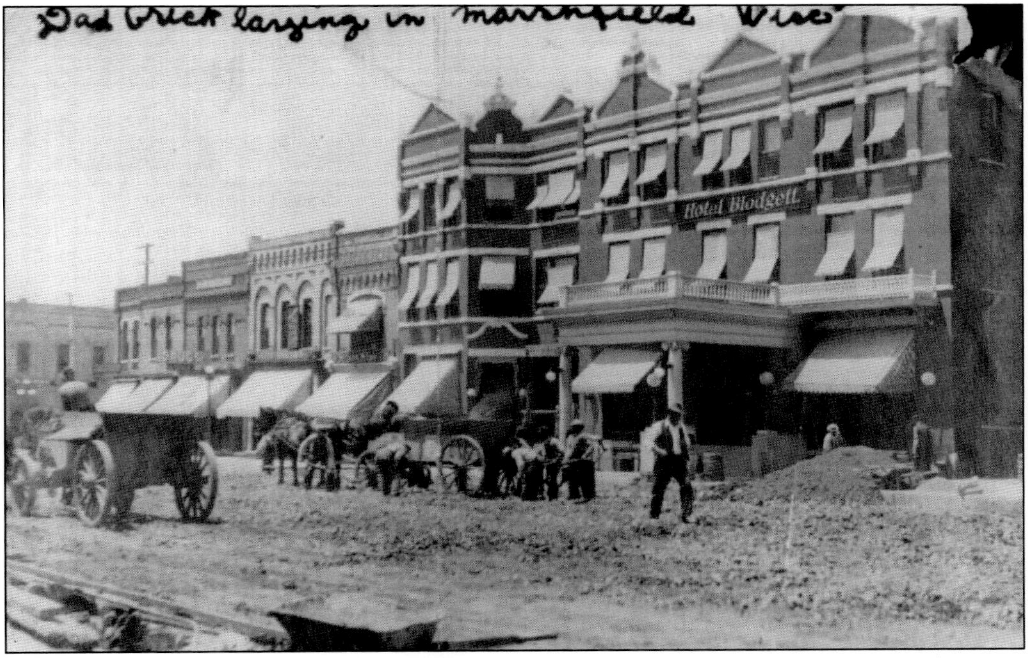

The brick paving of Central Avenue in the business district began in 1916. This section is between West Second and West Third Streets looking to the west at the Blodgett Hotel, one of the better hotels of the era. The street is having its base prepared for the next step in the laying of the brick. Brick streets were common across Wisconsin in the early 20th century.

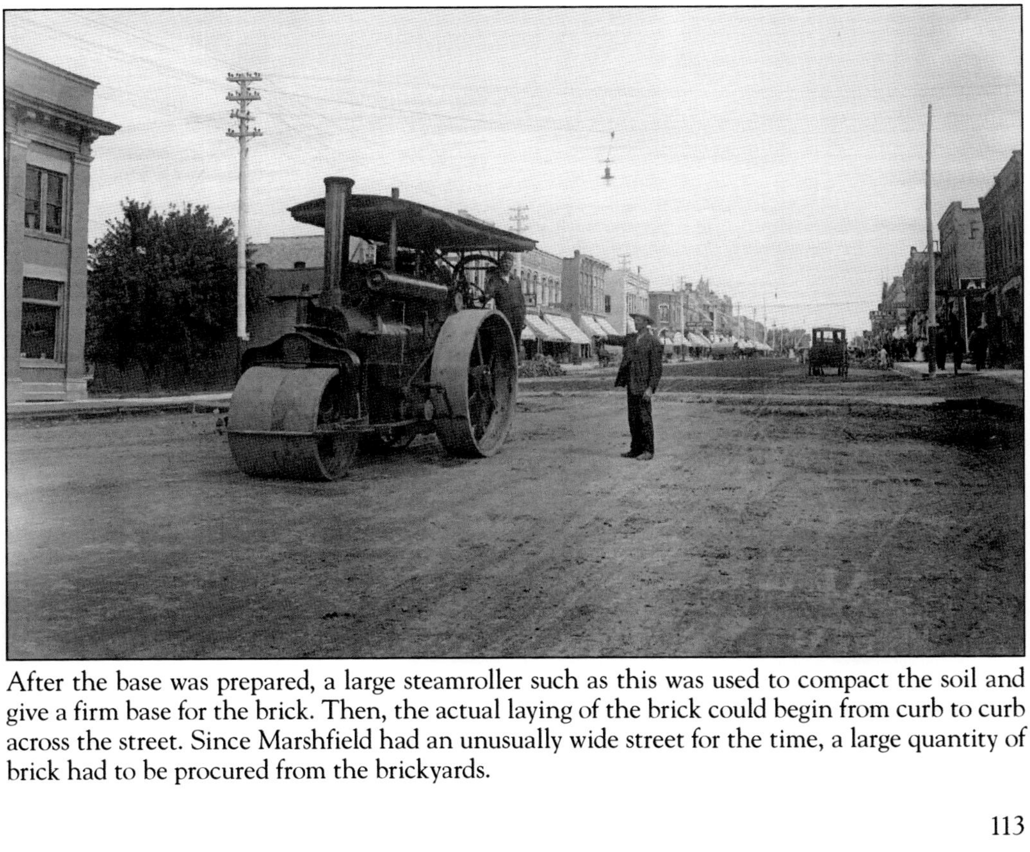

After the base was prepared, a large steamroller such as this was used to compact the soil and give a firm base for the brick. Then, the actual laying of the brick could begin from curb to curb across the street. Since Marshfield had an unusually wide street for the time, a large quantity of brick had to be procured from the brickyards.

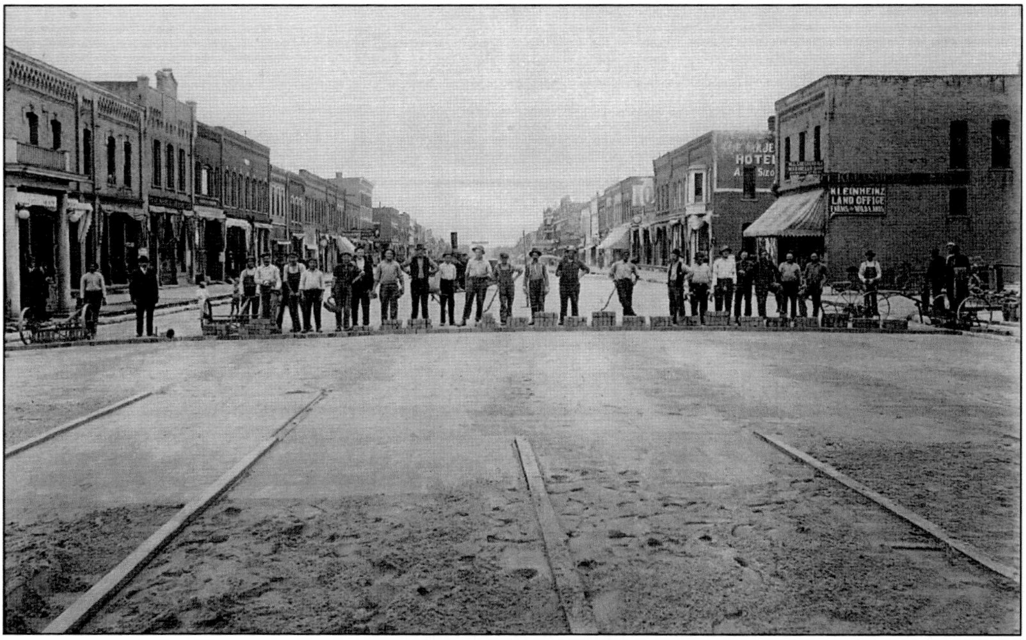

Men laid the brick from curb to curb across Central Avenue. This image looks south from the area of the Soo Line railroad tracks. The brick street would continue from Ninth Street across the tracks to A Street, today known as Arnold Street. The cost of the paving to the property owners and the city was $50,664.82.

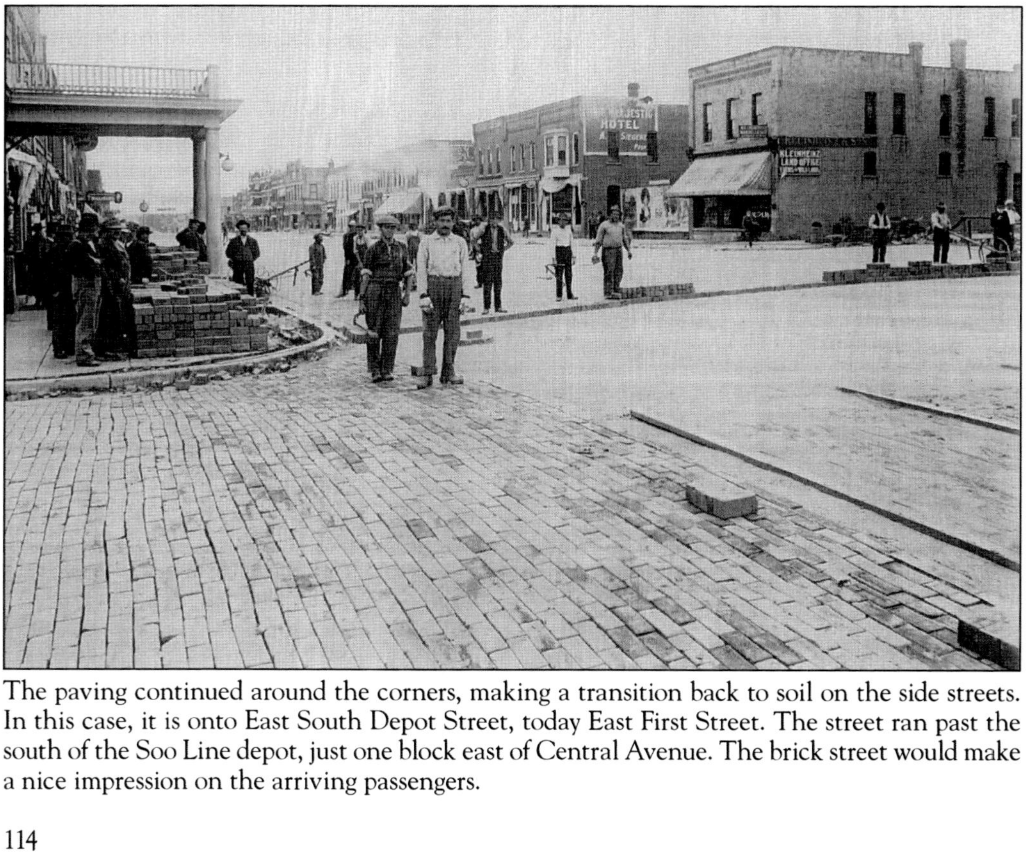

The paving continued around the corners, making a transition back to soil on the side streets. In this case, it is onto East South Depot Street, today East First Street. The street ran past the south of the Soo Line depot, just one block east of Central Avenue. The brick street would make a nice impression on the arriving passengers.

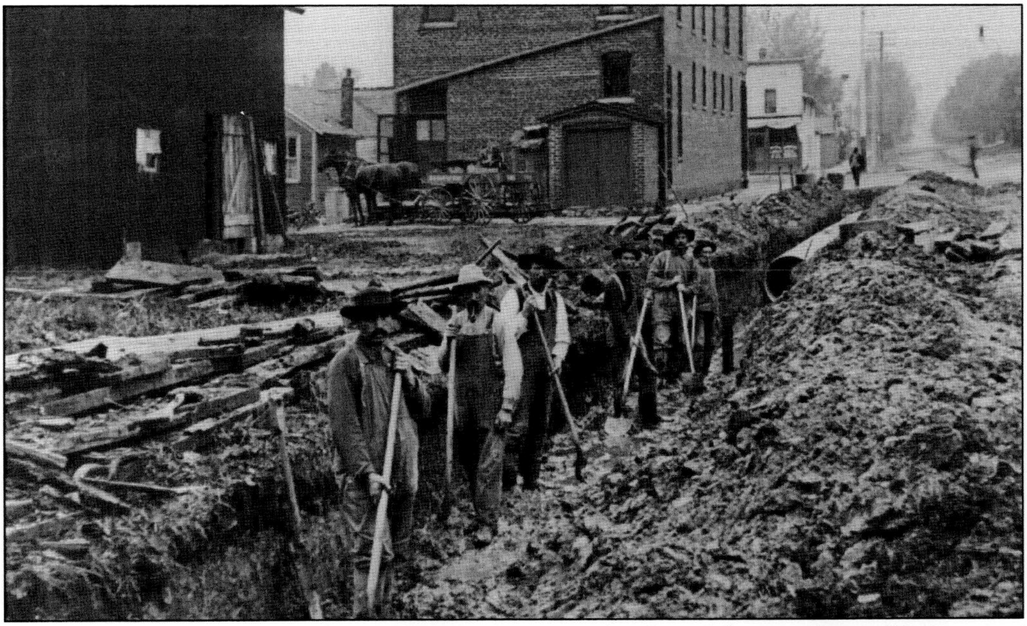

The laying of sanitary sewers along the side streets was also done following the establishment of a sewerage disposal plant in 1916. The sewer here is being laid along the south side of East Fifth Street. The building shown to the immediate left in the background is now Crabby Dave's Bar and Restaurant.

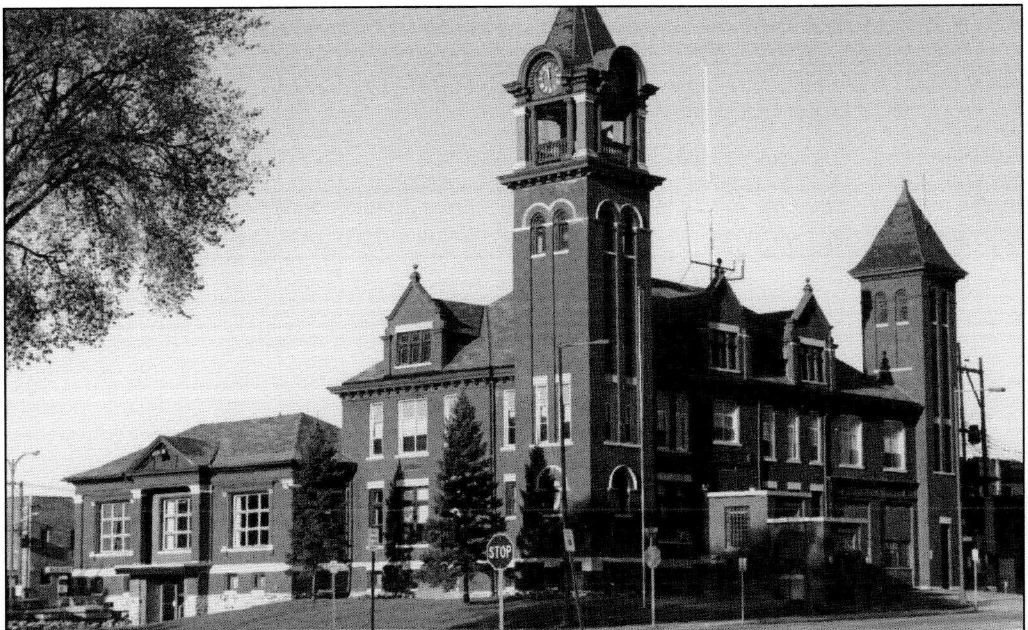

In 1901, the new Marshfield City Hall opened, located on the southwest corner of East Second Street and South Maple Street. Built on the east side of the building was the first Marshfield Public Library. The library no longer had to exist in various private businesses about the city. This was the result of a campaign waged by the Ladies' Travel Club. Della Ellinwood was the first librarian.

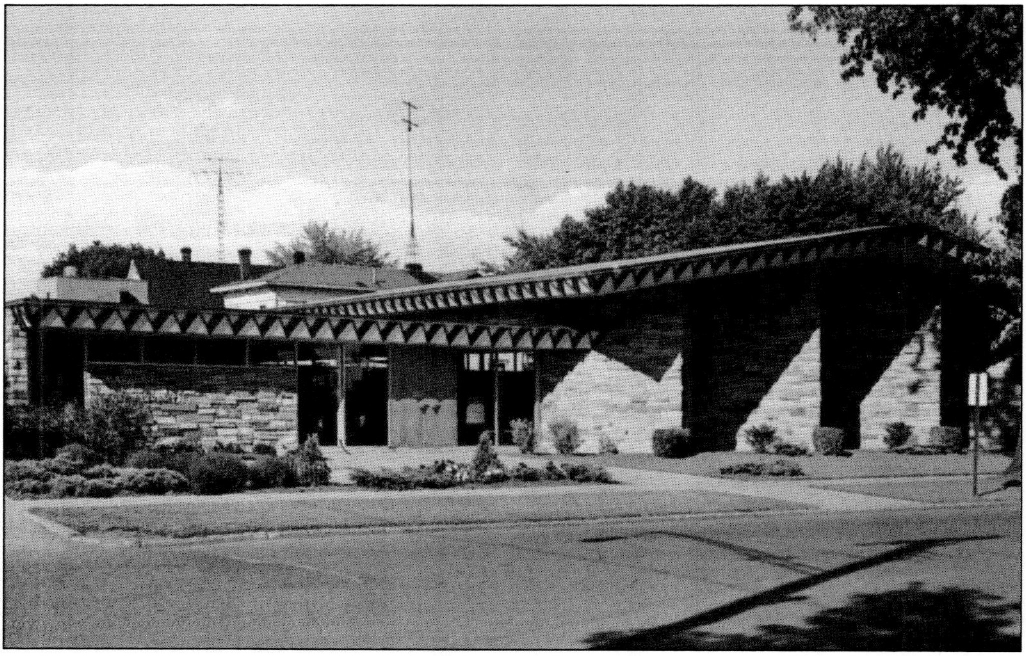

On July 17, 1960, a new Marshfield Public Library was dedicated. It is located near the northeast corner of East Second Street and South Maple Avenue. A unique display is found in the Beebee Forum Room: a collection of 140 species of Wisconsin birds that were collected and mounted in the 1920s by John Stierle.

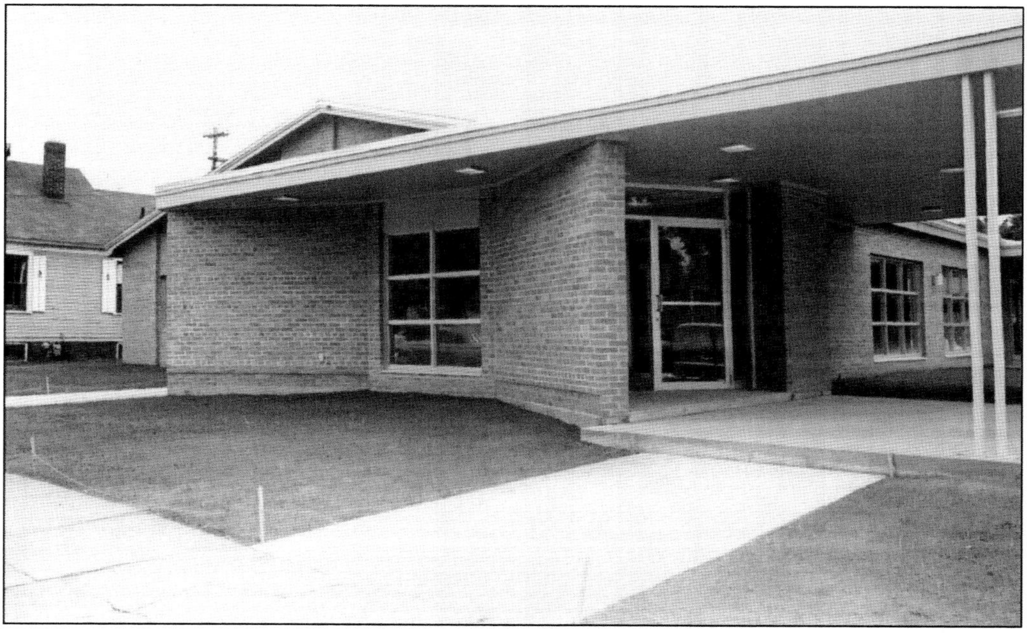

Sharing the library parking lot is the Marshfield Senior Community Center. Originally built as a youth center, it was converted for the seniors in 1984. Operated under the Marshfield Parks and Recreation Department, it is directed by the Senior Community Center Board, elected by the members. It is open to all over the age of 55. Activities range from cards and pool to computer and physical fitness classes.

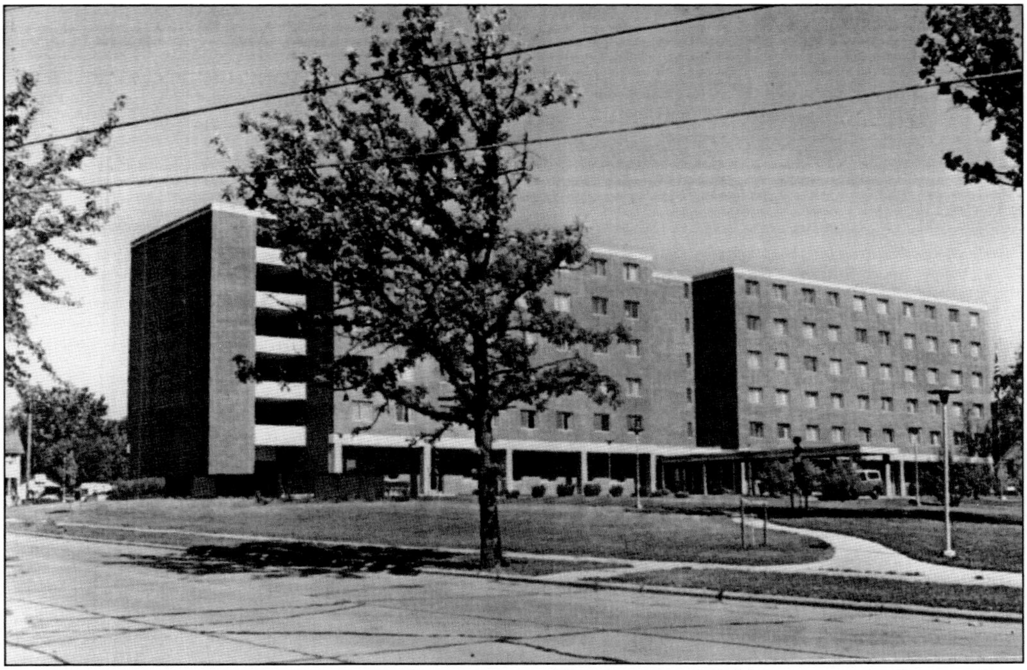

There are two senior apartment complexes operated by the Marshfield Housing Authority. One is Parkview Apartments, also referred to as the "High Rise." It overlooks Veterans Park and is a 97-unit, six-story complex. The first residents moved in in 1968. It has a mix of apartment sizes and has a beautiful sunroom reaching across the front of the building.

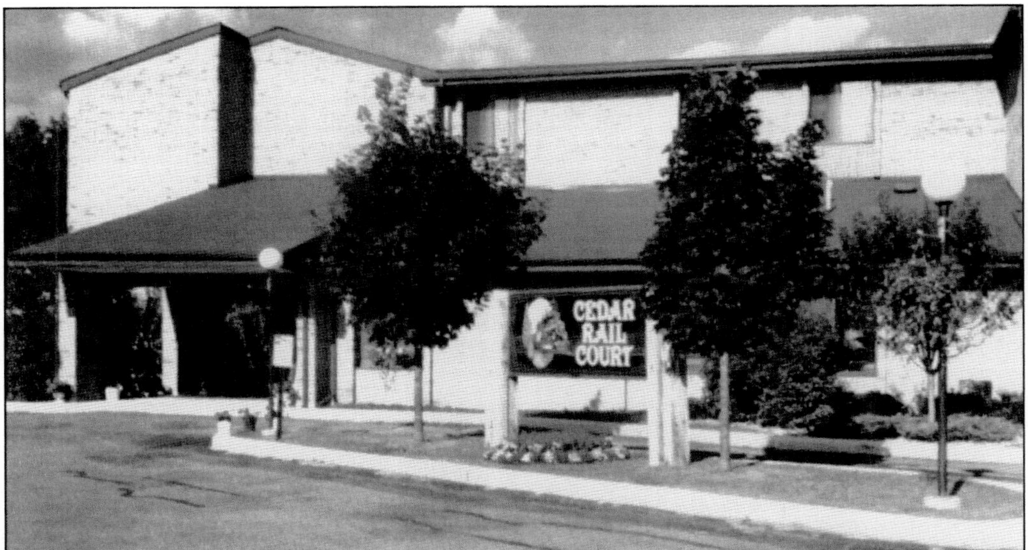

The second apartment complex is Cedar Rail Apartments, located on the east side of South Cedar Avenue, on the abandoned railroad right of way of the Chicago Northwestern Railroad. The complex opened in 1982 with 100 units. Since the right-of-way did not run perpendicular to the street, the building has an interesting design that resembles a series of boxes placed end to end in a staggered formation.

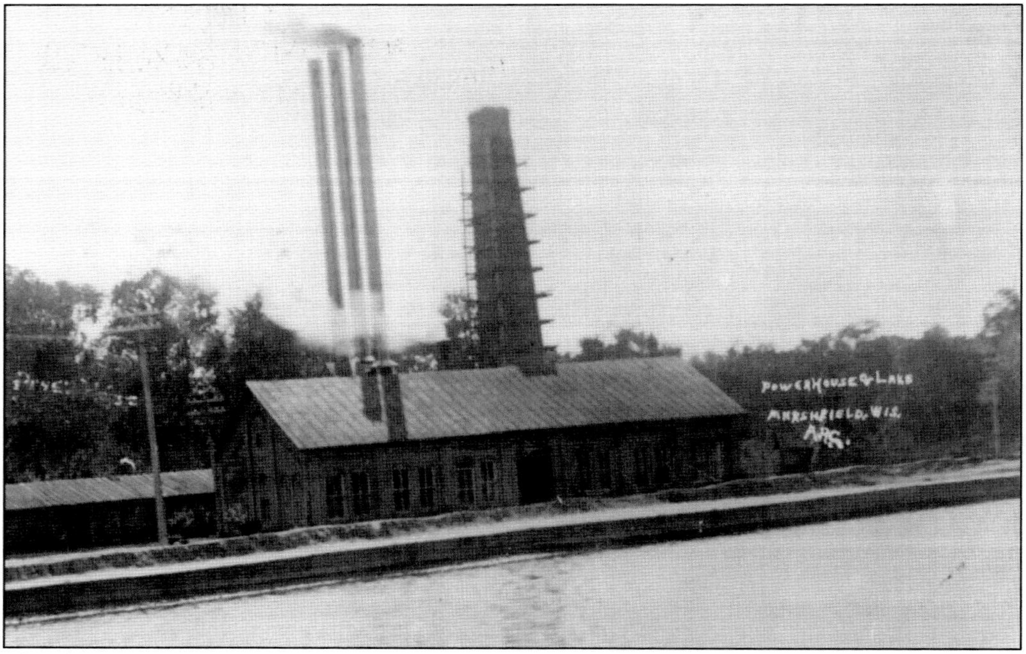

The electric power plant is located on the south side of the city. Built by William Upham, it was sold to the City of Marshfield in 1905. The plant, with many additions and modernizations, continues to provide power to the city from the same location. The Marshfield and Texas Railroad supplied the coal to fire the boilers until coal was no longer used.

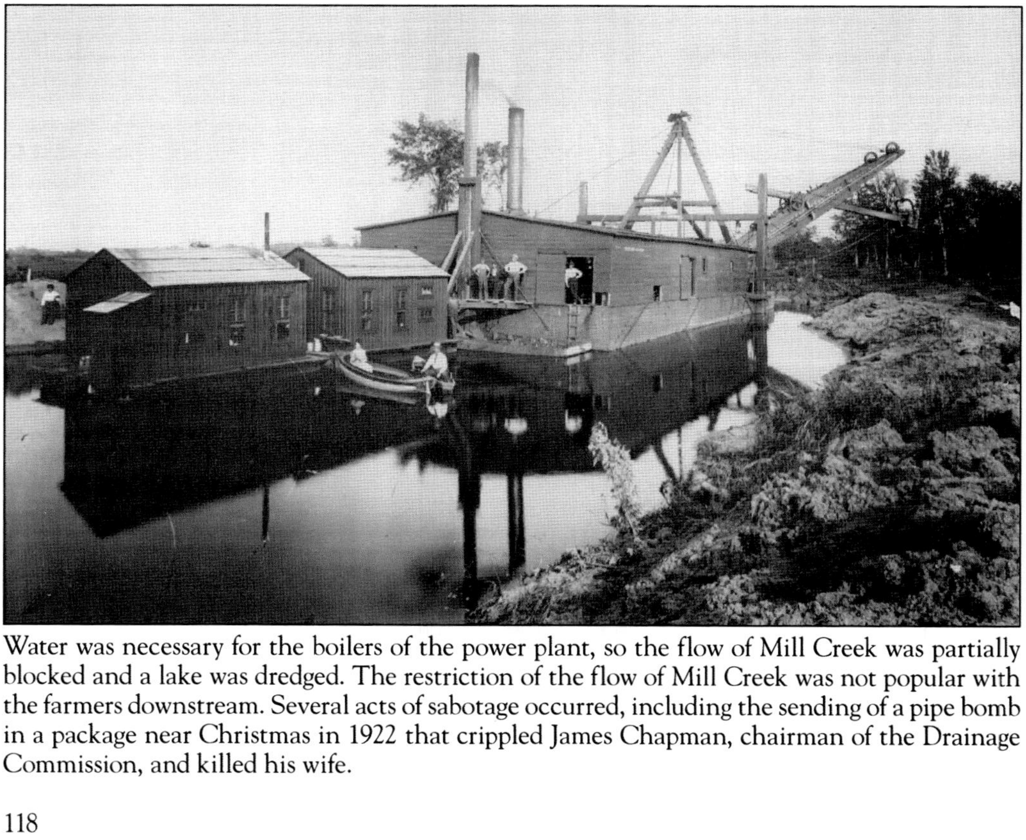

Water was necessary for the boilers of the power plant, so the flow of Mill Creek was partially blocked and a lake was dredged. The restriction of the flow of Mill Creek was not popular with the farmers downstream. Several acts of sabotage occurred, including the sending of a pipe bomb in a package near Christmas in 1922 that crippled James Chapman, chairman of the Drainage Commission, and killed his wife.

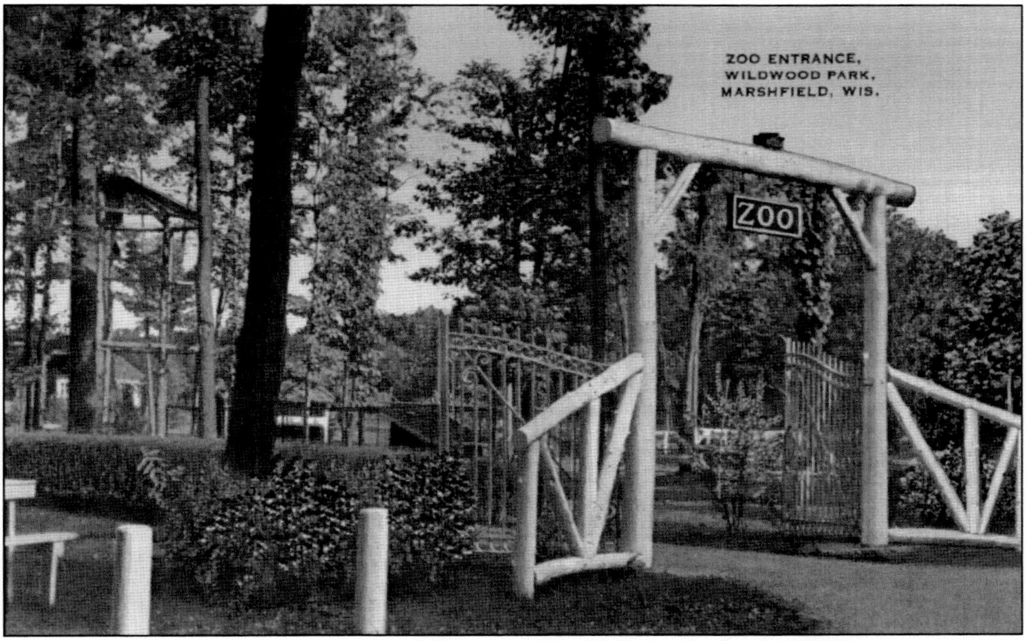

Wildwood Park has been located across the cooling pond from the power station since the 1920s. It is a very large park with two ponds, a large shelter house, playgrounds, and a very nice zoo. The zoo was added later and has grown to include a large variety of animals both native to the region and from other areas. It is a well laid-out and attractive facility.

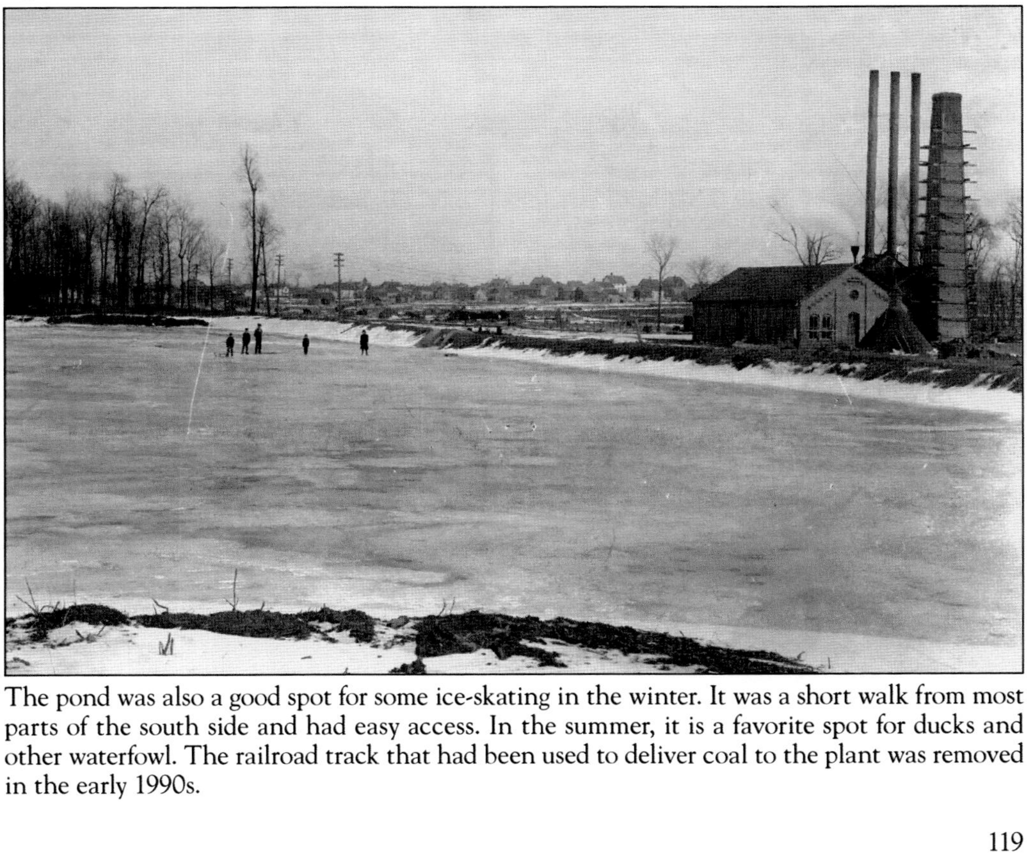

The pond was also a good spot for some ice-skating in the winter. It was a short walk from most parts of the south side and had easy access. In the summer, it is a favorite spot for ducks and other waterfowl. The railroad track that had been used to deliver coal to the plant was removed in the early 1990s.

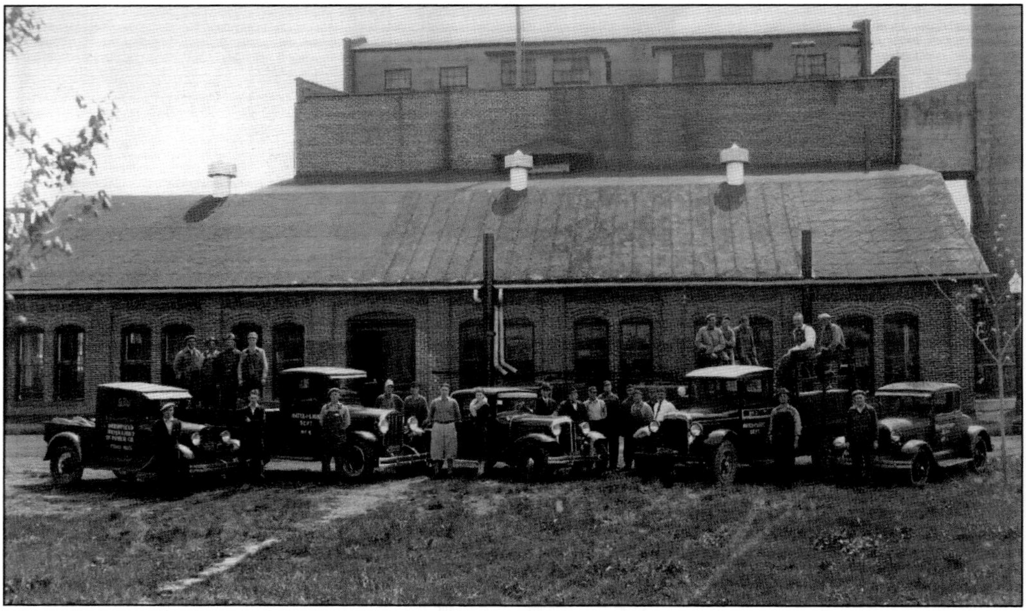

This photograph shows the Power and Light crew of 1931. Standing from left to right are Charles Marvin, Cliff Garten, Elmer Wistrom, Ed Schmitt, Peter Molter, Lambert Ruffing, Mrs. Lambert Ruffing, George Lawhead, George Marvin, Archie Lamere, Ray Lamere, Lloyd Spalding, Otto Meyer, Ed Kipp, and Julius Koenig. In the trucks from left to right are Lawrence Bartl, Joe Michalski, Henry Schmitt, Harold Spencer, Anton Adler, William Stauber, Walter, Ehrlick, and Alfred Kipp.

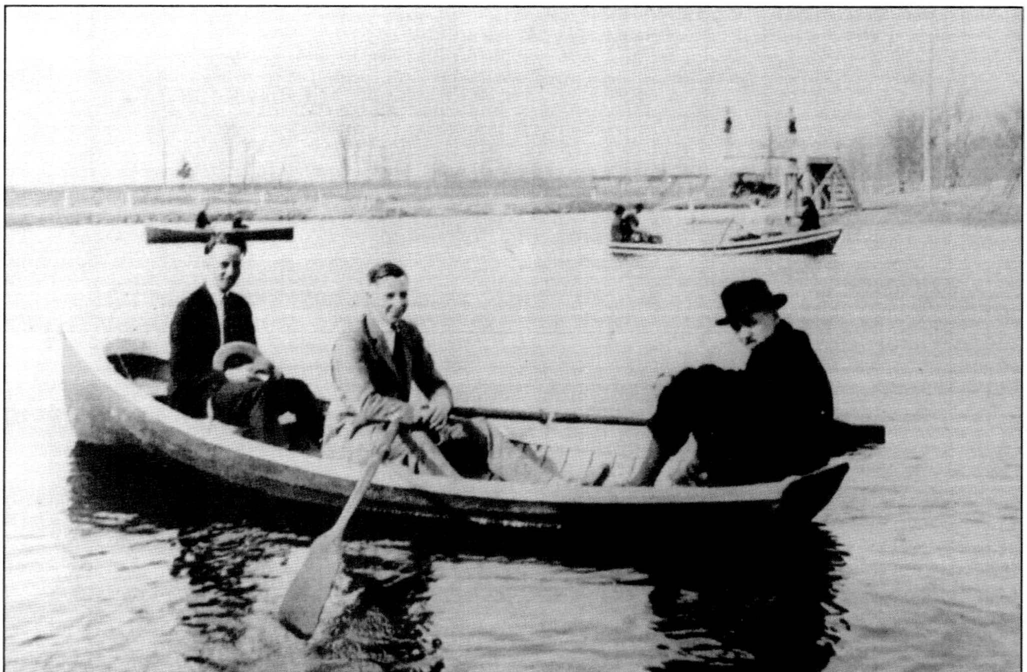

Because Marshfield had no natural water deep enough to swim in, few children learned to swim. The closest pond was west of the city, about four miles on the Yellow River at Blodgett's Pond, a long walk from town. On Memorial Day 1934, a swimming pool was opened in the city.

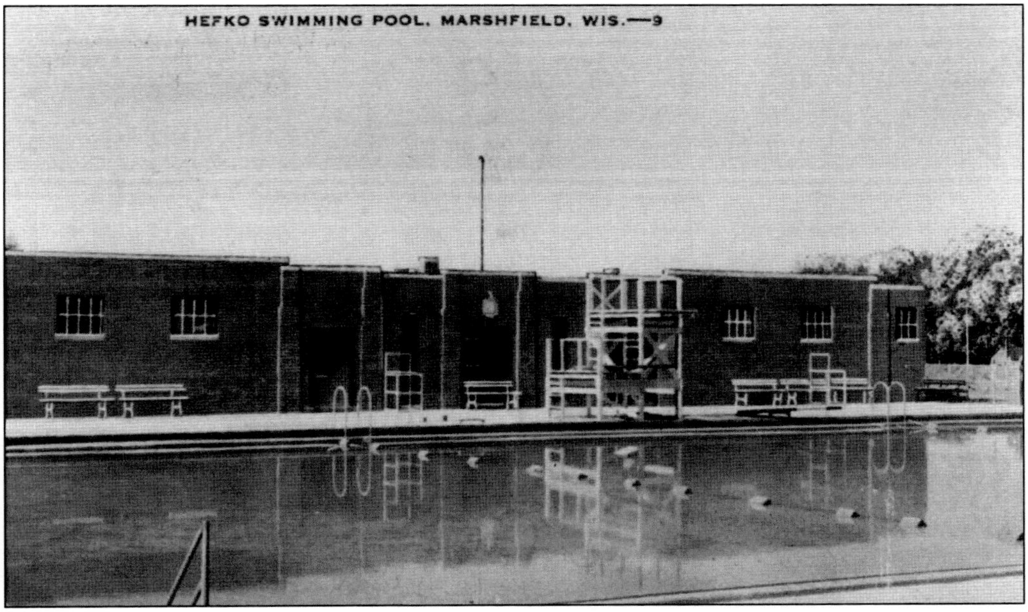

Hefko Pool was named after the mayor who managed to get federal money for the project. The pool was built on the edge of Wildwood Park and was staffed with lifeguards. The pool was free for children in the morning. In the afternoon, they were charged 50¢ and the adult admission charge was $1. The pool is still located in the same area but has undergone some alterations.

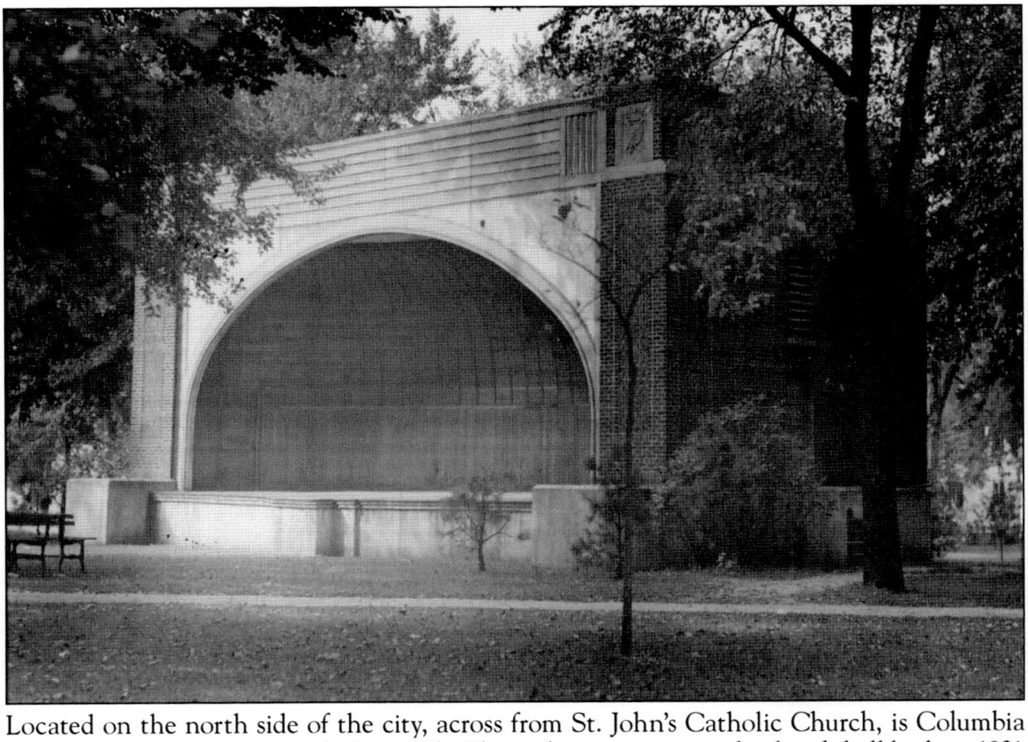

Located on the north side of the city, across from St. John's Catholic Church, is Columbia Park, once known as Northside City Park. The park contains a wooden band shell built in 1931 where summer band concerts were held. The tradition continues today, with concerts held each Wednesday evening during the summer.

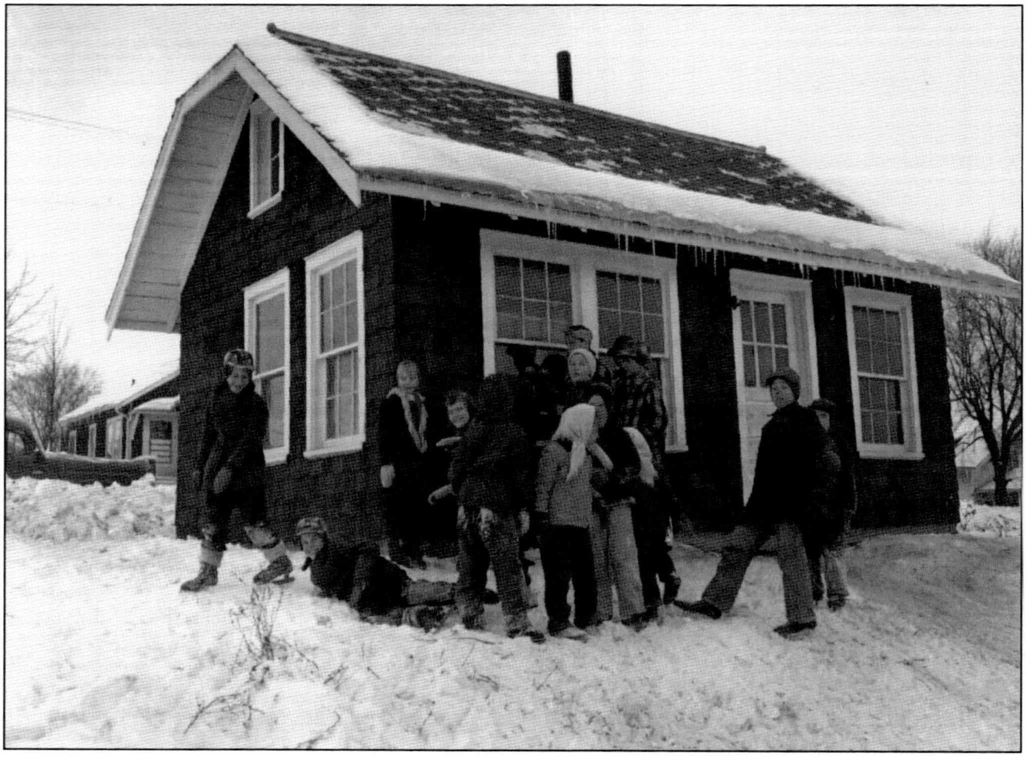

Several areas in the city were flooded and maintained for ice skating. This warming house is located at Pickle Pond on the northeast side of the city. It is located near where pickle vats once stood.

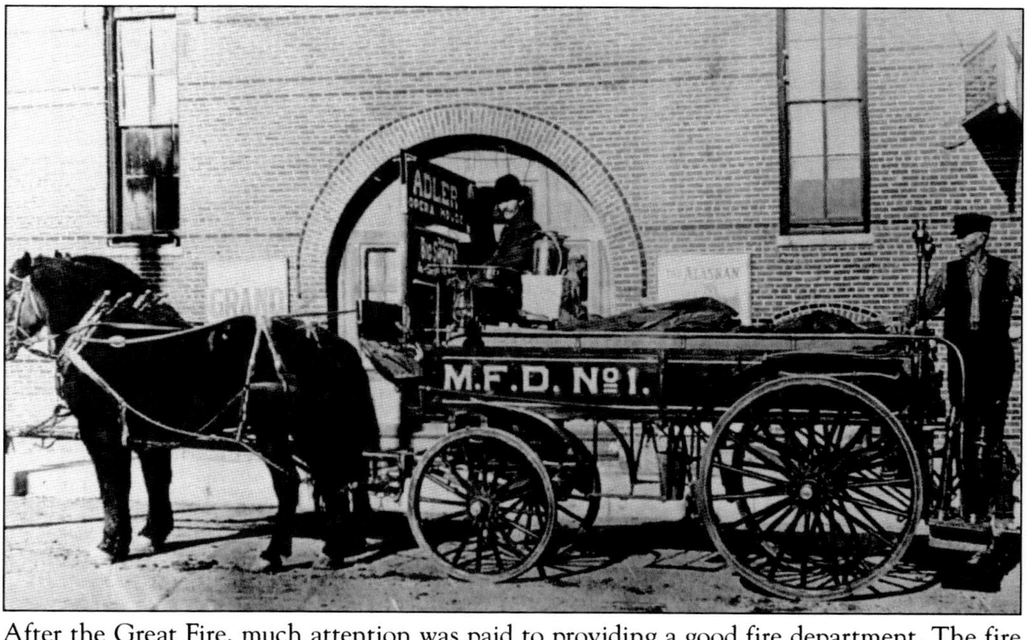

After the Great Fire, much attention was paid to providing a good fire department. The fire department moved into the new city hall in 1901 and remained there for the next 60 years. In 1898, the department purchased its first horse-drawn fire wagon after depending on human-drawn hose carts.

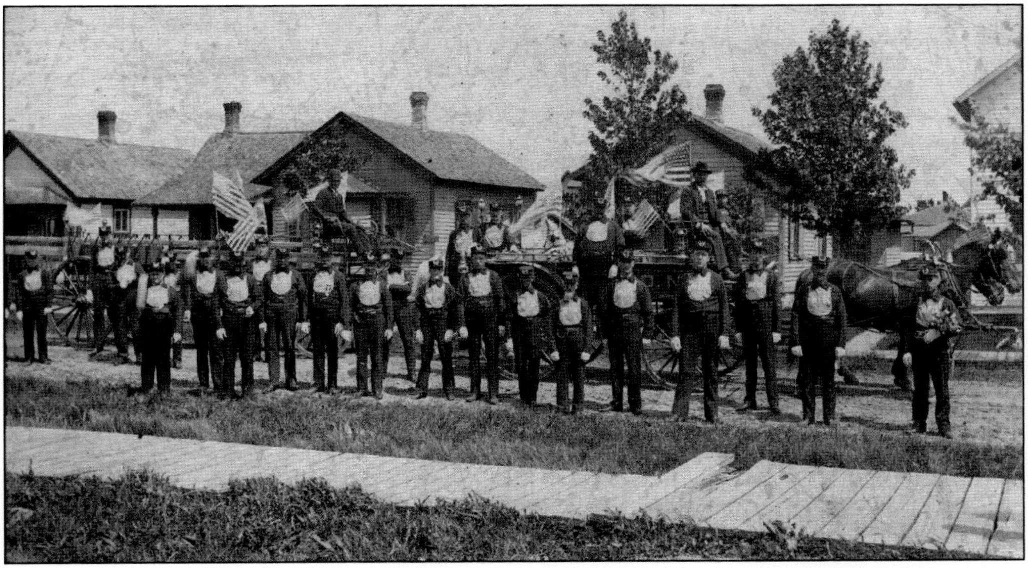

Members of the 1899 fire department are pictured with their two-hose carts. From left to right are Chief E.A. Upham, George Lang, Solon Reilu, Will Pflum, Otto Scharmann, D.C. Pickett, Ed Payne, E.E. Finney, Karl Mess, unidentified, Frank Ward, John Hoffman, Joe Pflum (rear), unidentified, Robert Schroeder, Lacy Gwinn (rear), Joe Morel, Will Kamps, Bert McLee, and two unidentified. Seated on the front truck is Ludolph Wolleson, driving. Next to him is the fire department mascot. Standing on the truck are Frank R. Upham, Phillip Scherr, unidentified, and C. Warfield. The person on the rear truck is unidentified.

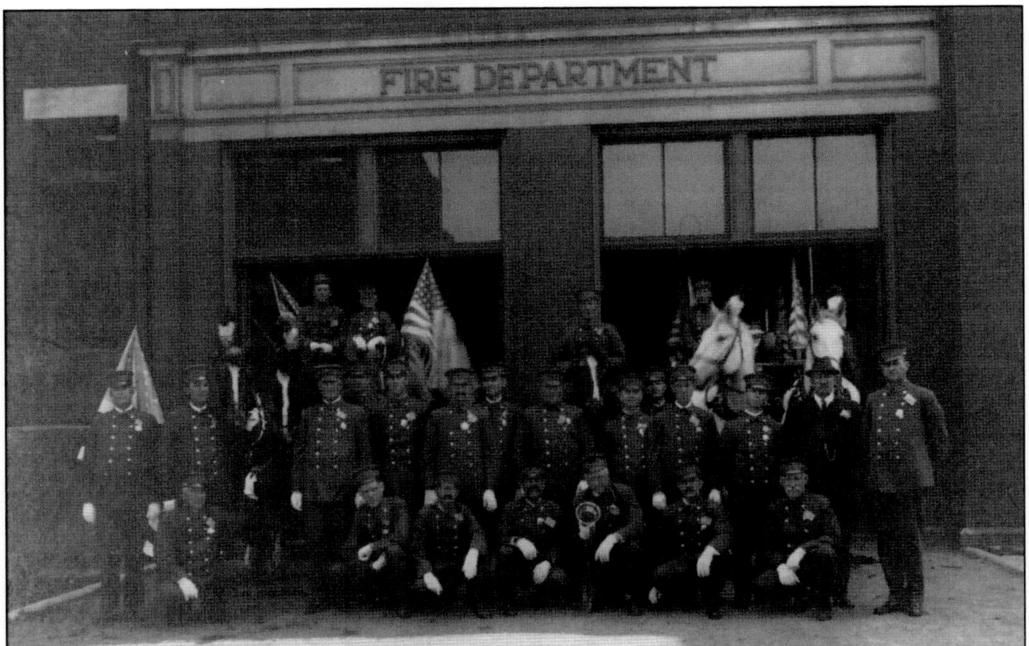

The pre-1920 volunteer firemen pose in front of the firehouse in city hall. The horses appear to be all decorated for a parade. As with today's trucks, a horse-drawn fire wagon was a popular feature in any parade. One of the firemen in the front row holds the warning horn used to clear the way of pedestrians and vehicles.

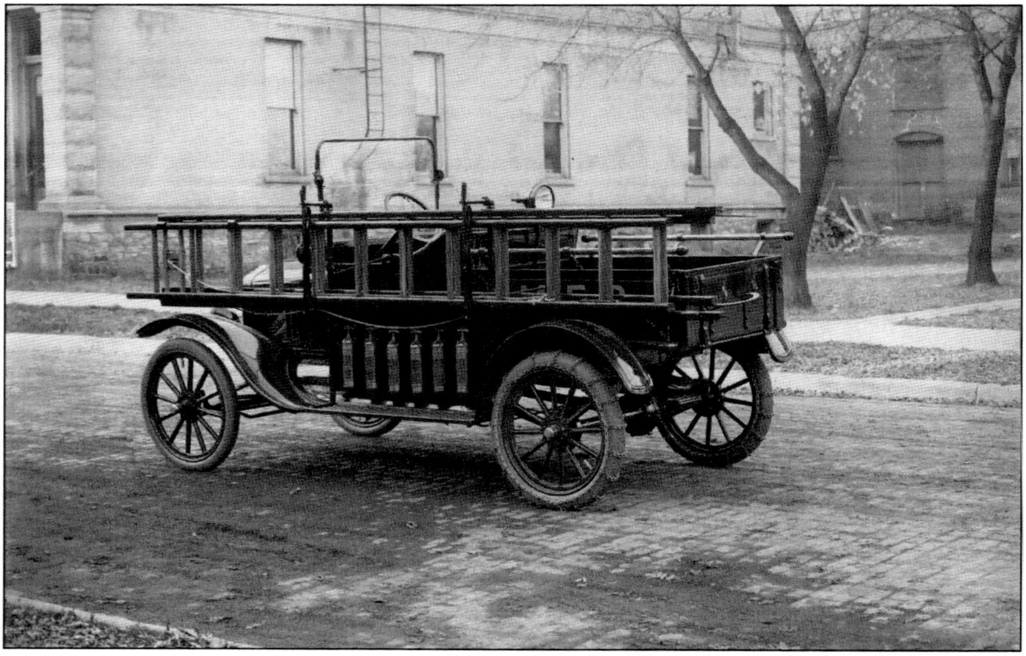

In 1920, the fire department bought its first motorized vehicle, a 750-gallon LaFrance Pumper. A year later, they bought a ladder truck that replaced this homemade vehicle. In 1937, they purchased a four-wheel-drive, 750-gallon pumper that could deliver water at the rate of 1,000 gallons per minute.

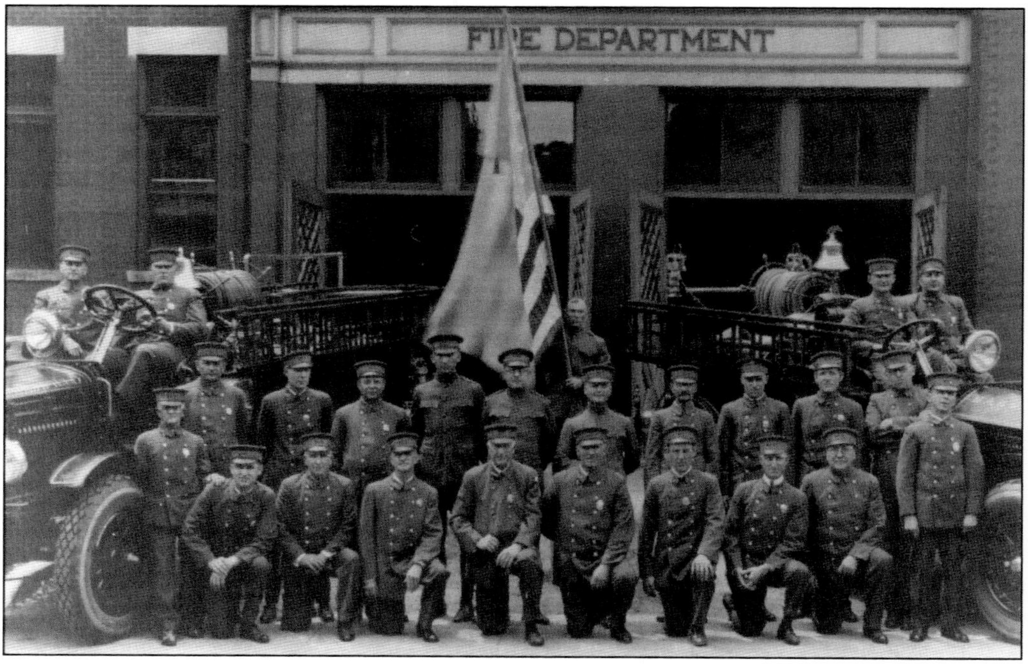

Marshfield remained a volunteer fire department until 1948. They had living quarters on the second floor of city hall. This photograph was taken in 1923 in front of city hall and shows the two new pieces of motorized equipment. Ambulance service was provided by two local funeral homes until 1964. The city purchased one of the vehicles and added emergency medical service.

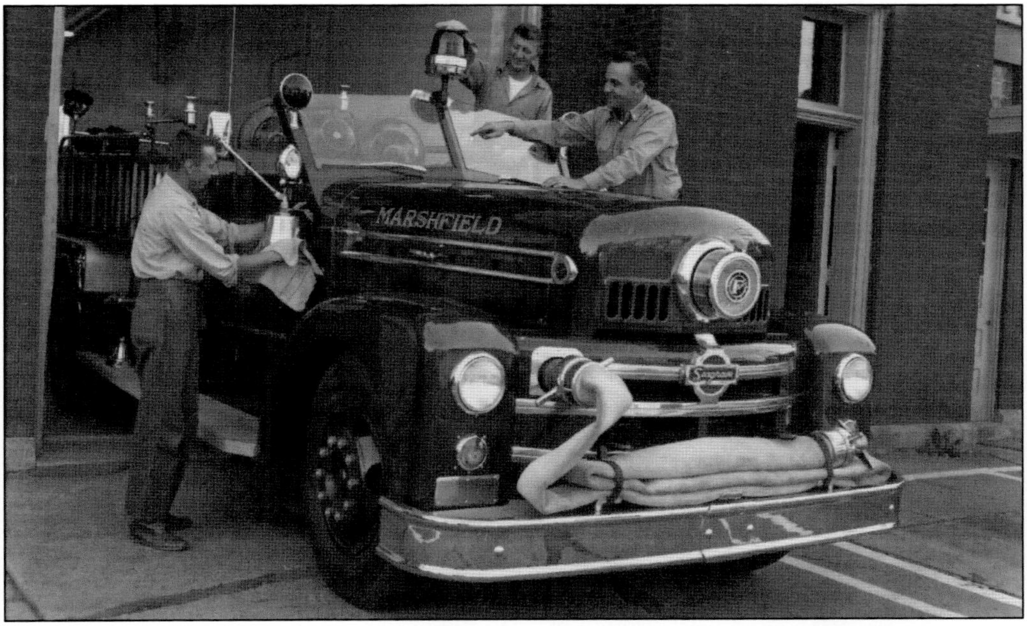

One time-honored activity of firemen is polishing the equipment between uses. This truck is a Seagraves chassis from Appleton. The photograph was taken before 1961, since it is still at the city hall location. In 1962, a new station opened on East Fourth Street and West Vine Avenue, at the site of the old Lincoln School.

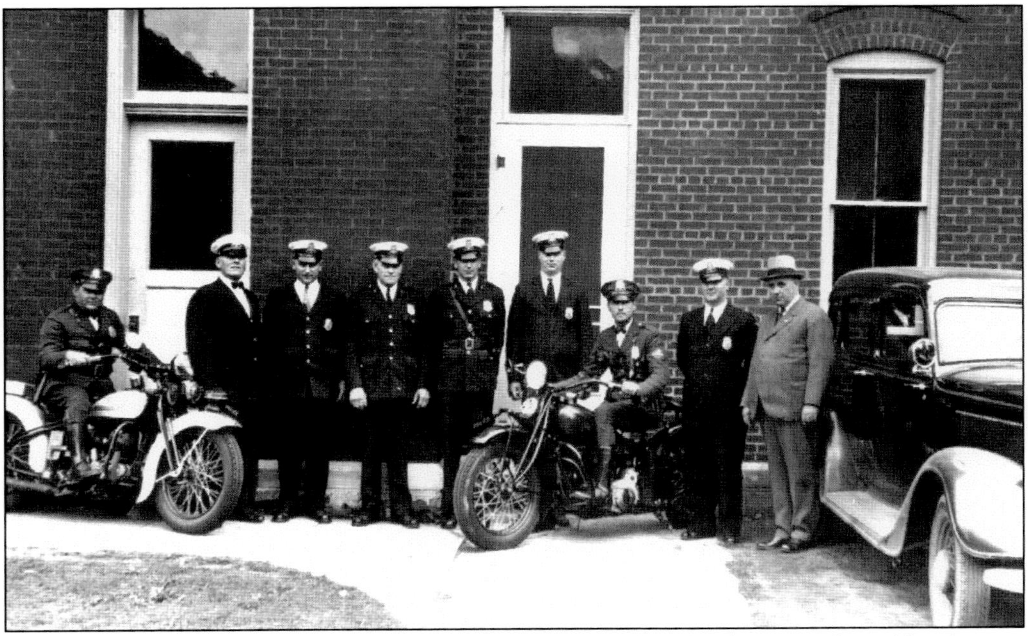

The police department began in 1883 with a city marshal and policeman elected by the city council. In 1902, call boxes were installed. In 1904, the force was increased to five men. The force in 1935 was, from left to right, Henry Kottmeyer on the white Harley-Davidson, George Fyksen, Ernest Crosset, Henry Mueller, Hubert Wegner, William Nelson, Joseph Gravitter on the red and black Indian, John Seidl, and Chief Joe Paape. The car, a 1934 Plymouth, was the first city-owned squad car. (Courtesy of Mike Meyers.)

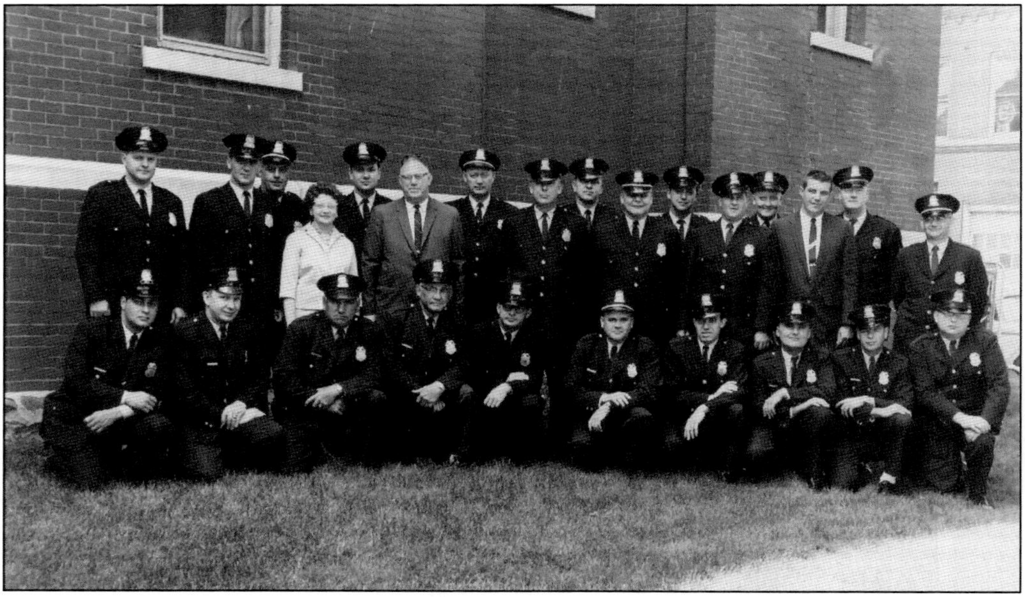

The police department had grown by 1963. From left to right are (first row, kneeling) Walt Kuhn, Bill Jahnke, Erv Schiebe, Lloyd Burt, Dick Blackburn, Lavern Reigel, Terry Rhodes, Bob Grayes, Leroy Schilling, and Jim Hanson; (second row, standing) Robert Woytasik, Mickey Bell, Clarence Reisner, Marion Jahr, Pat Madden, Chief Walter Wolfahrt, Joe Altman, Al Pautzke, Ray Blanchard, Walt Yokimkus, Dave Deitchman, Fred Bartsch, Jerry Thieme, Bill Wolhlfahrt, Ray Schmidt, and Rod Franke.

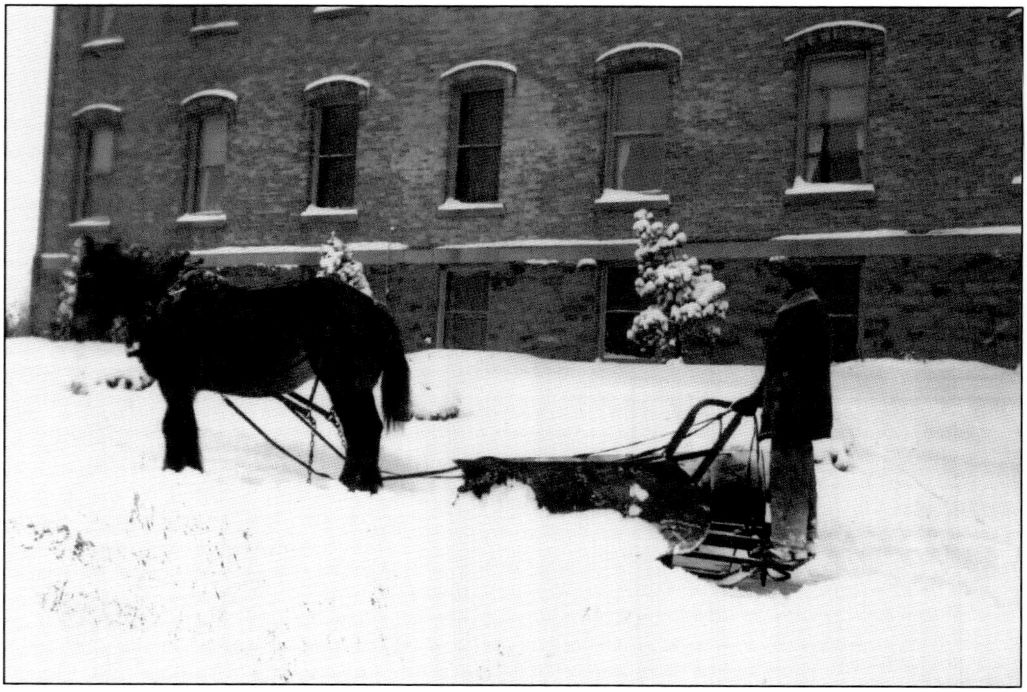

Horses were used to plow the sidewalks in the business area during World War II. It was done to conserve gasoline during the wartime rationing that occurred in the early 1940s. After the war, the horses were retired and snow removal methods became more mechanized.

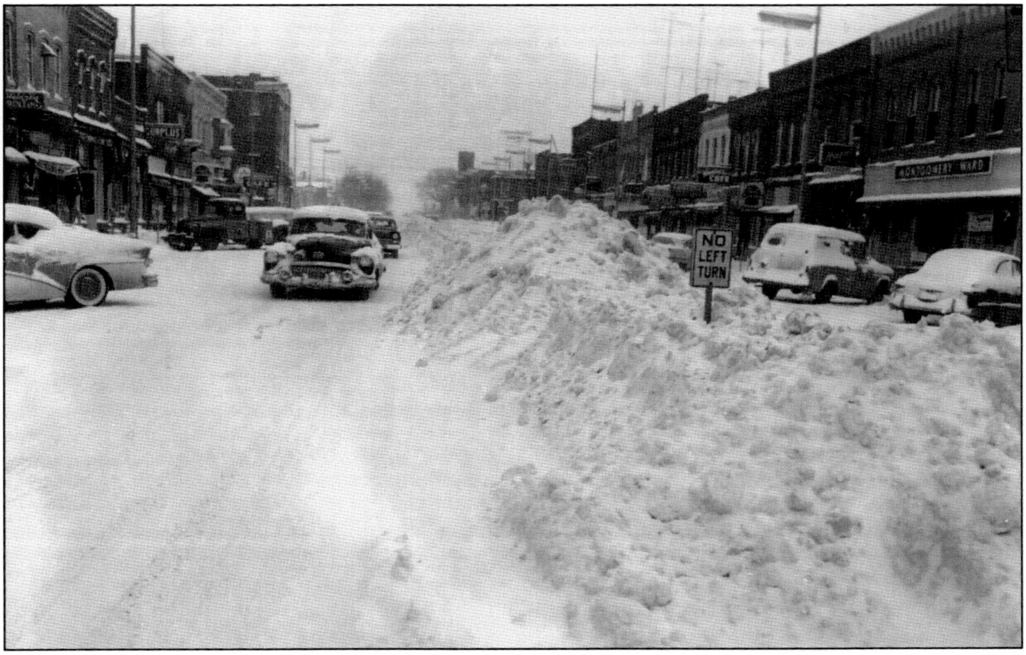

Snow removal in the business district has always presented a problem and continues to do so today. With the extra wide street, essentially four lanes plus a parking lane and a boulevard down the center, there is no place to move the snow except to the boulevard. This presents the problem of removing the piles from the center of the street in the busiest part of the city.

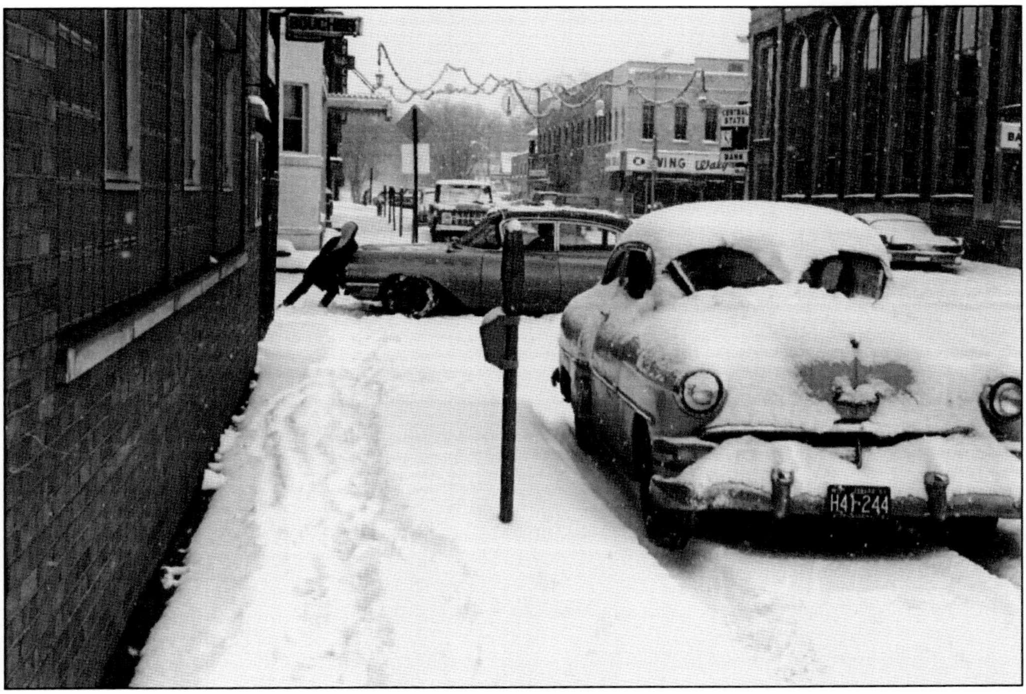

Snow was a problem on Central Avenue as well as on the side streets. Here, a motorist encounters a common problem for Central Wisconsin drivers: "Can you help? I need just a little push. Won't take much." "OK, just don't spin the wheels!"